DMZ

THE FIVE NATIONS OF NEW YORK

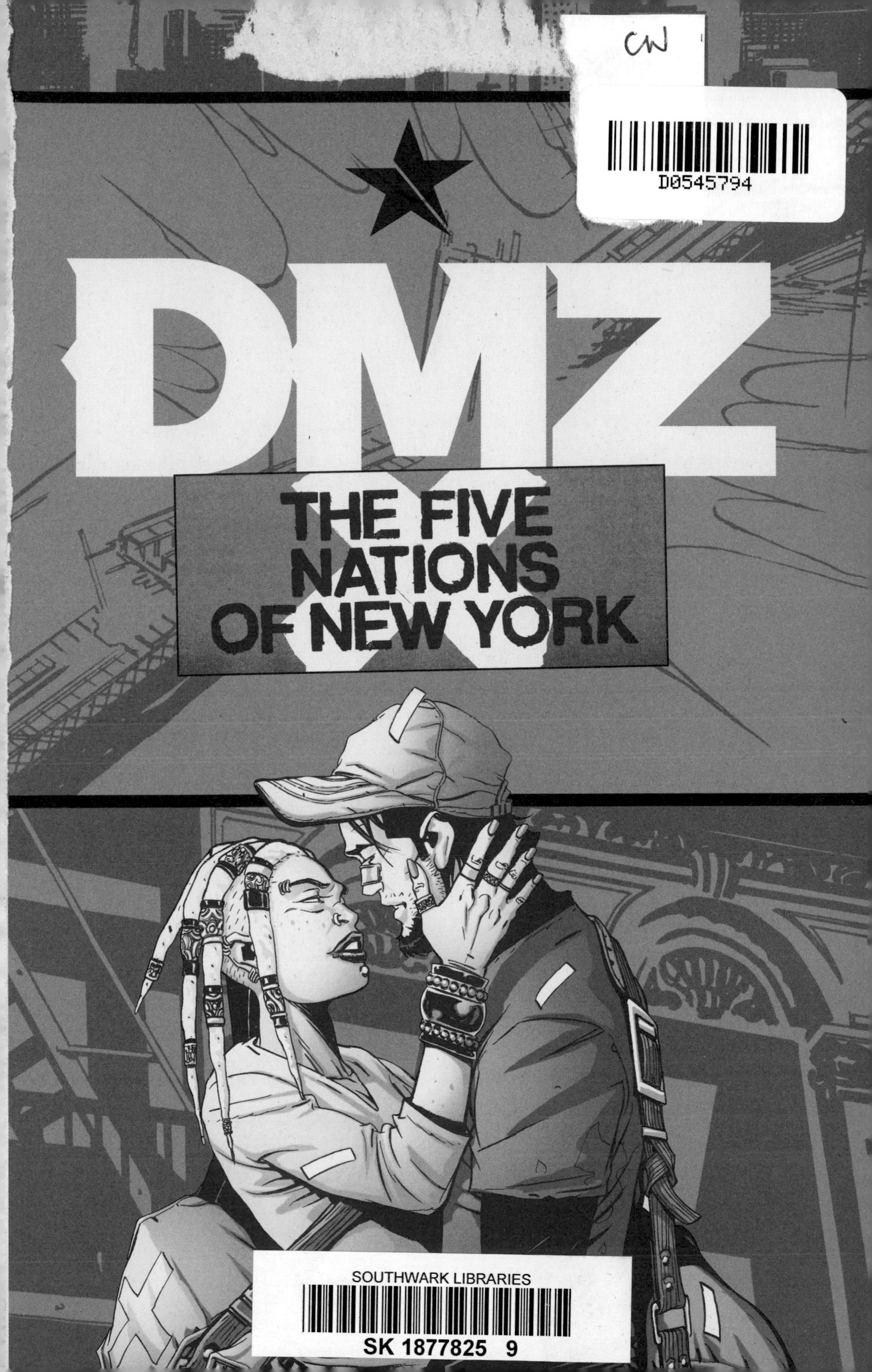

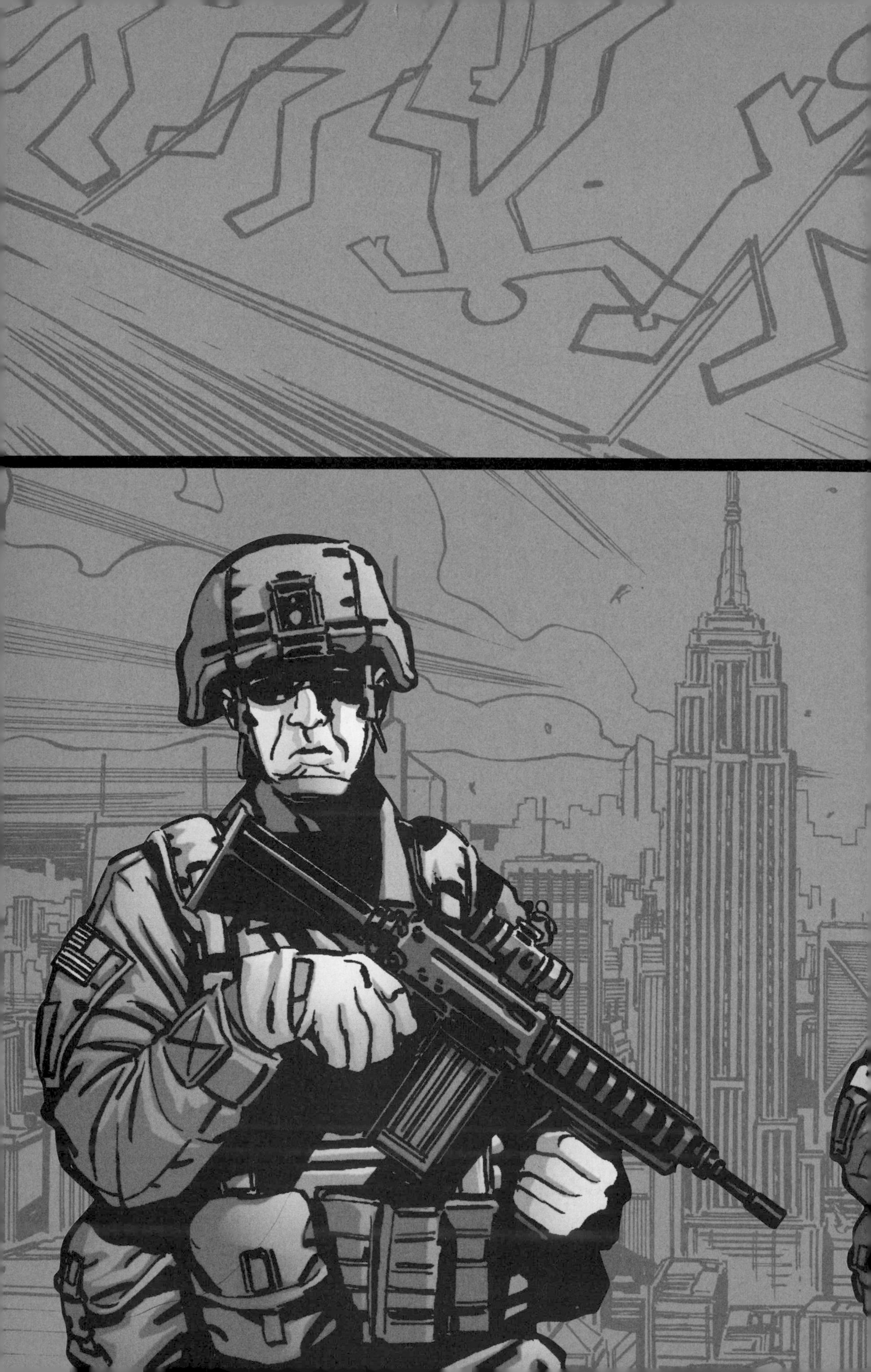

DMZ

THE FIVE NATIONS OF NEW YORK

BRIAN WOOD WRITER

RICCARDO BURCHIELLI ARTIST

JEROMY COX COLORIST

JARED K. FLETCHER LETTERER

ORIGINAL SERIES COVERS BY **JP LEON**

COLLECTION COVER BY **BRIAN WOOD**

DMZ CREATED BY **BRIAN WOOD** AND **RICCARDO BURCHIELLI**

Will Dennis Editor – Original Series
Mark Doyle Associate Editor – Original Series
Robin Wildman Editor
Robbin Brosterman Design Director – Books
Robbie Biederman Publication Design

Karen Berger Senior VP – Executive Editor, Vertigo
Bob Harras VP – Editor-in-Chief

Diane Nelson President
Dan DiDio and **Jim Lee** Co-Publishers
Geoff Johns Chief Creative Officer
John Rood Executive VP – Sales, Marketing and Business Development
Amy Genkins Senior VP – Business and Legal Affairs
Nairi Gardiner Senior VP – Finance
Jeff Boison VP – Publishing Operations
Mark Chiarello VP – Art Direction and Design
John Cunningham VP – Marketing
Terri Cunningham VP – Talent Relations and Services
Alison Gill Senior VP – Manufacturing and Operations
David Hyde VP – Publicity
Hank Kanalz Senior VP – Digital
Jay Kogan VP – Business and Legal Affairs, Publishing
Jack Mahan VP – Business Affairs, Talent
Nick Napolitano VP – Manufacturing Administration
Sue Pohja VP – Book Sales
Courtney Simmons Senior VP – Publicity
Bob Wayne Senior VP – Sales

DMZ: THE FIVE NATIONS OF NEW YORK
Published by DC Comics. Cover and compilation Copyright © 2012 Brian Wood
and Riccardo Burchielli. All Rights Reserved.

Originally published in single magazine form in DMZ 67-72 Copyright © 2011,
2012 Brian Wood and Riccardo Burchielli. All Rights Reserved. VERTIGO is a trademark
of DC Comics. All characters, their distinctive likenesses and related elements featured
in this publication are trademarks of DC Comics. The stories, characters and incidents
featured in this publication are entirely fictional. DC Comics does not read or accept
unsolicited ideas, stories or artwork.

DC Comics, 1700 Broadway, New York, NY 10019
A Warner Bros. Entertainment Company.
Printed in the USA. 5/4/12. First Printing.
ISBN: 978-1-4012-3479-9

Library of Congress Cataloging-in-Publication Data

Wood, Brian, 1972-
   DMZ. The five nations of New York / Brian Wood, Riccardo Burchielli.
      p. cm. – (DMZ ; v. 12)
   "Originally published in single magazine form in DMZ 67-72" – T.p. verso.
   ISBN 978-1-4012-3479-9
   1. Militia movements–United States–Comic books, strips, etc. 2. Manhattan (New York, N.Y.)–
Fiction. 3. Graphic novels. I. Burchielli, Riccardo. II. Title. III. Title: Five nations of New York.

PN6727.W59D577 2012
741.5'973–dc23
                                                                2012010317

WHEN SOMEONE HANDED ME A COPY OF BRIAN WOOD'S FIRST BOOK,
CHANNEL ZERO, **BACK IN THE LATE '90S, LITTLE DID I KNOW IT WOULD BE
A HERALD OF THINGS TO COME.**

Brian came out of nowhere and was immediately a writer I identified with. His style was intrinsically indie, not having come up through traditional comic book channels. He emerged as one of the most important creative voices of the last 15 years, crisply articulating the zeitgeist of our generation. He captured the sense of optimism we'd learned from our Greatest Generation grandparents, tempered it with the counterculture of our 1960s activist parents, and then framed it all within the socially aware sensibility of our own generation. *Channel Zero* was young, brash, DIY art terrorism. It was fiercely low-fi. Brian would use the term "analog." I just thought it was cool. It *looked* cool. It *read* cool. Reading a Brian Wood book was empowering; it made you feel like you could change the world. In many ways, *Channel Zero* was the spiritual precursor to *DMZ.* If that first shot fired was an acute reaction to some very specific politics in New York City, then *DMZ* took on a broader message about the crumbling U.S. cultural identity and our position on the global stage.

As the end of 2001 approached, I'd been out of college a few years, worked a short time in federal law enforcement and settled into a long career in corporate security and emergency management at a Fortune 100 company. That Tuesday morning in September shocked the senses. I found myself staffing an Emergency Operations Center, evacuating hundreds of staffers from Manhattan, and then dealing with the direct impact — my company quickly confirmed that we had an employee aboard American Airlines Flight 77. Even from the heart of Silicon Valley, I already felt a painful affinity with the spirit of New York City, four years before the first issue of *DMZ* even shipped. The world had changed. In my line of work, we used to say that every day would now be September 12th.

In the earliest sequence of *DMZ,* Brian instantly set the tone by daring to say that *"Every Day is 9/11."* Brian once told me that he never consciously decided *DMZ* was going to be his official response to 9/11, but that's what it became. It was an unflinching "what if?" exercise that kept hammering away at a singular idea. *What if the unthinkable kept happening?* What if the elective desert campaigns never stopped? What if the disenfranchised reached a volatile tipping point? What if they were armed, organized, and among us? What if they rolled Federal Reserve Banks, National Guard Armories, and FBI Field Offices as they swept east? What if the U.S. was so busy nation-building abroad that it crumbled at home? What if this string of events catapulted the United States of America and a new entity, the Free States of America, into the Second American Civil War? What if Manhattan was the combat front for this ideological divide? Most important, what if the one guy who couldn't even find himself suddenly found his way into the middle of this mess?

Enter Matthew Roth.

Matty wasn't a superhero. Matty wasn't a hero. Matty wasn't even an everyman. In fact, he was kind of an idiot at first. He pissed off his family, his friends, and the city. He made mistakes. He even got people killed. Only Brian would make his protagonist unlikable at times. He did it with Megan in *Local,* he did it with the subversive kids in *DV8: Gods & Monsters,* and he certainly did it when he dropped Matty Roth into the DMZ. It was intellectually honest for the development of the character. It might take longer. It might not be easy. It might not be popular. But he did it anyway, because it was the right thing to do. That's the definition of integrity.

I've long advocated that one of the keys to understanding Brian's body of work is acknowledging that he pushes his characters right through Joseph Campbell's threshold of monomythic self-discovery and sends them off on an identity quest. There are a couple recurring traits in his work I'm fond of, but the identity theme is the underlying connective tissue that binds them all together. Matthew Roth is no exception. He entered the DMZ as a spoiled kid looking for something to do, looking to transcend his outsider status, and ultimately looking to find himself. But before he can exit as a man, every mistake he's made must be reckoned with. It's every sloppy order he issued, every time he got played, and every time he posed as something he wasn't. Overwhelmed by physical risk and mental exhaustion, somehow, in the middle of a war, he found himself.

It's a minor miracle that any modern series enjoys a critically acclaimed six-year run and hits 72 consecutive issues. That longevity is a testament to the fact that *DMZ,* while certainly politically minded, was always a character-driven human story first. It's easy to get distracted by the frenetic action of the rolling tanks, the helicopter flyovers, and Wilson's raging parties down on Mott Street. Matty's journey ends, the war ends, and so, the series ends with *The Five Nations of New York.* But as Brian tells us in the final issue and love letter to the great metropolis, the culture and resiliency of New York City will live on eternally.

Brian's worked with so many skilled collaborators, running the gamut of the venture, from Will Dennis, Jeromy Cox, and Jared Fletcher, to John Paul Leon, Kristian Donaldson, and Nikki Cook. But, there's one who deserves special acknowledgment for his steadfast creative output. Riccardo Burchielli rode shotgun since day one, and it's impossible to imagine the book existing without his dire aesthetic. Riccardo always captured the personal emotion hiding in the grit and grime of the city. From Stuy-Town to Chinatown, from Midtown to Central Park, his hand is ever-present. *Riccardo works hard.* He never stops the artistic generosity. It's the way a piece of clothing hangs from a weary soldier on Day 204, the texture of a steaming bowl of noodles in a secluded kitchen, or the simple power of "*Every Day is 9/11*" scrawled in background graffiti. With Riccardo's dynamic line, the city breathes on the page with an authenticity seldom seen in the medium.

DMZ has proven to be such a prescient powder keg that it's easy to forget how ahead of the times it was. Brian's creations are always one step ahead, about five years out as leading indicators of the ideas woven deep within our generational consciousness. If *Channel Zero* was a spiritual precursor to *DMZ*, then special attention should be paid to the next shot fired, to the spiritual successor to *DMZ*. Everyone likes being in on the secret before it becomes breaking news. Odds are that Brian will be writing about it in diligently researched, forward-thinking, and emotionally charged stories. Remember that the next time he writes.

Remember that before the political landscape became so divisive, this book existed. Before the global financial calamities and unrelenting media spin, this book existed. Before the first African-American President, there was Decade Later, The Delgado Nation, and Radio Free DMZ. Before an Illinois Governor thought he had the juice of Michael Corleone and tried to sell a Senate seat, there was *DMZ*. Before it began to feel like the tapestry of the country was going to unravel into something apocalyptic, *DMZ* was unraveling it for you. Before anything was declared Too Big To Fail, before The Arab Spring, before The Occupy Movement…

You saw it here first.

In pop culture, poli-sci and sci-fi are commonly used, but "poli-fi" is a term rarely heard. The hybrid genre of political fiction is an underutilized storytelling engine, particularly when the speculative scenarios provoke, entertain, and resonate as strongly as *DMZ*. We're at a precarious time when the national ethos and personal identity impact our collective future. Before easy answers can be hurled out by the talking heads on TV, consider that complex issues require hard-earned immersive understanding and independent analysis. We learn these lessons vicariously through the experiences of Matthew Roth.

DMZ is the most relevant political allegory in early 21st century fiction. It captures a defining moment in the history of our generation, by the writer of our generation.

JUSTIN GIAMPAOLI
San Diego
February 2012

Justin Giampaoli has written several mini-comics, including The Mercy Killing, Silicon Valley Blues *and* Blood Orange. *He has blogged about comics since 2005 at the award-winning* Thirteen Minutes *and hosts interviews and behind-the-scenes content at* LIVE FROM THE DMZ, *the only site dedicated to Brian Wood's contemporary classic.*

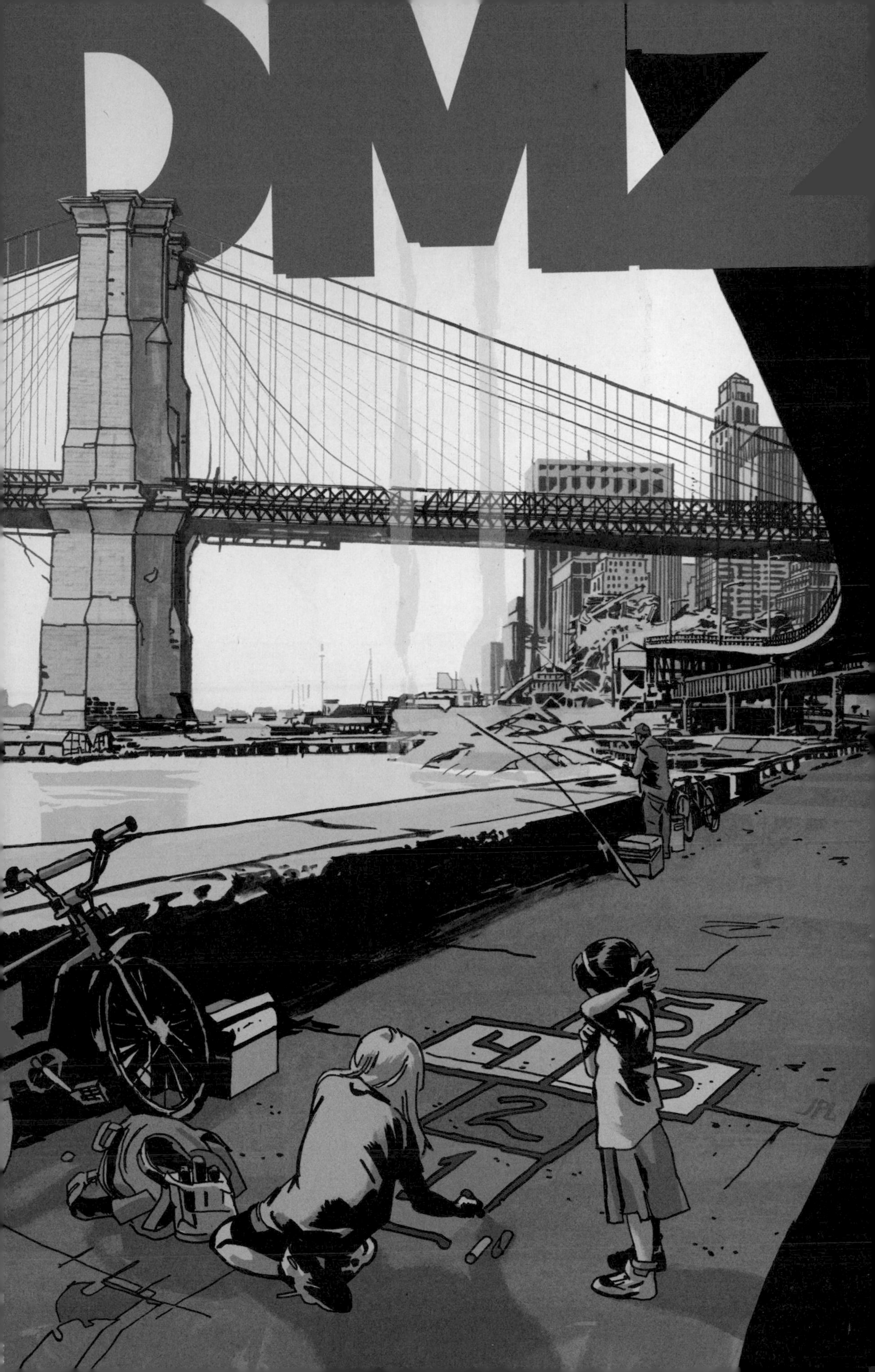
DMZ

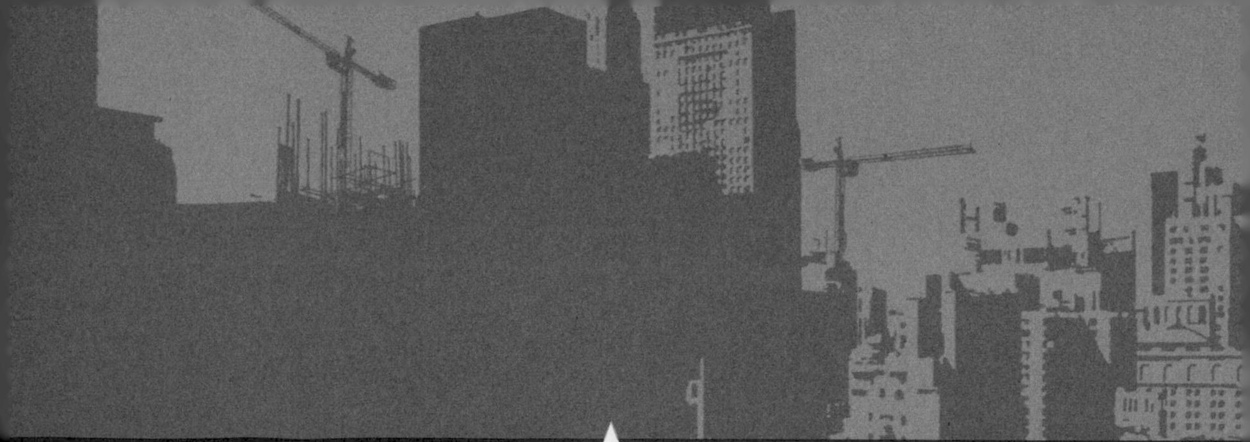

DMZ

THE FIVE NATIONS OF NEW YORK

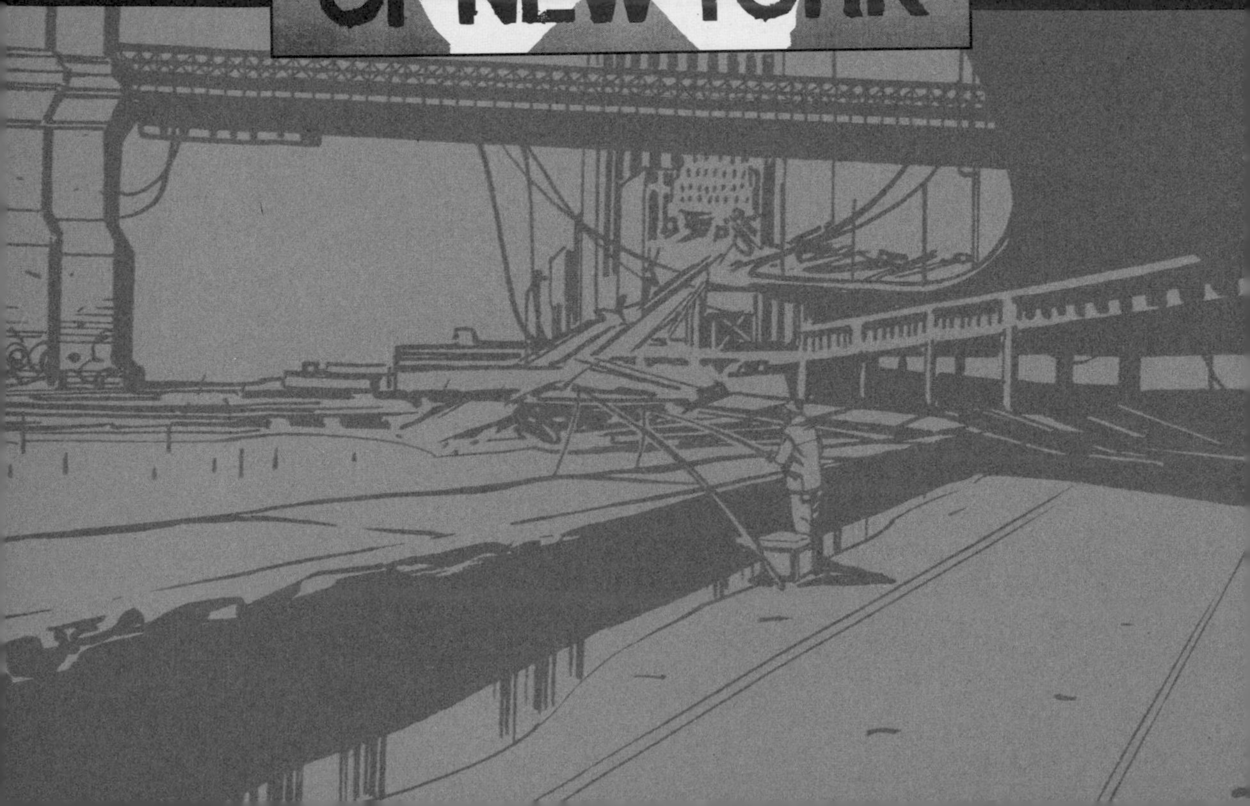

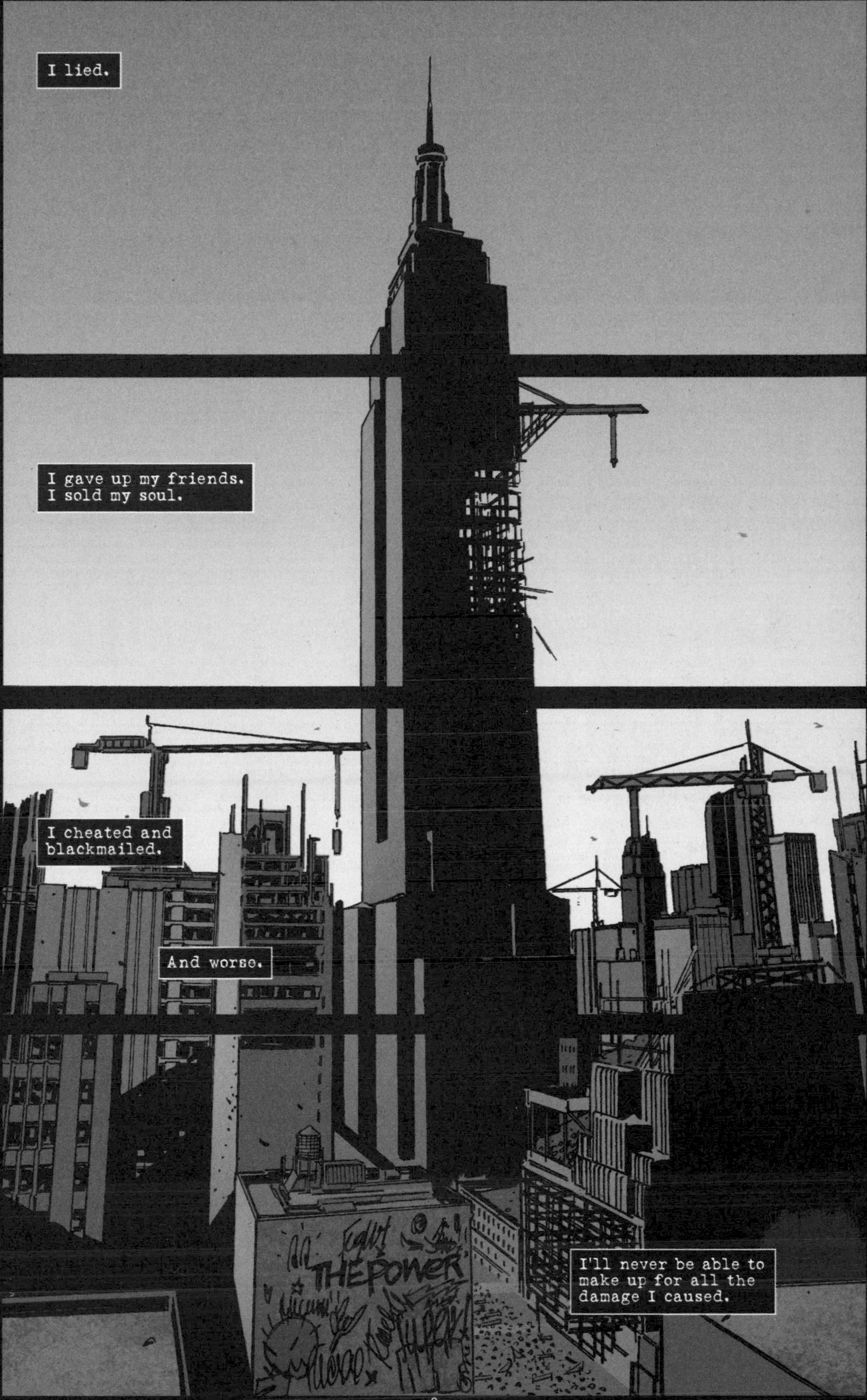
I lied.
I gave up my friends. I sold my soul.
I cheated and blackmailed.
And worse.
THE POWER
I'll never be able to make up for all the damage I caused.

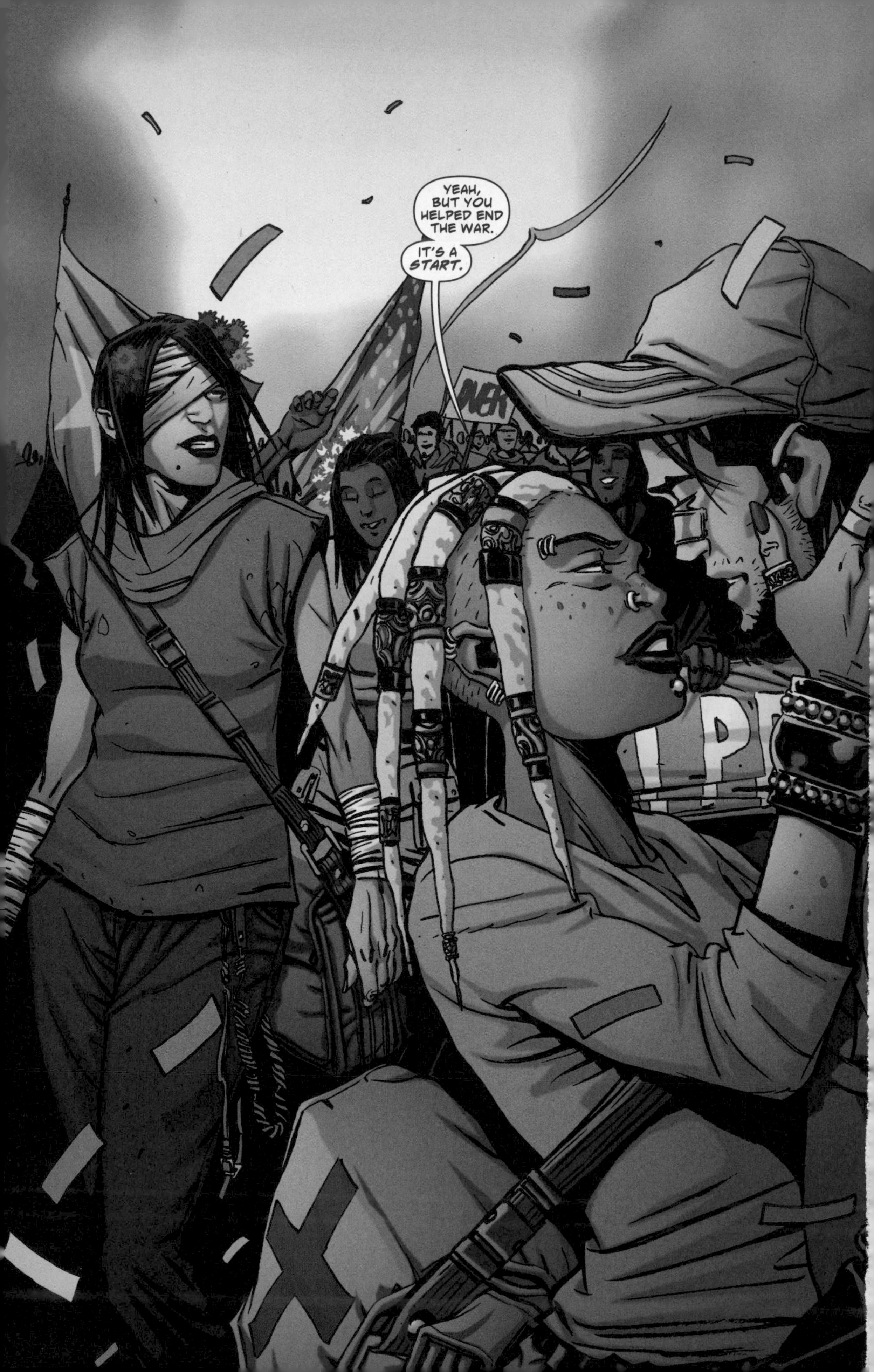
YEAH, BUT YOU HELPED END THE WAR.
IT'S A START.

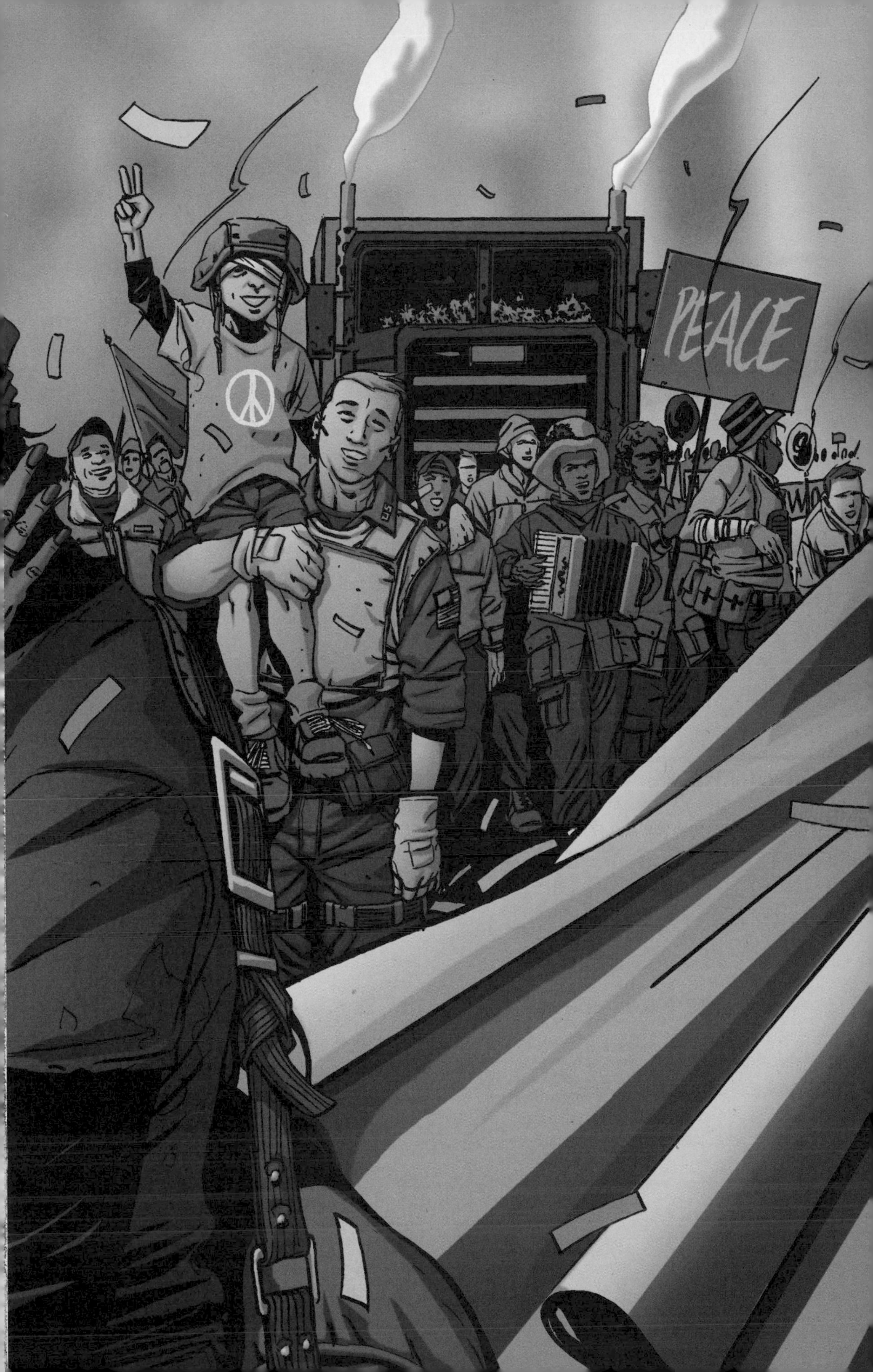
PEACE

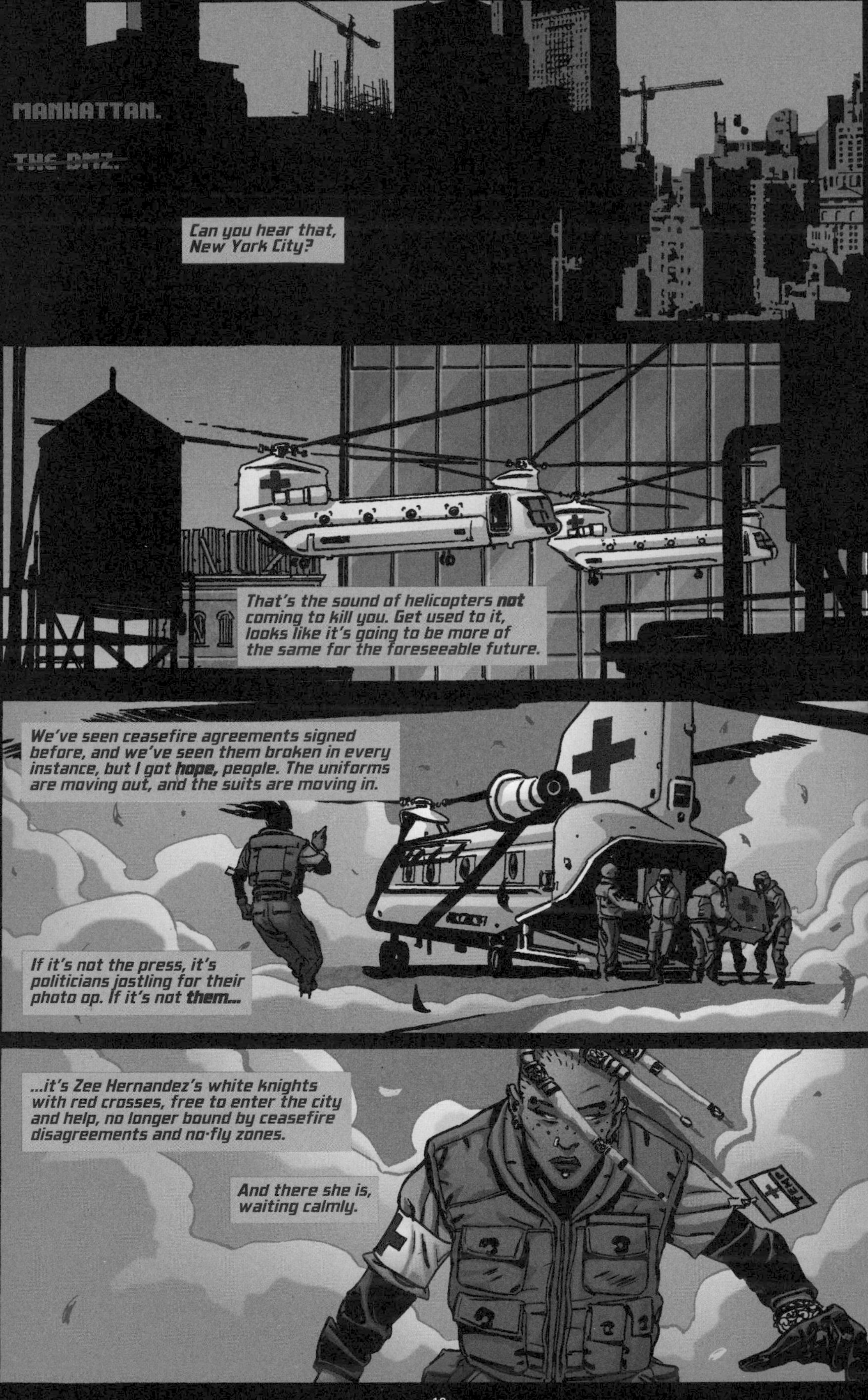
MANHATTAN.
THE DMZ.
Can you hear that, New York City?
That's the sound of helicopters **not** coming to kill you. Get used to it, looks like it's going to be more of the same for the foreseeable future.
We've seen ceasefire agreements signed before, and we've seen them broken in every instance, but I got **hope,** people. The uniforms are moving out, and the suits are moving in.
If it's not the press, it's politicians jostling for their photo op. If it's not **them...**
...it's Zee Hernandez's white knights with red crosses, free to enter the city and help, no longer bound by ceasefire disagreements and no-fly zones.
And there she is, waiting calmly.

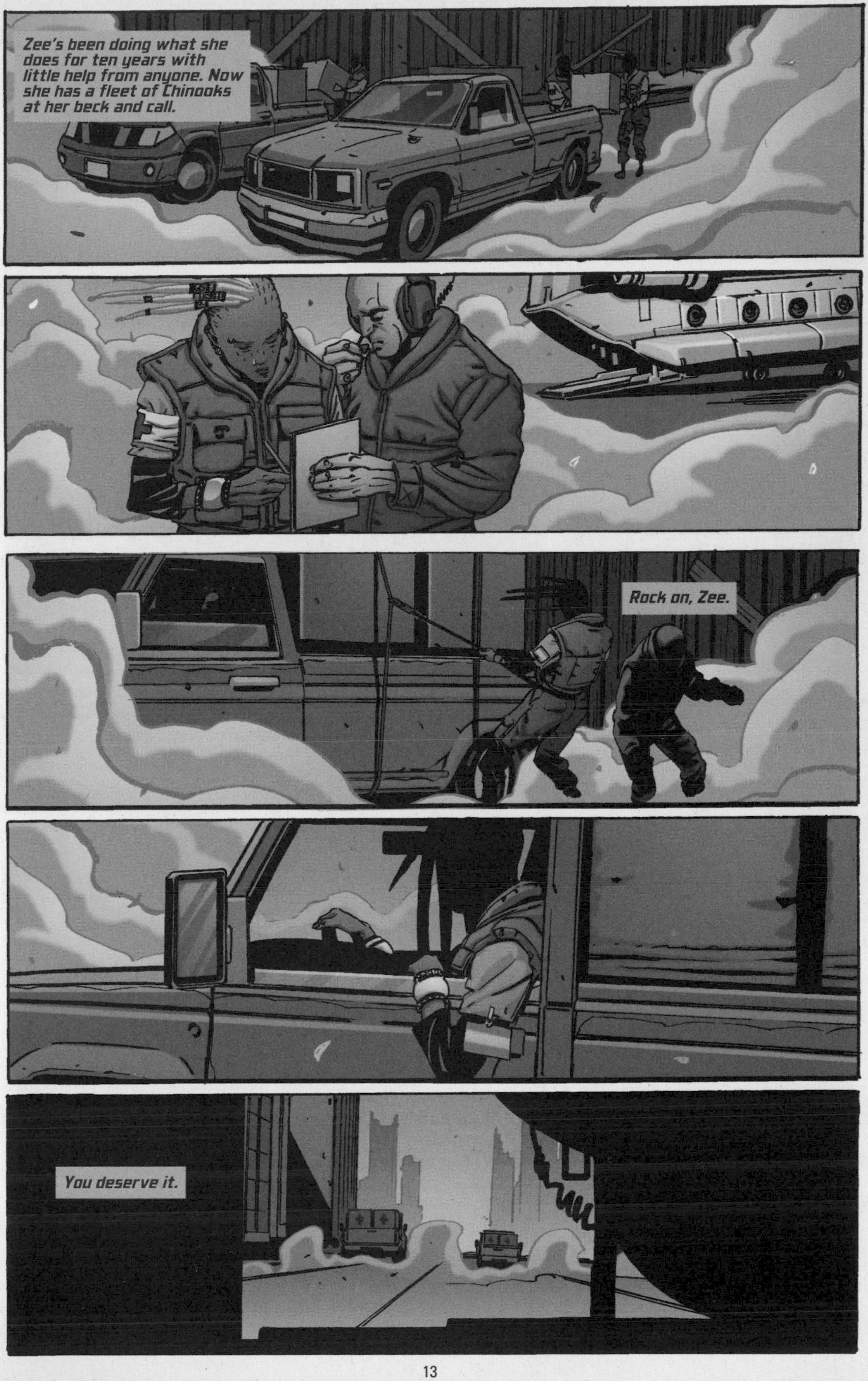

Zee's been doing what she does for ten years with little help from anyone. Now she has a fleet of Chinooks at her beck and call.
Rock on, Zee.
You deserve it.

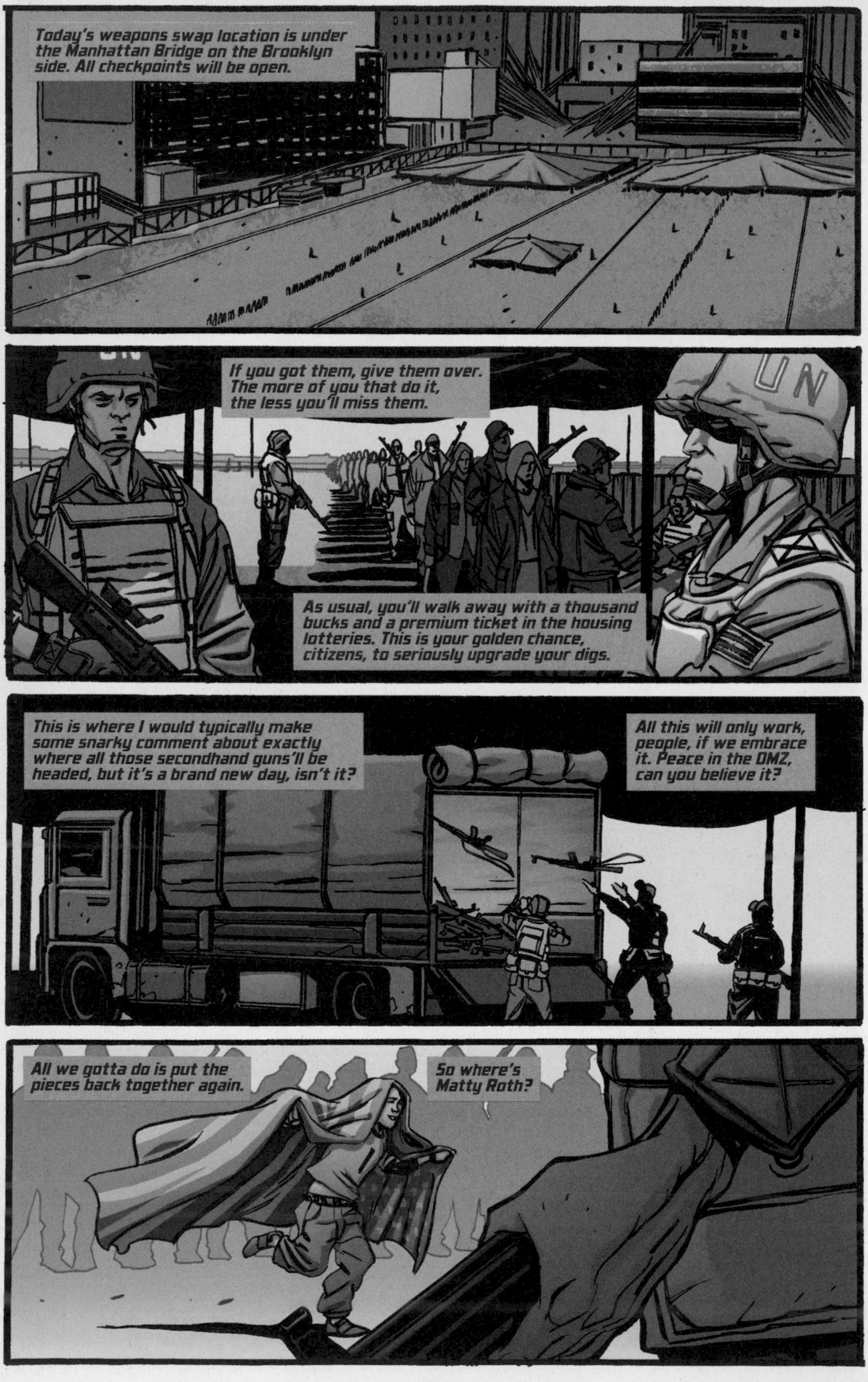
Today's weapons swap location is under the Manhattan Bridge on the Brooklyn side. All checkpoints will be open.
UN
If you got them, give them over. The more of you that do it, the less you'll miss them.
UN
As usual, you'll walk away with a thousand bucks and a premium ticket in the housing lotteries. This is your golden chance, citizens, to seriously upgrade your digs.
This is where I would typically make some snarky comment about exactly where all those secondhand guns'll be headed, but it's a brand new day, isn't it?
All this will only work, people, if we embrace it. Peace in the DMZ, can you believe it?
All we gotta do is put the pieces back together again.
So where's Matty Roth?

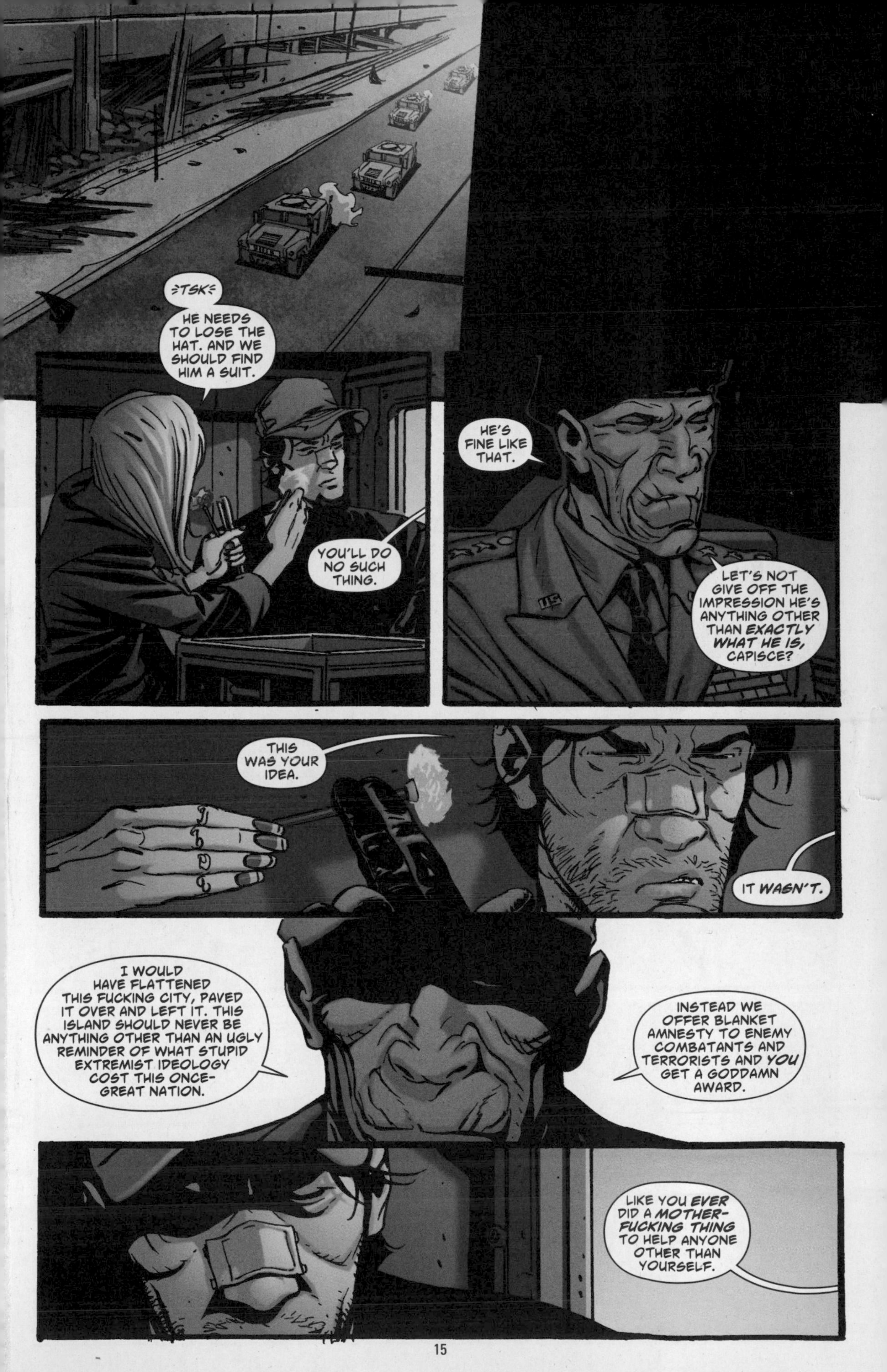
TSK
HE NEEDS TO LOSE THE HAT. AND WE SHOULD FIND HIM A SUIT.
YOU'LL DO NO SUCH THING.
HE'S FINE LIKE THAT.
LET'S NOT GIVE OFF THE IMPRESSION HE'S ANYTHING OTHER THAN EXACTLY WHAT HE IS, CAPISCE?
THIS WAS YOUR IDEA.
IT WASN'T.
I WOULD HAVE FLATTENED THIS FUCKING CITY, PAVED IT OVER AND LEFT IT. THIS ISLAND SHOULD NEVER BE ANYTHING OTHER THAN AN UGLY REMINDER OF WHAT STUPID EXTREMIST IDEOLOGY COST THIS ONCE-GREAT NATION.
INSTEAD WE OFFER BLANKET AMNESTY TO ENEMY COMBATANTS AND TERRORISTS AND YOU GET A GODDAMN AWARD.
LIKE YOU EVER DID A MOTHER-FUCKING THING TO HELP ANYONE OTHER THAN YOURSELF.

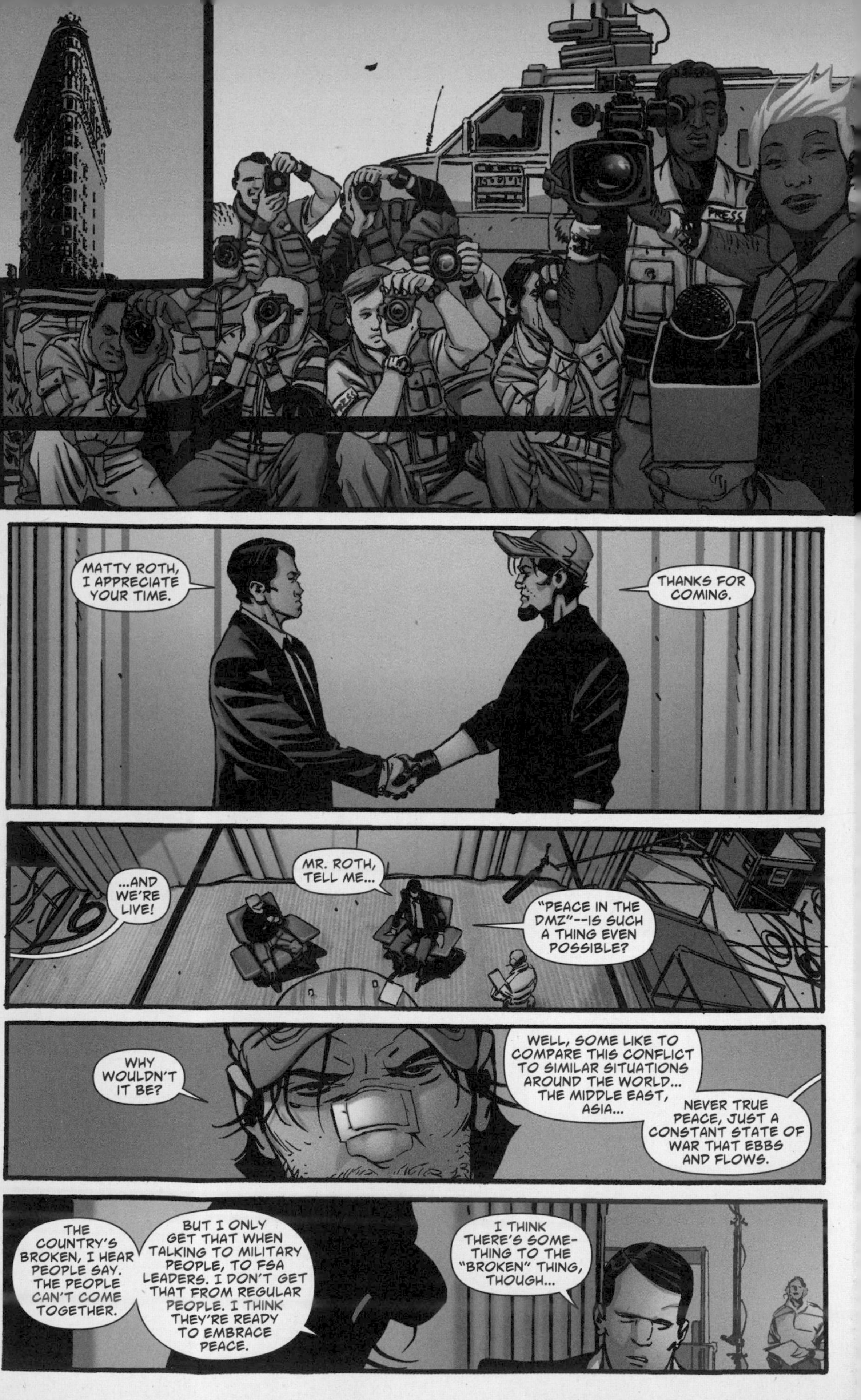

PRESS
MATTY ROTH, I APPRECIATE YOUR TIME.
THANKS FOR COMING.
...AND WE'RE LIVE!
MR. ROTH, TELL ME...
"PEACE IN THE DMZ"--IS SUCH A THING EVEN POSSIBLE?
WHY WOULDN'T IT BE?
WELL, SOME LIKE TO COMPARE THIS CONFLICT TO SIMILAR SITUATIONS AROUND THE WORLD... THE MIDDLE EAST, ASIA...
NEVER TRUE PEACE, JUST A CONSTANT STATE OF WAR THAT EBBS AND FLOWS.
THE COUNTRY'S BROKEN, I HEAR PEOPLE SAY. THE PEOPLE CAN'T COME TOGETHER.
BUT I ONLY GET THAT WHEN TALKING TO MILITARY PEOPLE, TO FSA LEADERS. I DON'T GET THAT FROM REGULAR PEOPLE. I THINK THEY'RE READY TO EMBRACE PEACE.
I THINK THERE'S SOME-THING TO THE "BROKEN" THING, THOUGH...

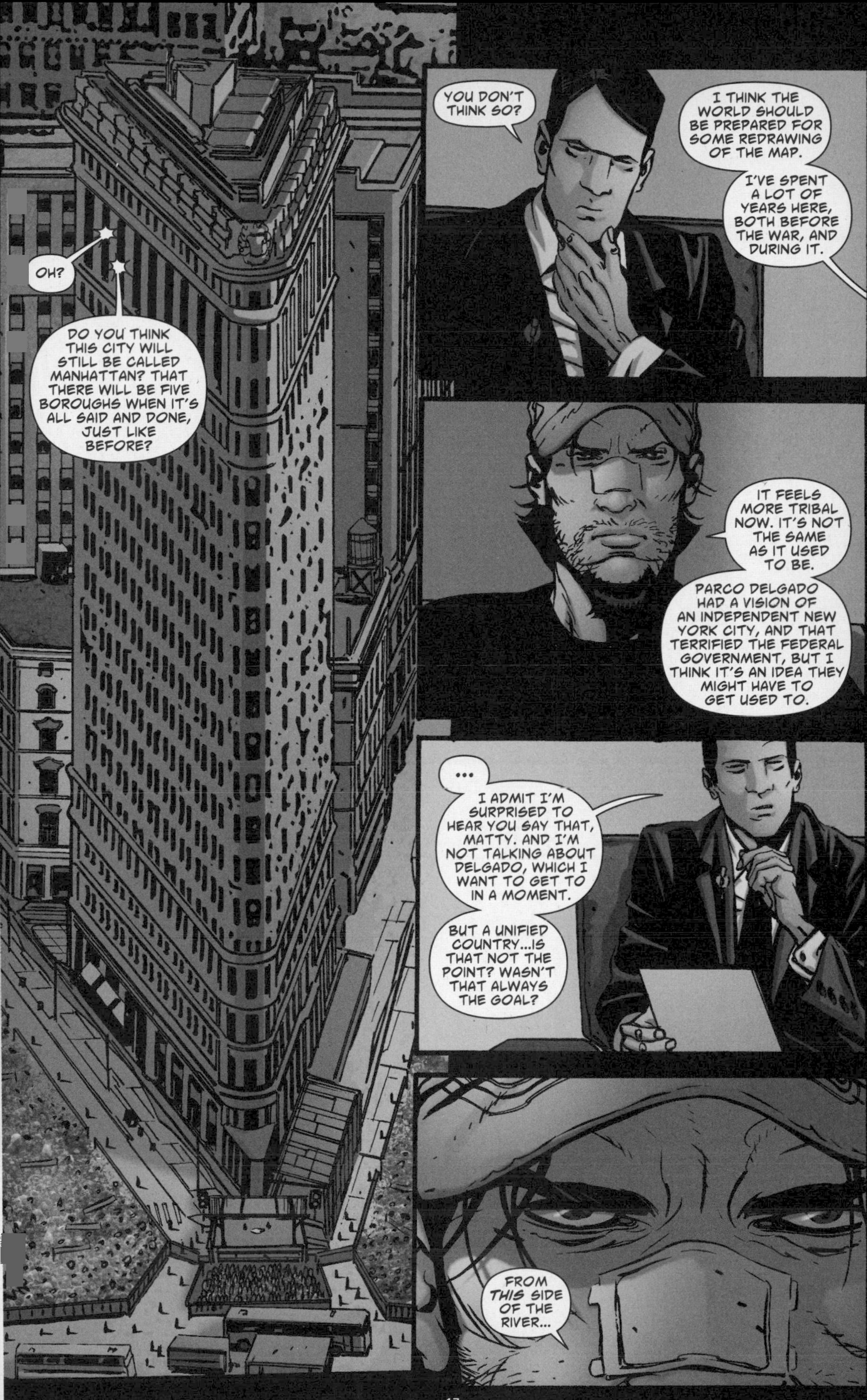
OH?
DO YOU THINK THIS CITY WILL STILL BE CALLED MANHATTAN? THAT THERE WILL BE FIVE BOROUGHS WHEN IT'S ALL SAID AND DONE, JUST LIKE BEFORE?
YOU DON'T THINK SO?
I THINK THE WORLD SHOULD BE PREPARED FOR SOME REDRAWING OF THE MAP.
I'VE SPENT A LOT OF YEARS HERE, BOTH BEFORE THE WAR, AND DURING IT.
IT FEELS MORE TRIBAL NOW. IT'S NOT THE SAME AS IT USED TO BE.
PARCO DELGADO HAD A VISION OF AN INDEPENDENT NEW YORK CITY, AND THAT TERRIFIED THE FEDERAL GOVERNMENT, BUT I THINK IT'S AN IDEA THEY MIGHT HAVE TO GET USED TO.
...
I ADMIT I'M SURPRISED TO HEAR YOU SAY THAT, MATTY. AND I'M NOT TALKING ABOUT DELGADO, WHICH I WANT TO GET TO IN A MOMENT.
BUT A UNIFIED COUNTRY...IS THAT NOT THE POINT? WASN'T THAT ALWAYS THE GOAL?
FROM THIS SIDE OF THE RIVER...

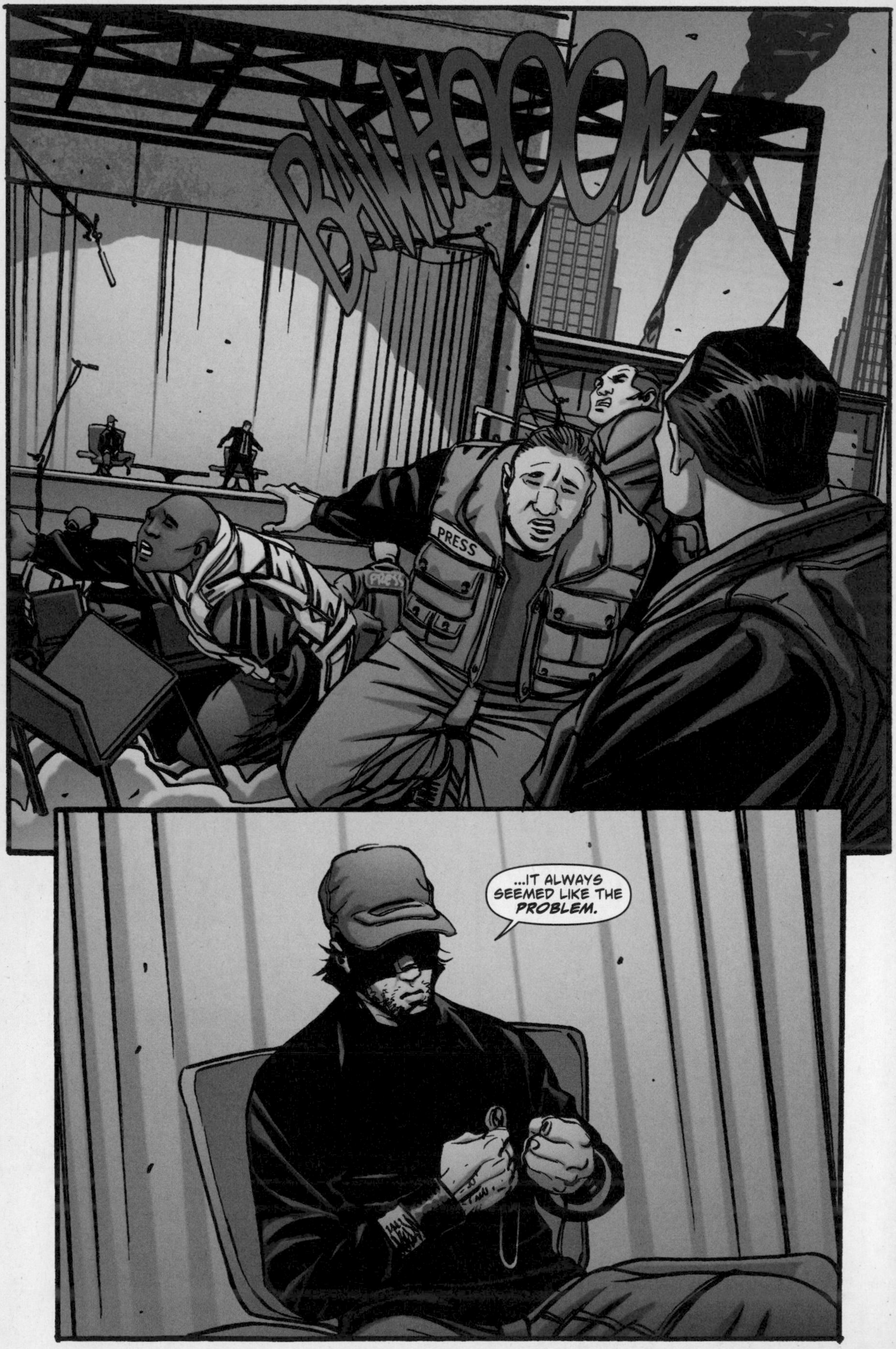
BAWHOOOM
PRESS
...IT ALWAYS SEEMED LIKE THE *PROBLEM*.

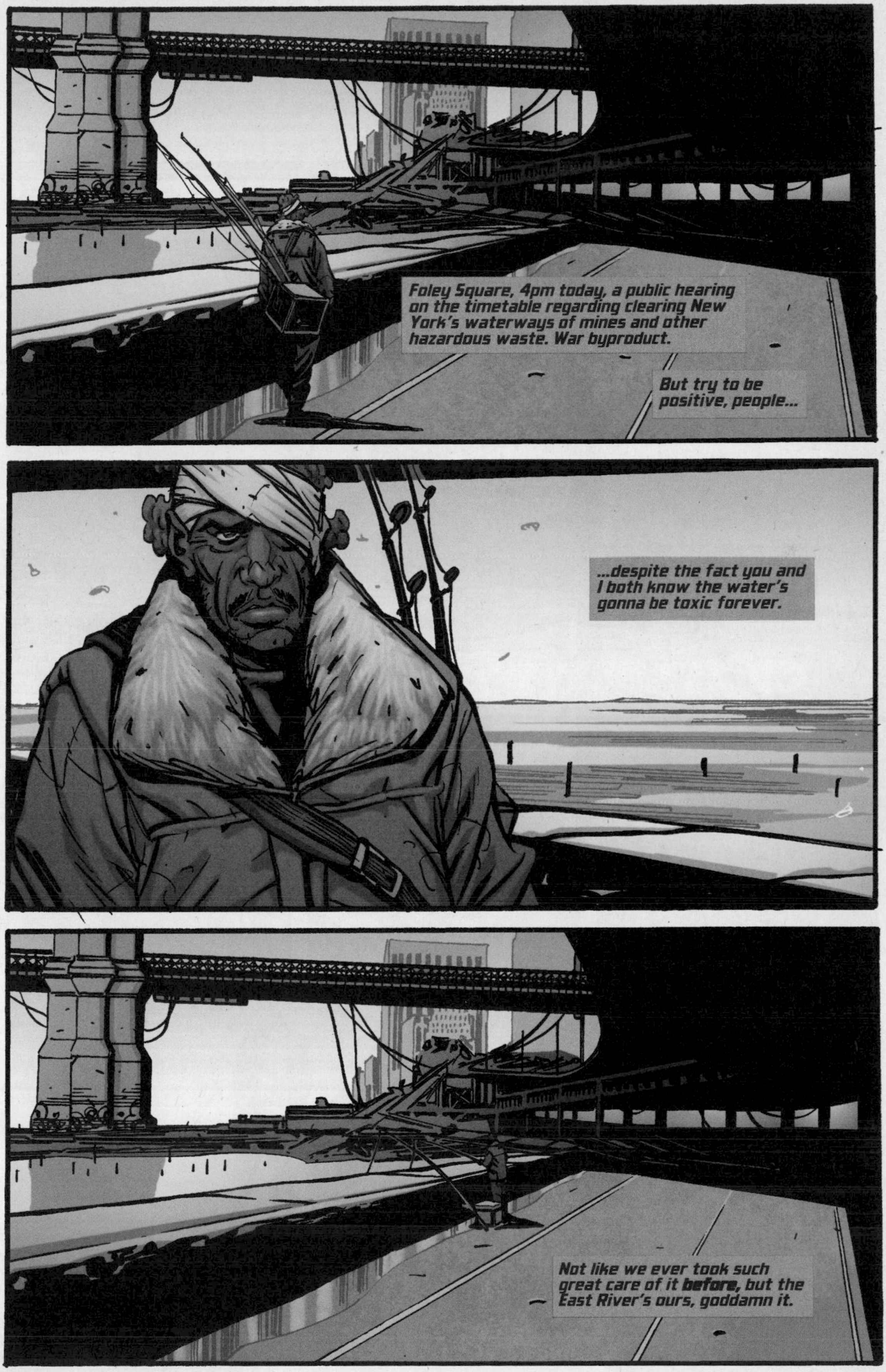

Foley Square, 4pm today, a public hearing on the timetable regarding clearing New York's waterways of mines and other hazardous waste. War byproduct.
But try to be positive, people...
...despite the fact you and I both know the water's gonna be toxic forever.
Not like we ever took such great care of it **before**, but the East River's ours, goddamn it.

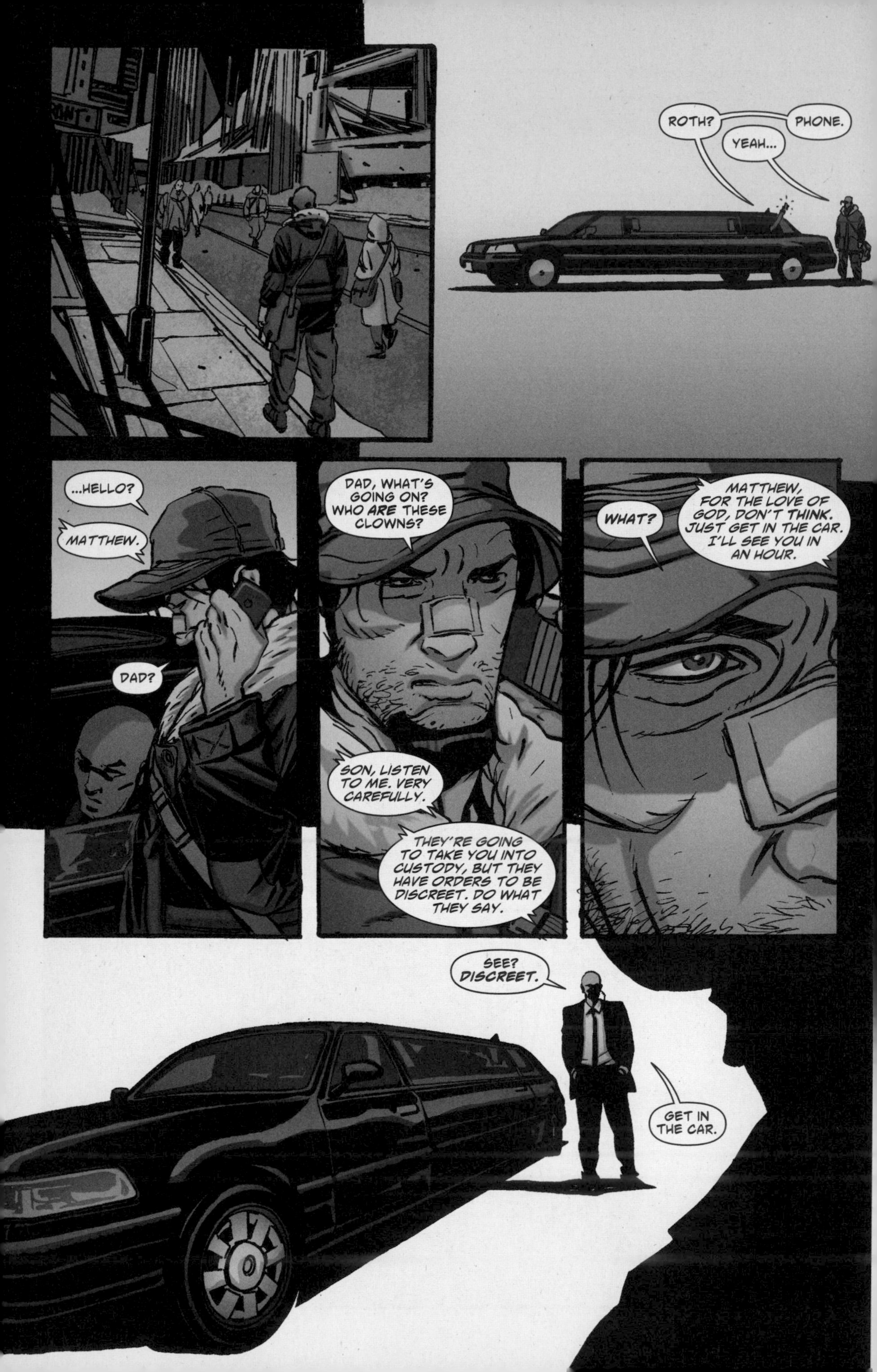
ROTH?
YEAH...
PHONE.
...HELLO?
MATTHEW.
DAD?
DAD, WHAT'S GOING ON? WHO ARE THESE CLOWNS?
SON, LISTEN TO ME. VERY CAREFULLY.
THEY'RE GOING TO TAKE YOU INTO CUSTODY, BUT THEY HAVE ORDERS TO BE DISCREET. DO WHAT THEY SAY.
WHAT?
MATTHEW, FOR THE LOVE OF GOD, DON'T THINK. JUST GET IN THE CAR. I'LL SEE YOU IN AN HOUR.
SEE? DISCREET.
GET IN THE CAR.

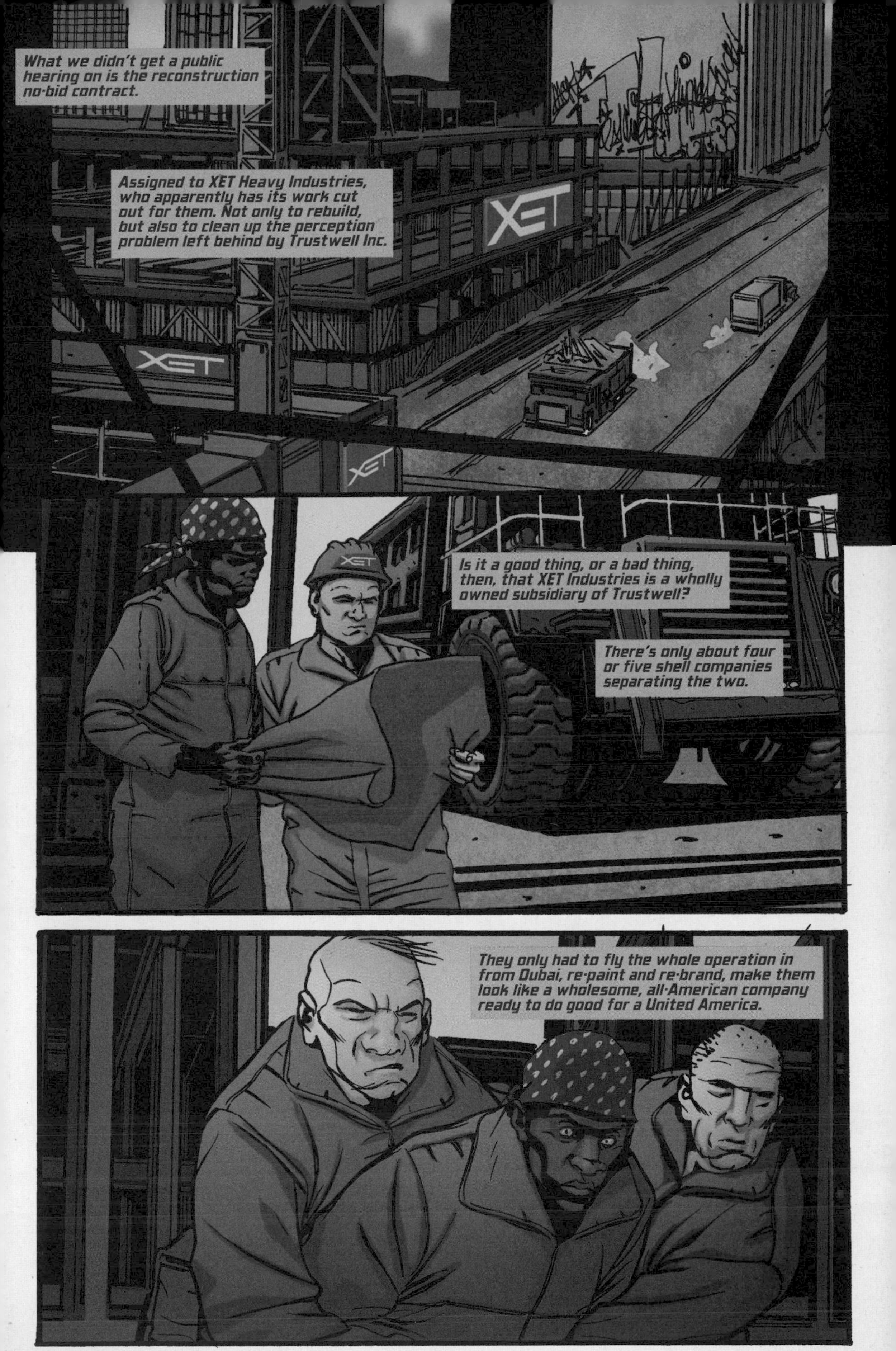
What we didn't get a public hearing on is the reconstruction no-bid contract.
Assigned to XET Heavy Industries, who apparently has its work cut out for them. Not only to rebuild, but also to clean up the perception problem left behind by Trustwell Inc.
XET
XET
XET
XET
Is it a good thing, or a bad thing, then, that XET Industries is a wholly owned subsidiary of Trustwell?
There's only about four or five shell companies separating the two.
They only had to fly the whole operation in from Dubai, re-paint and re-brand, make them look like a wholesome, all-American company ready to do good for a United America.

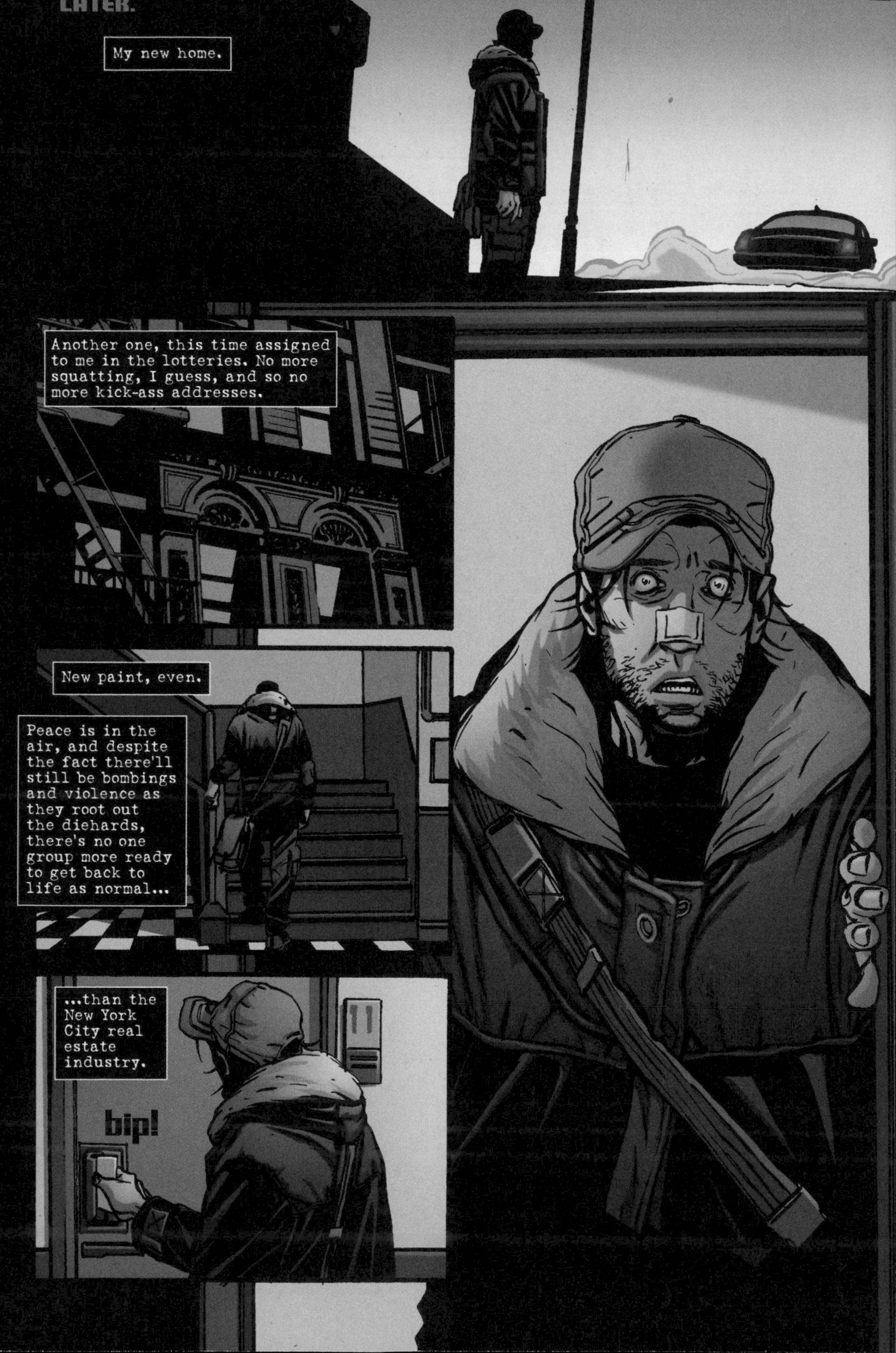
LATER.
My new home.
Another one, this time assigned to me in the lotteries. No more squatting, I guess, and so no more kick-ass addresses.
New paint, even.
Peace is in the air, and despite the fact there'll still be bombings and violence as they root out the diehards, there's no one group more ready to get back to life as normal...
...than the New York City real estate industry.
bip!

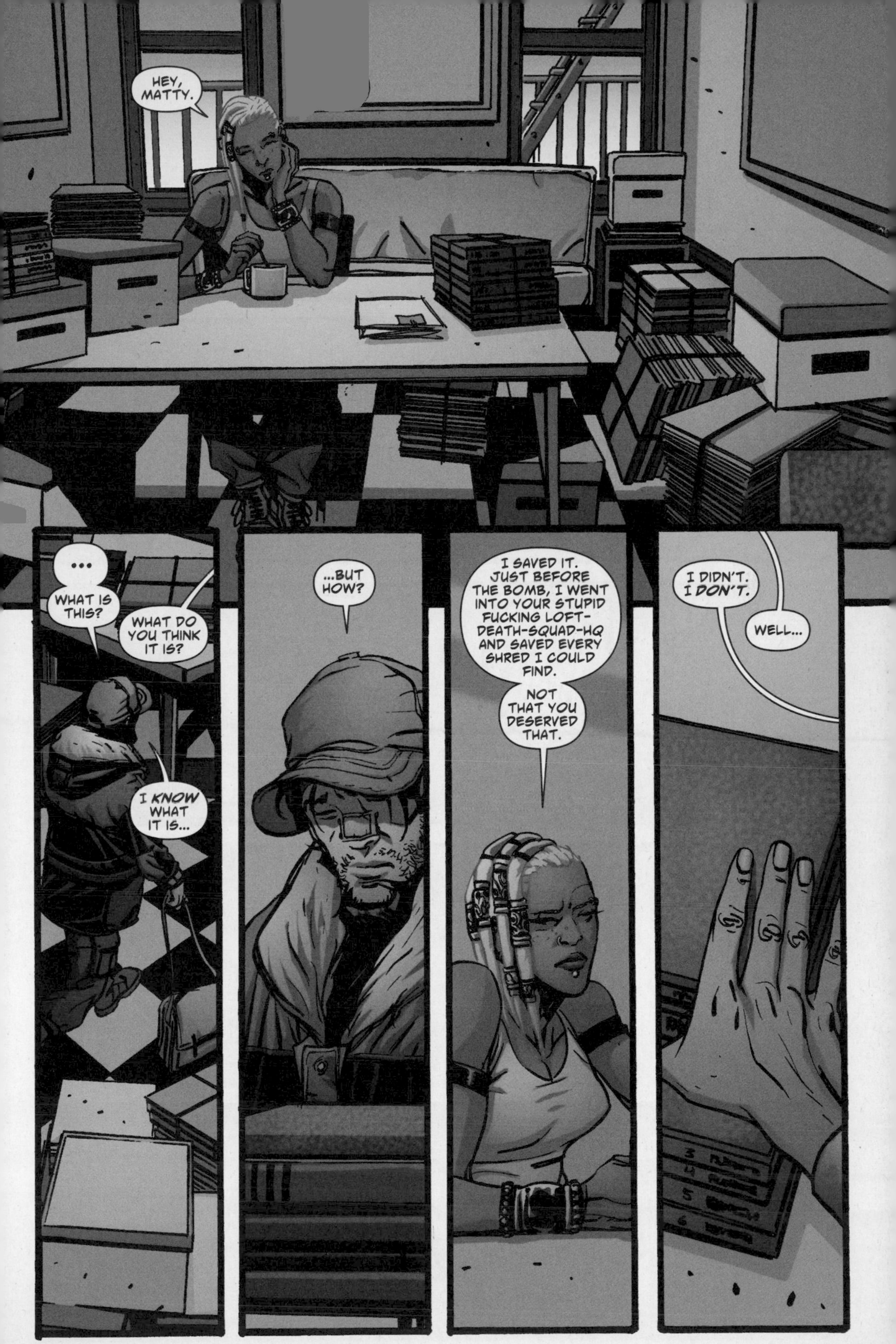
HEY, MATTY.
...
WHAT IS THIS?
WHAT DO YOU THINK IT IS?
I KNOW WHAT IT IS...
...BUT HOW?
I SAVED IT. JUST BEFORE THE BOMB, I WENT INTO YOUR STUPID FUCKING LOFT-DEATH-SQUAD-HQ AND SAVED EVERY SHRED I COULD FIND.
NOT THAT YOU DESERVED THAT.
I DIDN'T. I DON'T.
WELL...

...SOMEDAY YOU MIGHT.

AND EVEN IF YOU NEVER DID, IT'S NOT ALL ABOUT YOU, ROTH.

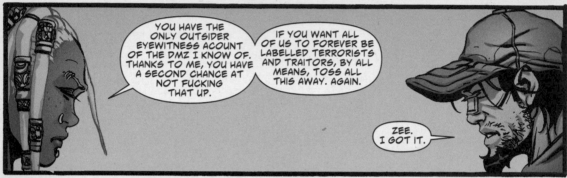

YOU HAVE THE ONLY OUTSIDER EYEWITNESS ACOUNT OF THE DMZ I KNOW OF. THANKS TO ME, YOU HAVE A SECOND CHANCE AT NOT FUCKING THAT UP.

IF YOU WANT ALL OF US TO FOREVER BE LABELLED TERRORISTS AND TRAITORS, BY ALL MEANS, TOSS ALL THIS AWAY. AGAIN.

ZEE. I GOT IT.

I HATED YOU. FOR A LONG TIME AND FOR PRETTY GOOD REASONS, I HATED YOUR GUTS.

AT SOME POINT, THOUGH, I FIGURED IN A CITY FULL OF SELF-OBSESSED, GUN-CARRYING ASSHOLES, YOU WERE KIND OF A LAME SPECIMEN. AND WHAT *MADE* YOU SO LAME...

...IS YOUR HEART WAS NEVER IN IT.

ONCE I FIGURED THAT OUT, IT WASN'T A MATTER OF IF, BUT *WHEN* YOU'D COME BACK AROUND.

SEE YOU LATER.

YOU CAN DECIDE IF YOU WANT TO TELL ME ABOUT THE GOONS IN THE TOWNCAR OR NOT.

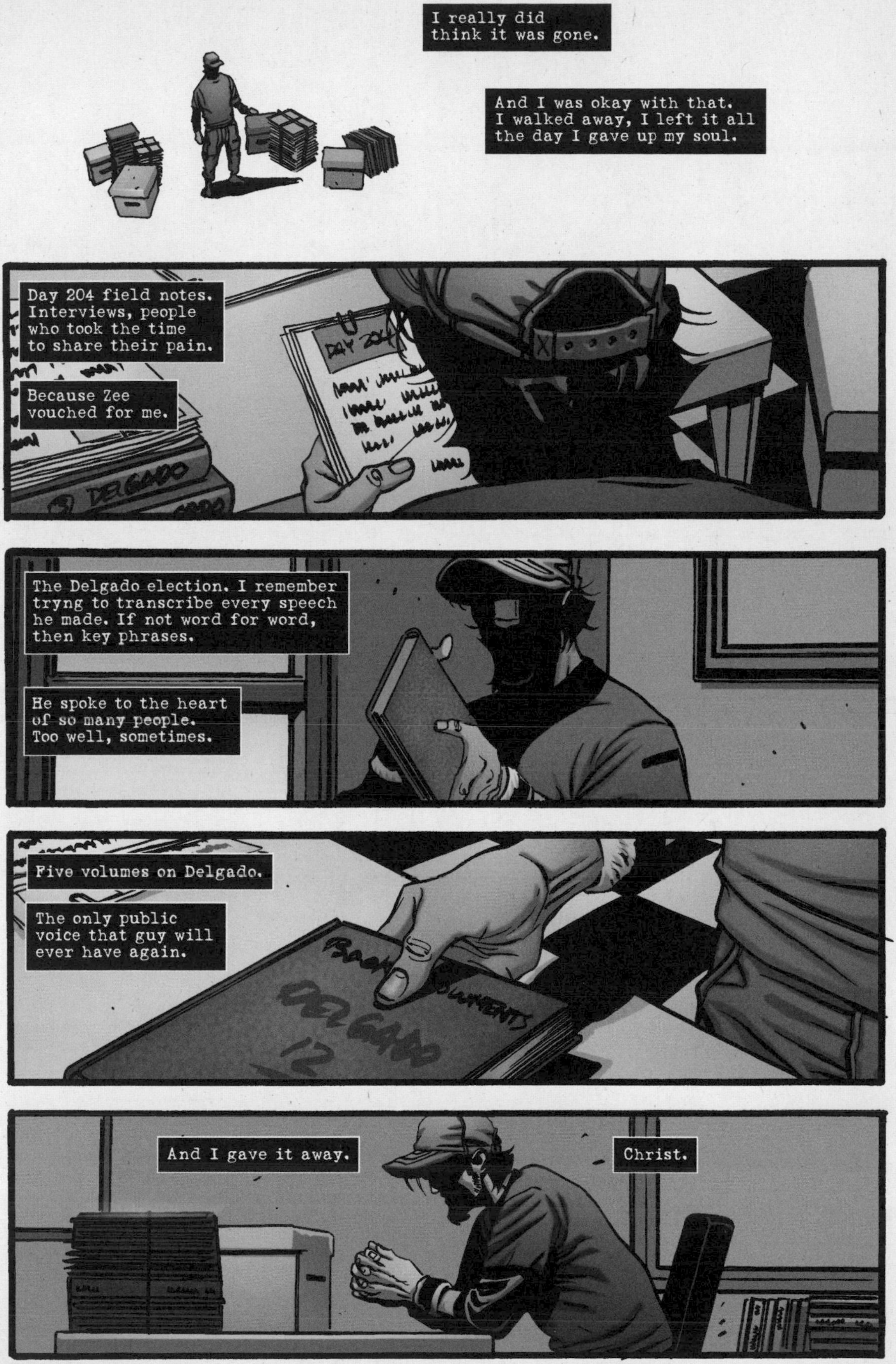
I really did think it was gone.
And I was okay with that. I walked away, I left it all the day I gave up my soul.
Day 204 field notes. Interviews, people who took the time to share their pain.
Because Zee vouched for me.
The Delgado election. I remember tryng to transcribe every speech he made. If not word for word, then key phrases.
He spoke to the heart of so many people. Too well, sometimes.
Five volumes on Delgado.
The only public voice that guy will ever have again.
And I gave it away.
Christ.

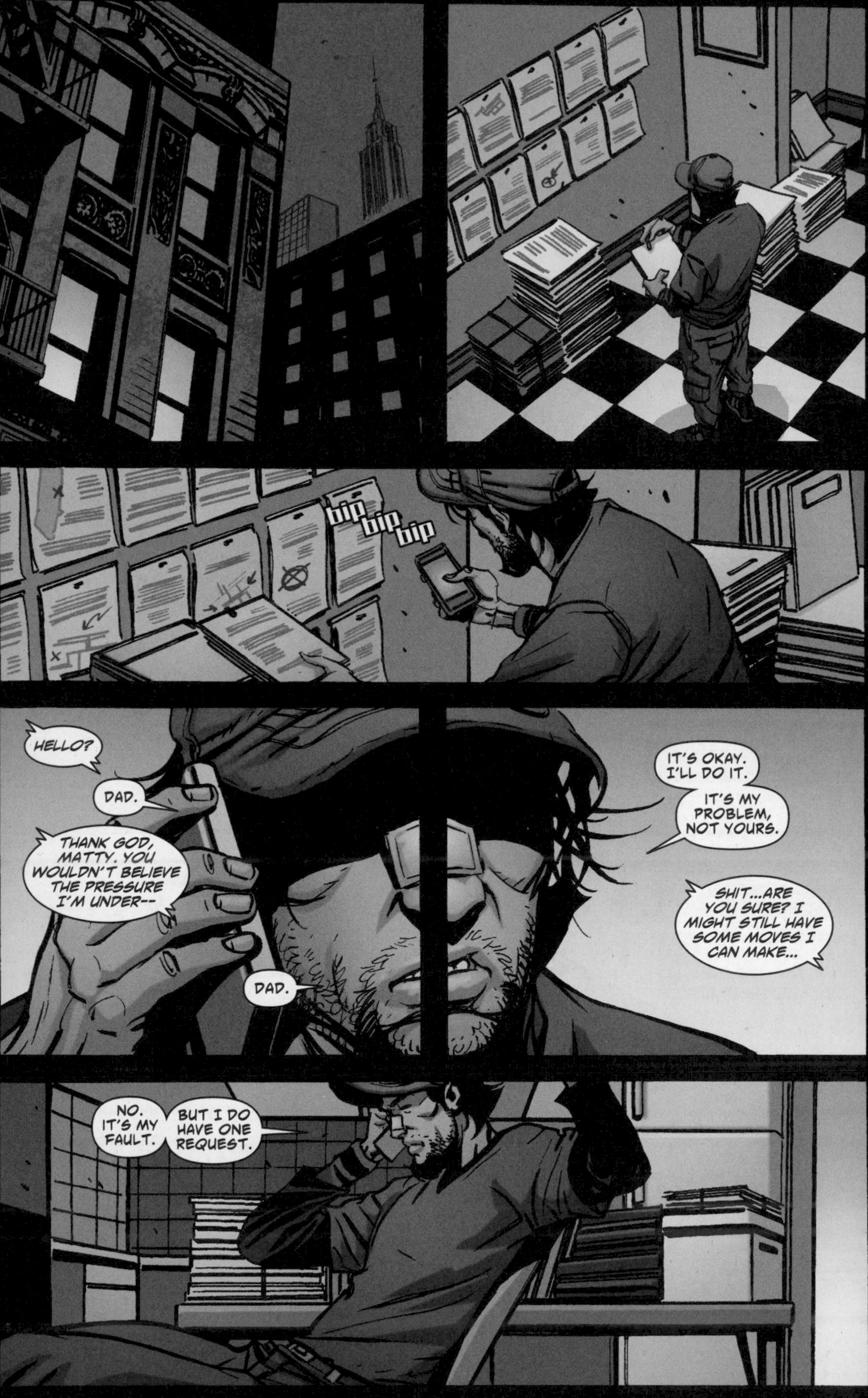
bip bip bip
HELLO?
DAD.
THANK GOD, MATTY. YOU WOULDN'T BELIEVE THE PRESSURE I'M UNDER--
DAD.
IT'S OKAY. I'LL DO IT.
IT'S MY PROBLEM, NOT YOURS.
SHIT...ARE YOU SURE? I MIGHT STILL HAVE SOME MOVES I CAN MAKE...
NO. IT'S MY FAULT.
BUT I DO HAVE ONE REQUEST.

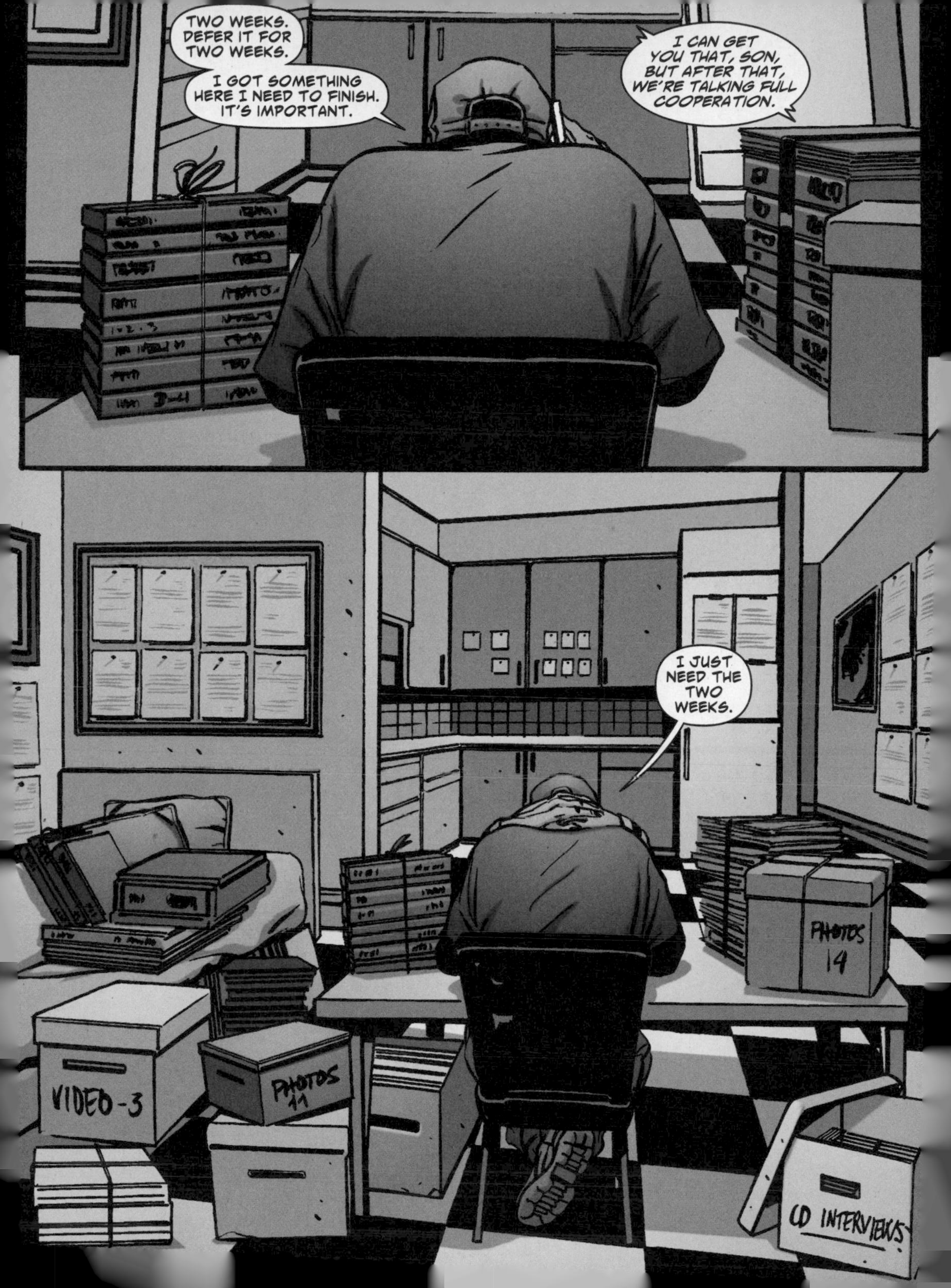
TWO WEEKS. DEFER IT FOR TWO WEEKS.
I GOT SOMETHING HERE I NEED TO FINISH. IT'S IMPORTANT.
I CAN GET YOU THAT, SON, BUT AFTER THAT, WE'RE TALKING FULL COOPERATION.
I JUST NEED THE TWO WEEKS.
PHOTOS 14
VIDEO-3
PHOTOS 11
CD INTERVIEWS

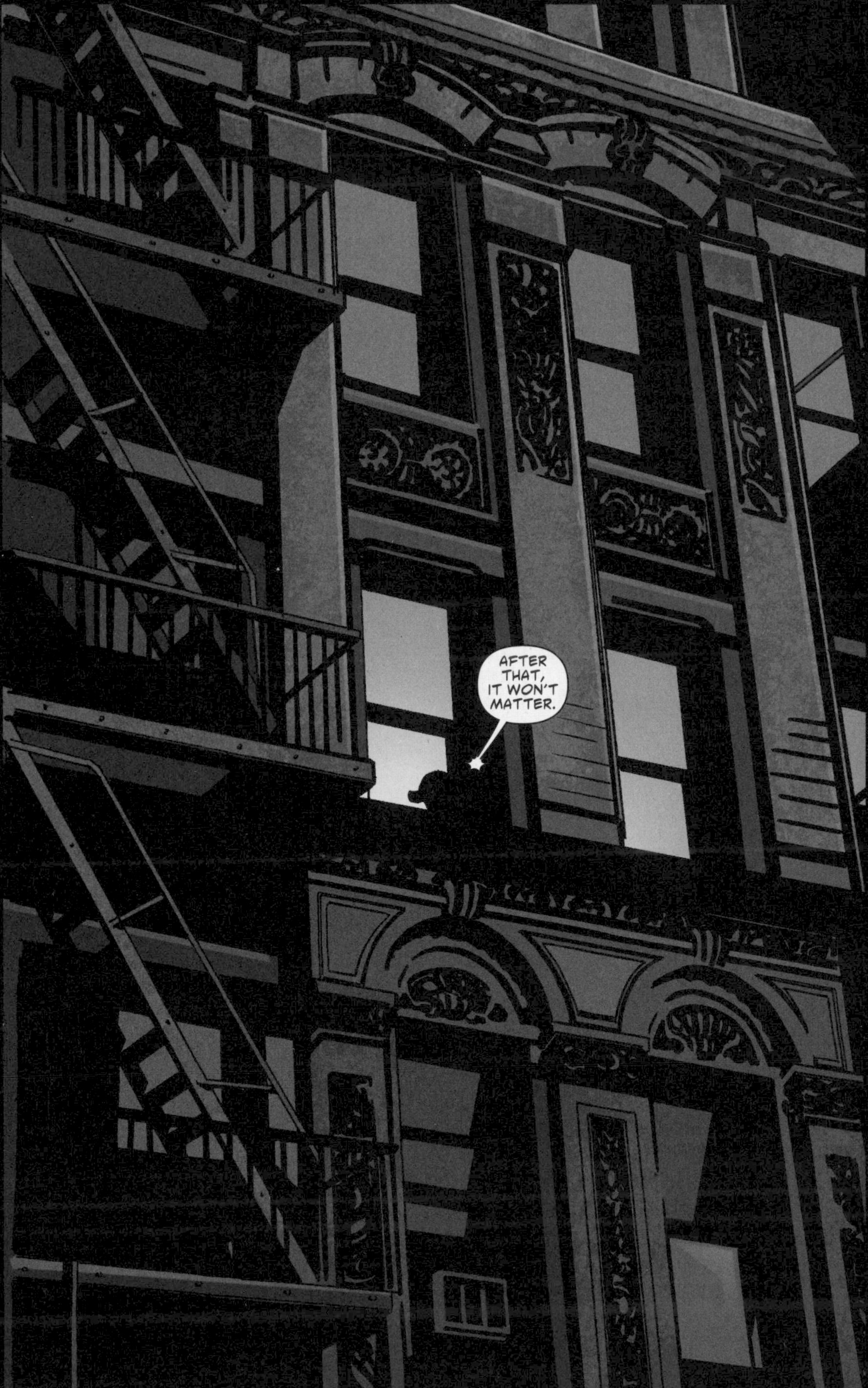
AFTER THAT, IT WON'T MATTER.

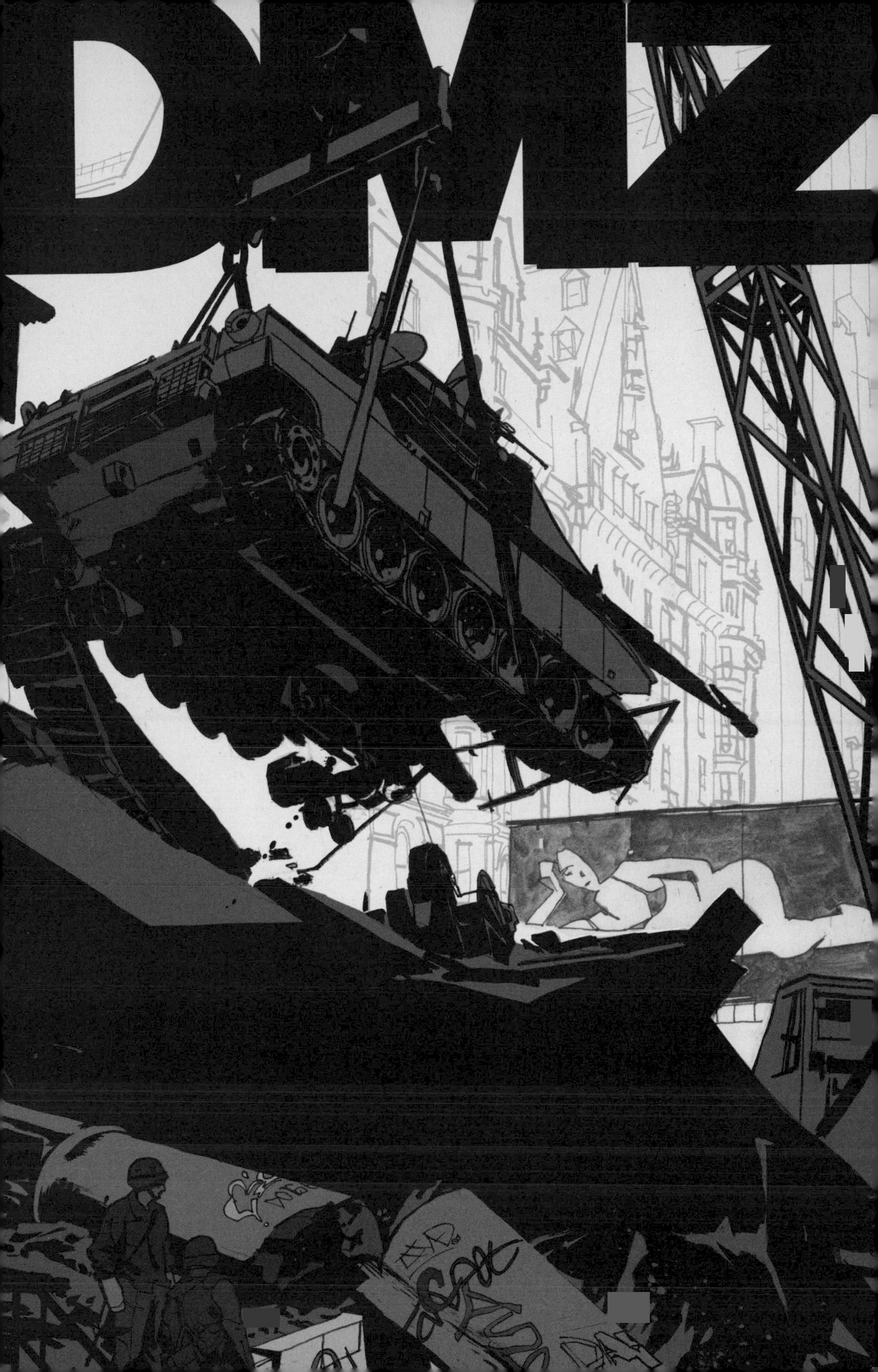
DMZ

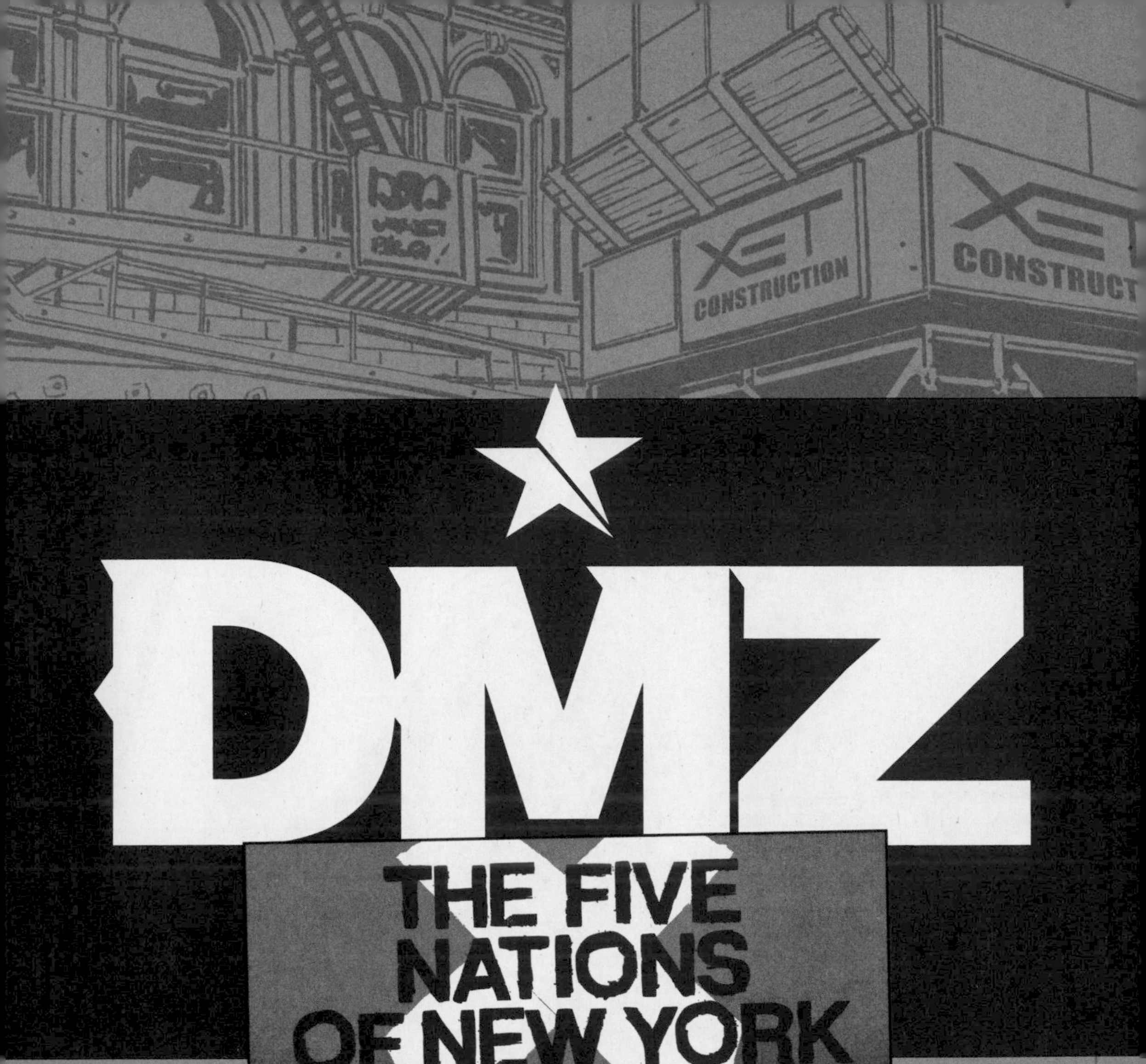
CONSTRUCTION
CONSTRUCT

DMZ

THE FIVE NATIONS OF NEW YORK

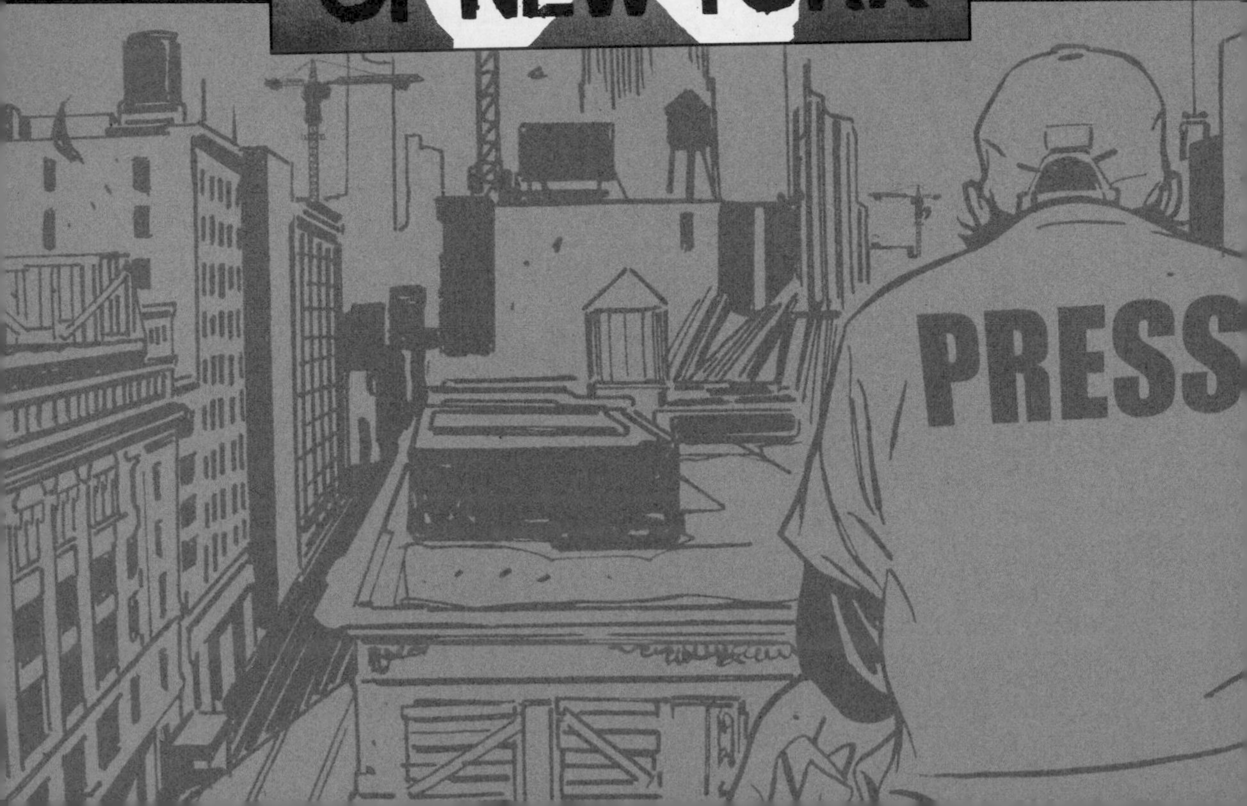
PRESS

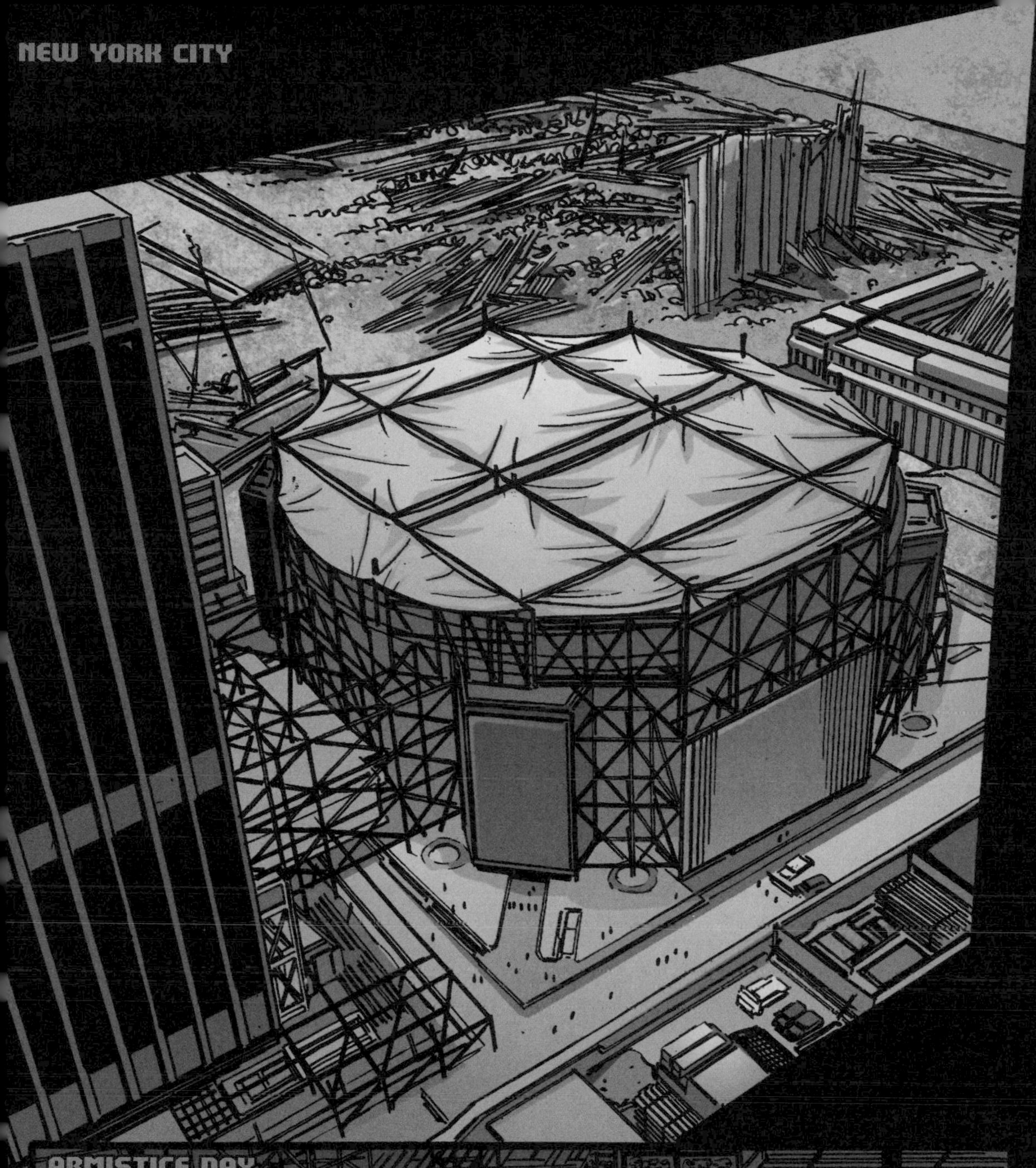
NEW YORK CITY

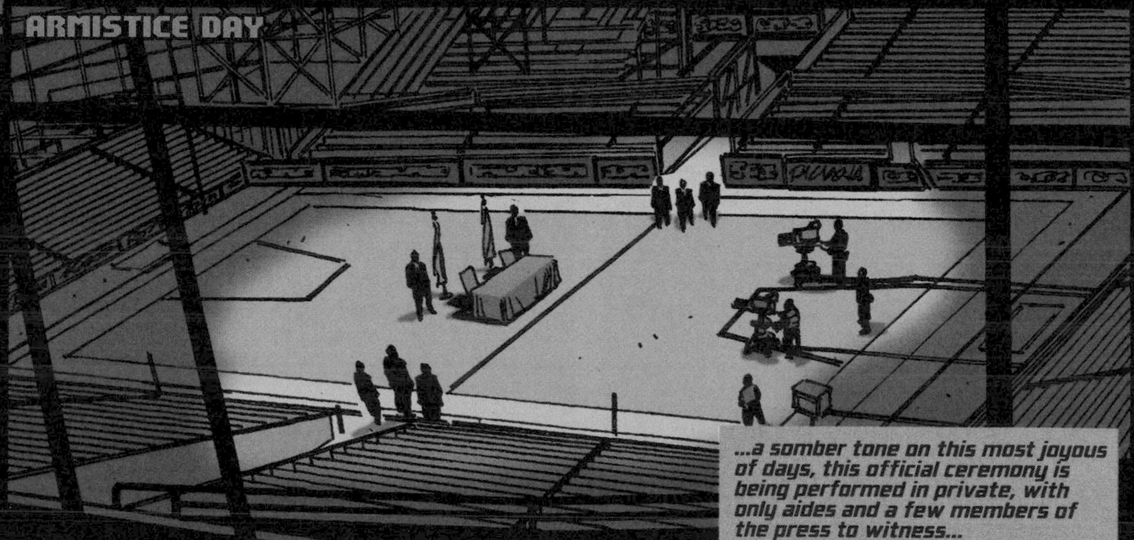
ARMISTICE DAY
...a somber tone on this most joyous of days, this official ceremony is being performed in private, with only aides and a few members of the press to witness...

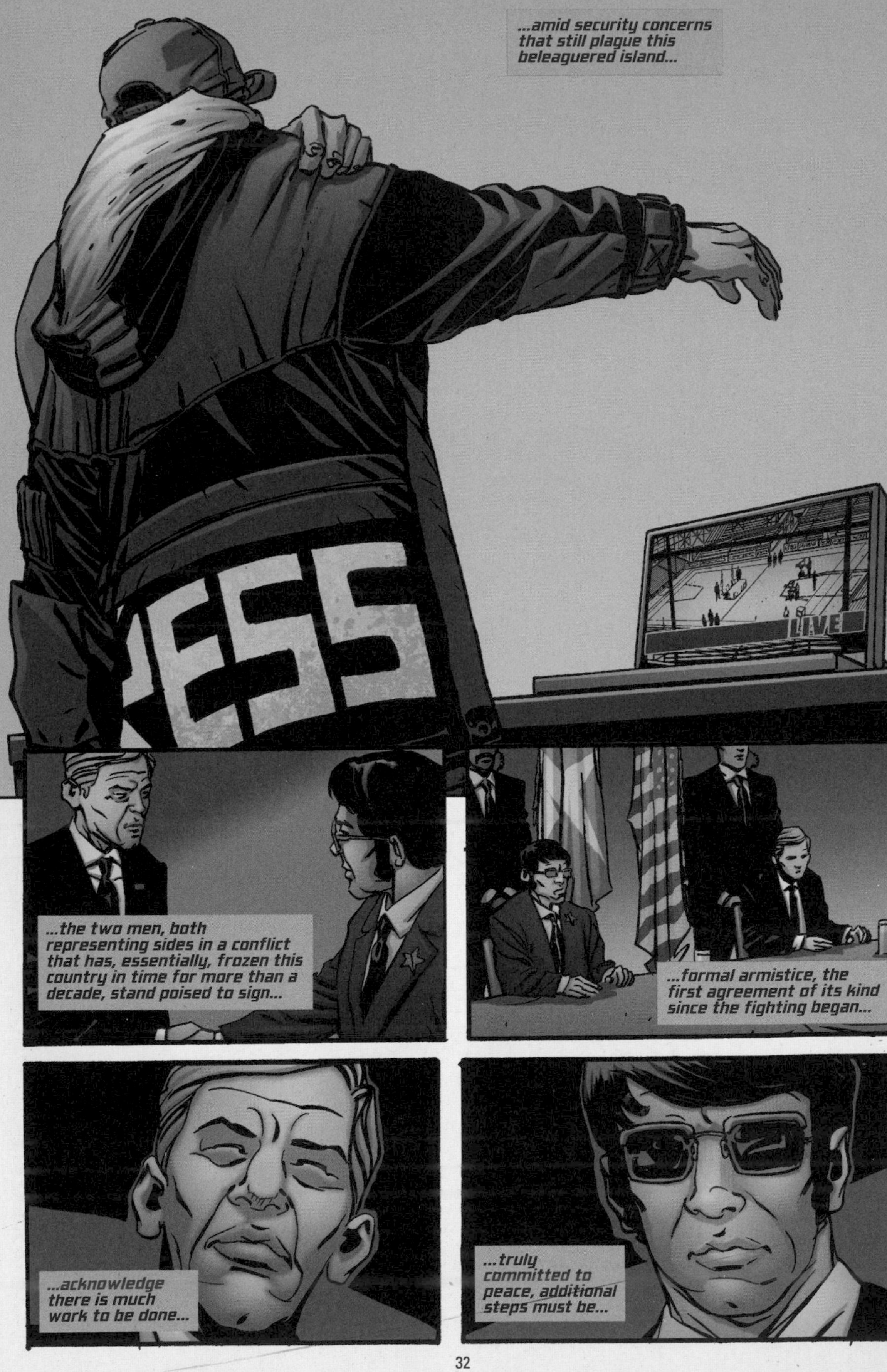
...amid security concerns that still plague this beleaguered island...
PESS
LIVE
...the two men, both representing sides in a conflict that has, essentially, frozen this country in time for more than a decade, stand poised to sign...
...formal armistice, the first agreement of its kind since the fighting began...
...acknowledge there is much work to be done...
...truly committed to peace, additional steps must be...

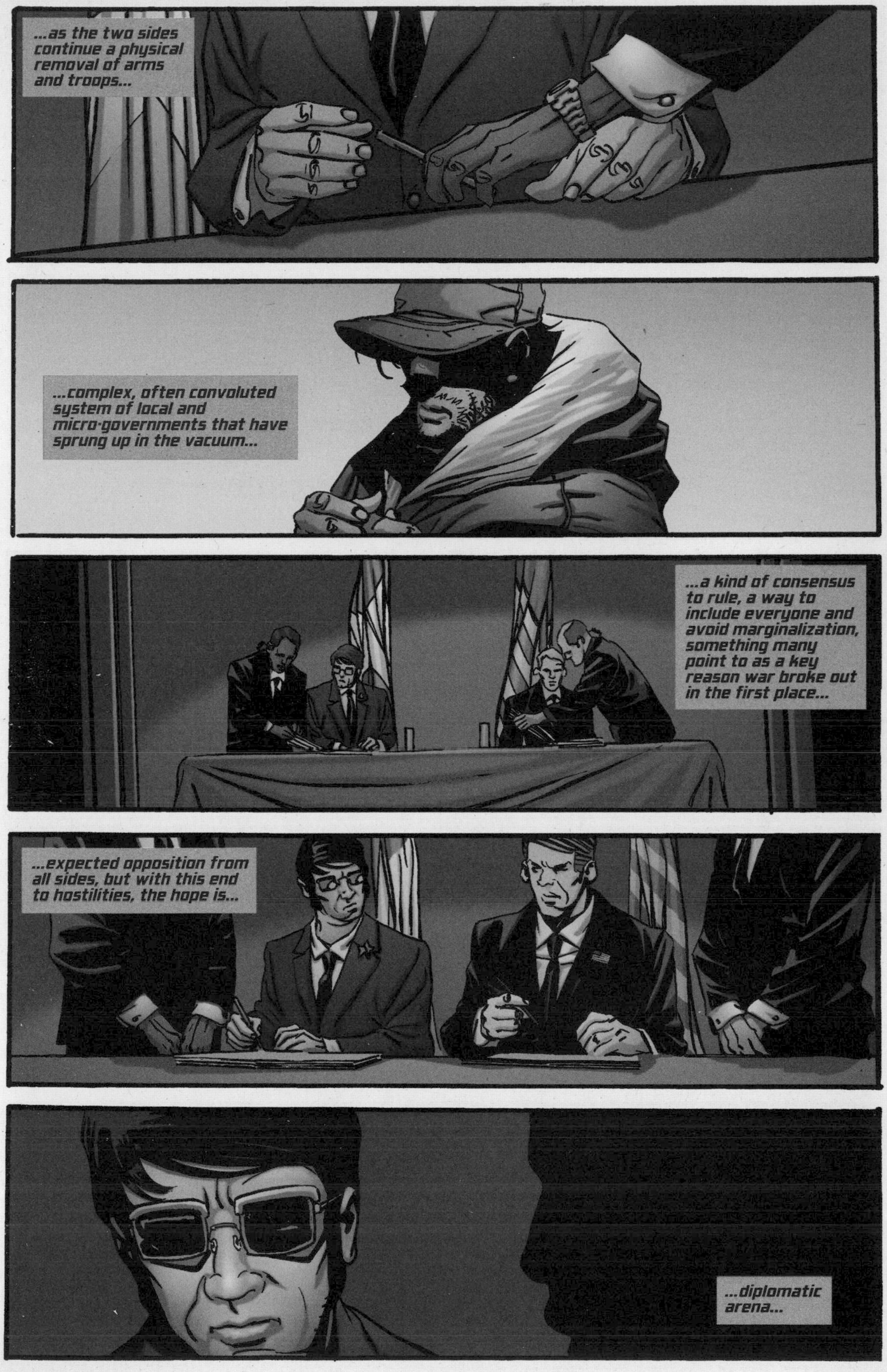
...as the two sides continue a physical removal of arms and troops...
...complex, often convoluted system of local and micro-governments that have sprung up in the vacuum...
...a kind of consensus to rule, a way to include everyone and avoid marginalization, something many point to as a key reason war broke out in the first place...
...expected opposition from all sides, but with this end to hostilities, the hope is...
...diplomatic arena...

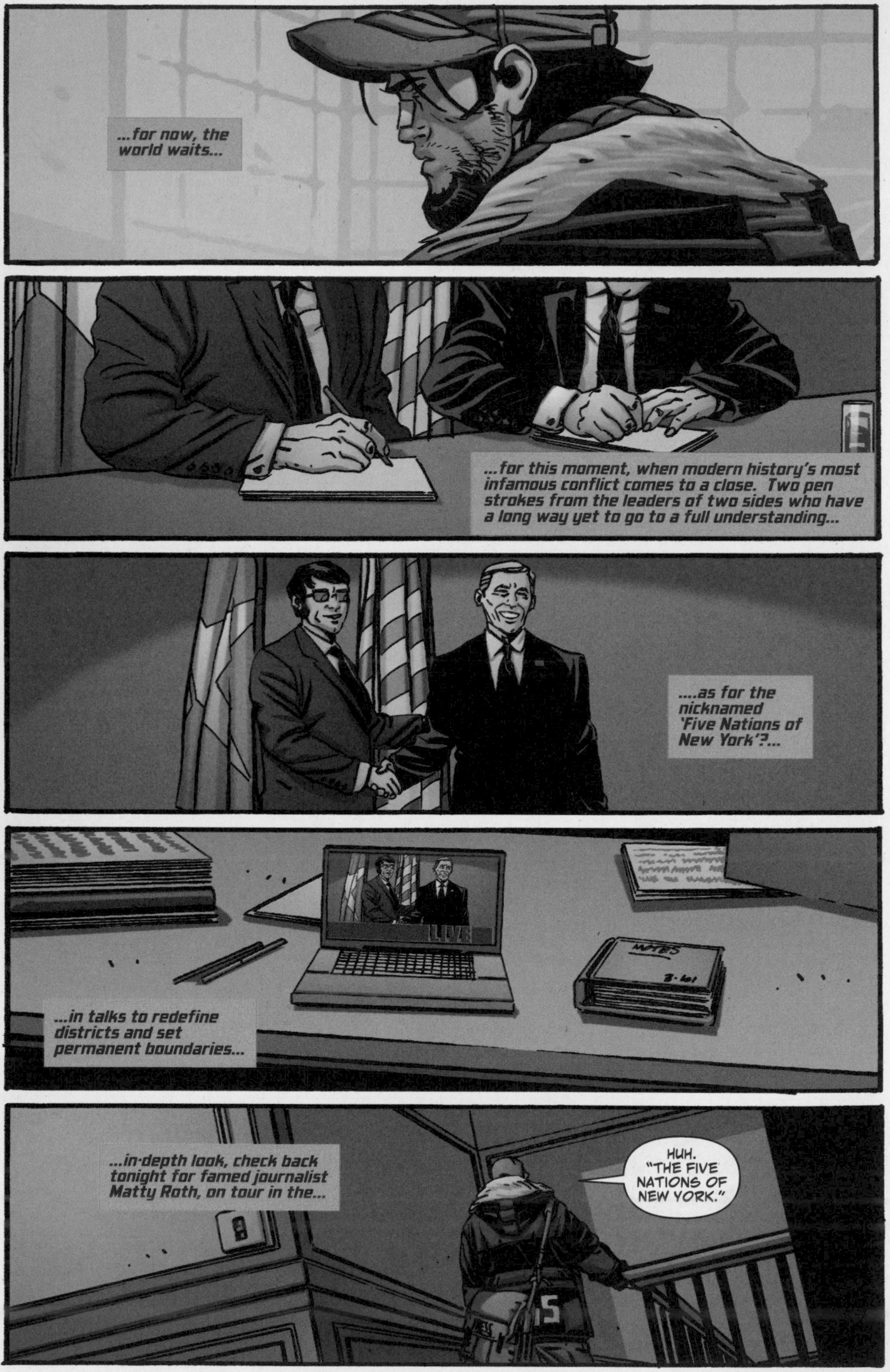
...for now, the world waits...
...for this moment, when modern history's most infamous conflict comes to a close. Two pen strokes from the leaders of two sides who have a long way yet to go to a full understanding...
....as for the nicknamed 'Five Nations of New York'?...
...in talks to redefine districts and set permanent boundaries...
...in-depth look, check back tonight for famed journalist Matty Roth, on tour in the...
HUH. "THE FIVE NATIONS OF NEW YORK."

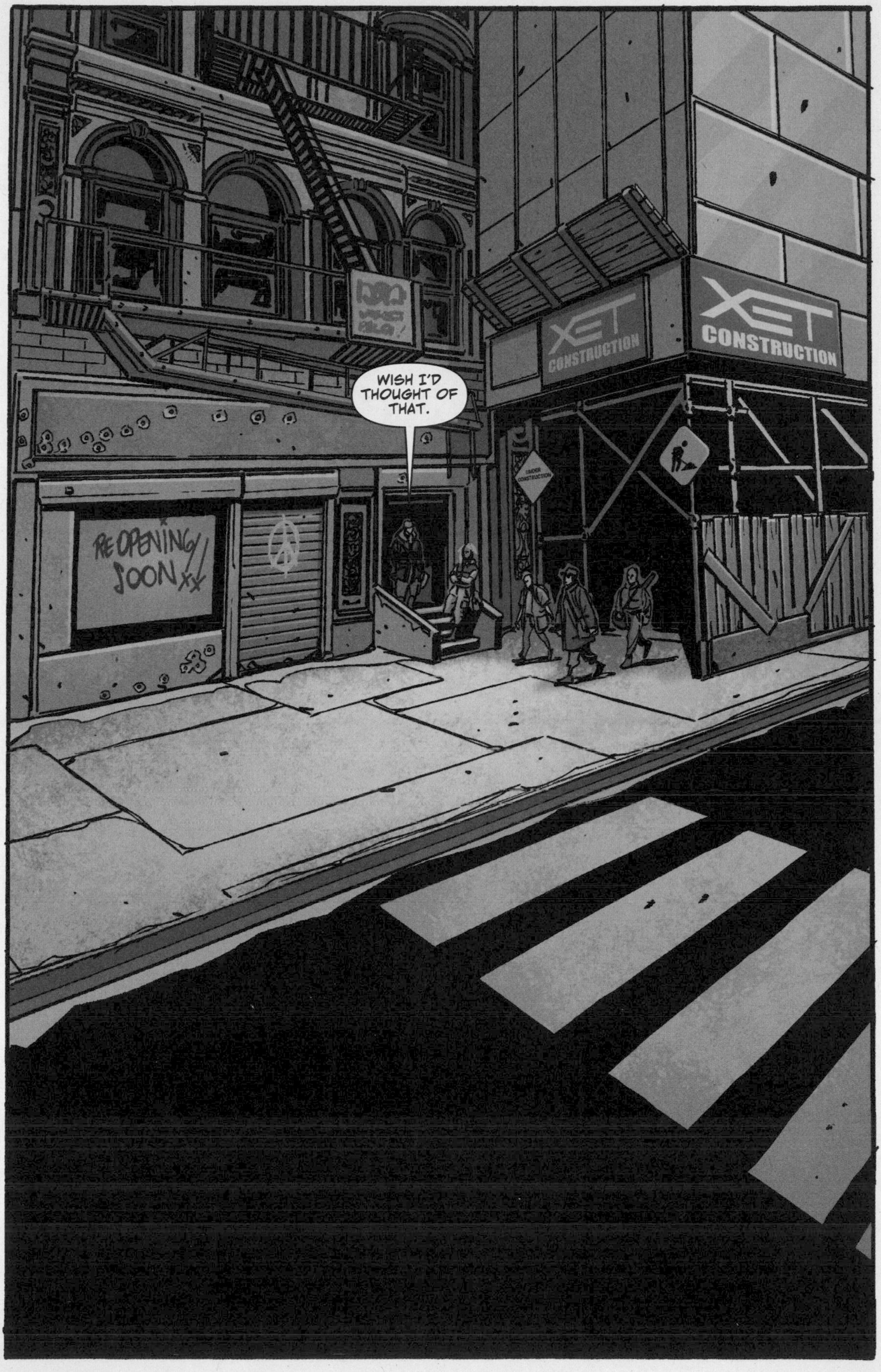
WISH I'D THOUGHT OF THAT.
RE OPENING SOON xx
XET CONSTRUCTION
XET CONSTRUCTION
UNDER CONSTRUCTION

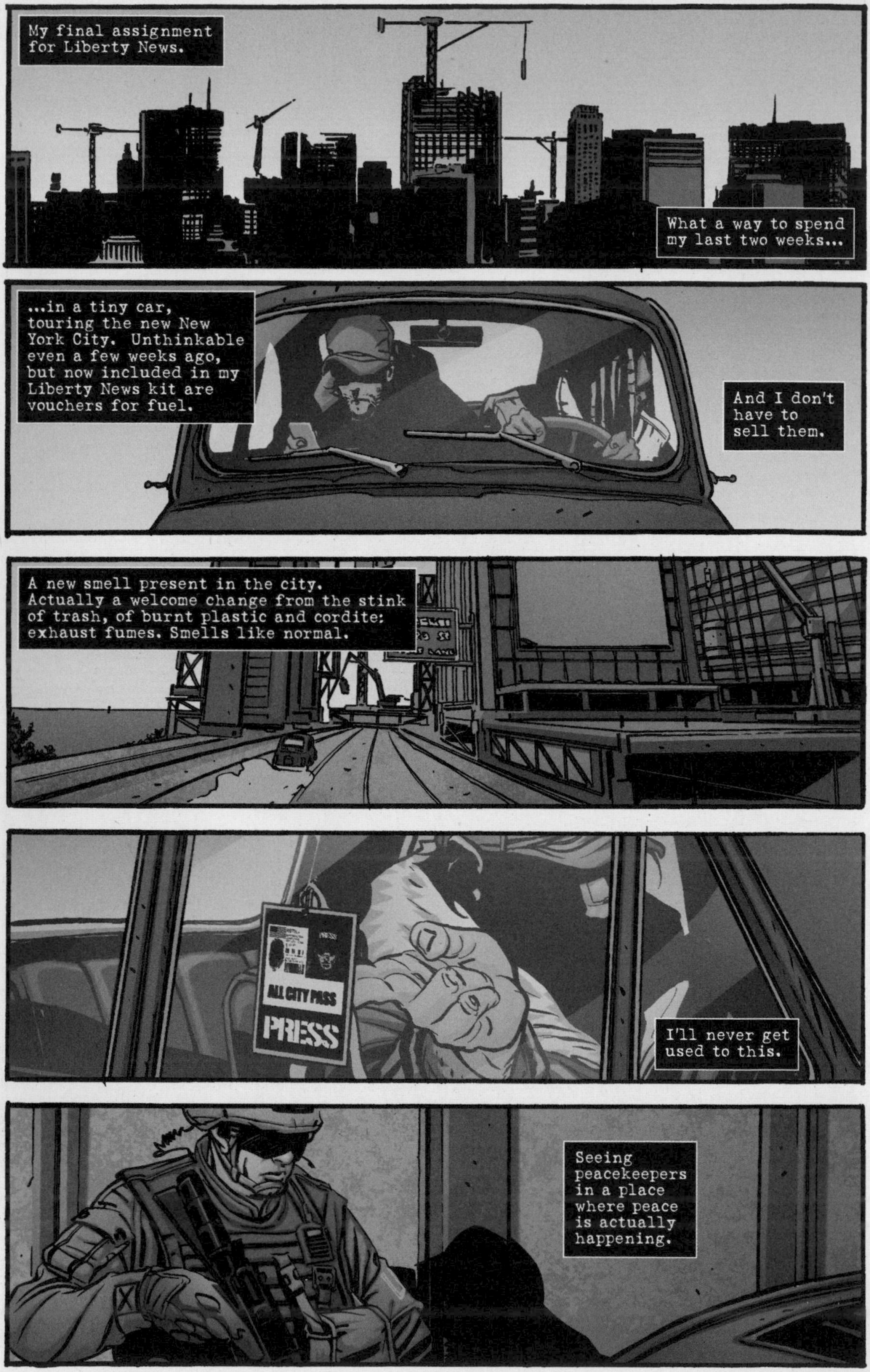

My final assignment for Liberty News.
What a way to spend my last two weeks...
...in a tiny car, touring the new New York City. Unthinkable even a few weeks ago, but now included in my Liberty News kit are vouchers for fuel.
And I don't have to sell them.
A new smell present in the city. Actually a welcome change from the stink of trash, of burnt plastic and cordite: exhaust fumes. Smells like normal.
PRESS
ALL CITY PASS
PRESS
I'll never get used to this.
Seeing peacekeepers in a place where peace is actually happening.

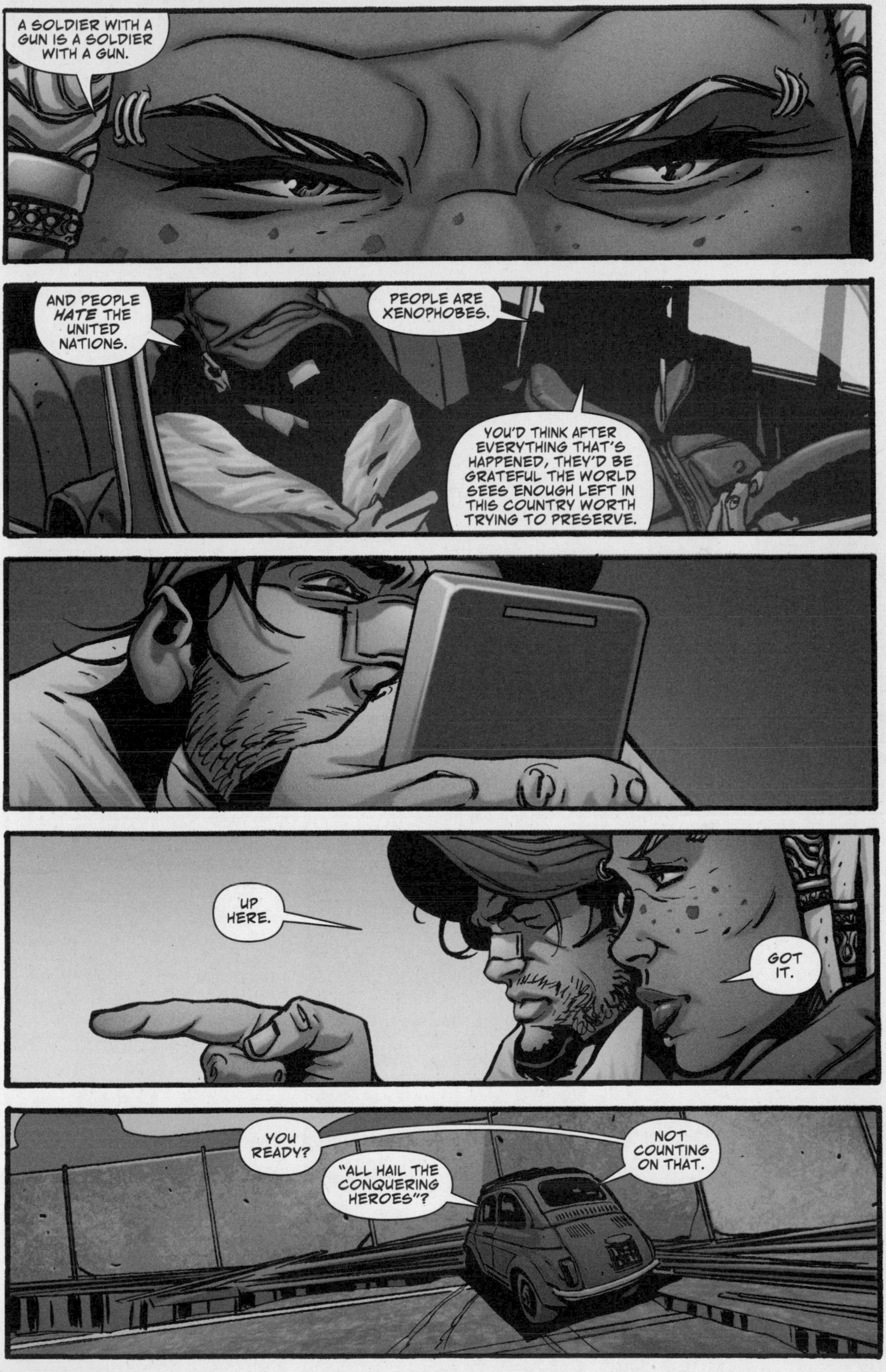
A SOLDIER WITH A GUN IS A SOLDIER WITH A GUN.
AND PEOPLE *HATE* THE UNITED NATIONS.
PEOPLE ARE XENOPHOBES.
YOU'D THINK AFTER EVERYTHING THAT'S HAPPENED, THEY'D BE GRATEFUL THE WORLD SEES ENOUGH LEFT IN THIS COUNTRY WORTH TRYING TO PRESERVE.
UP HERE.
GOT IT.
YOU READY?
"ALL HAIL THE CONQUERING HEROES"?
NOT COUNTING ON THAT.

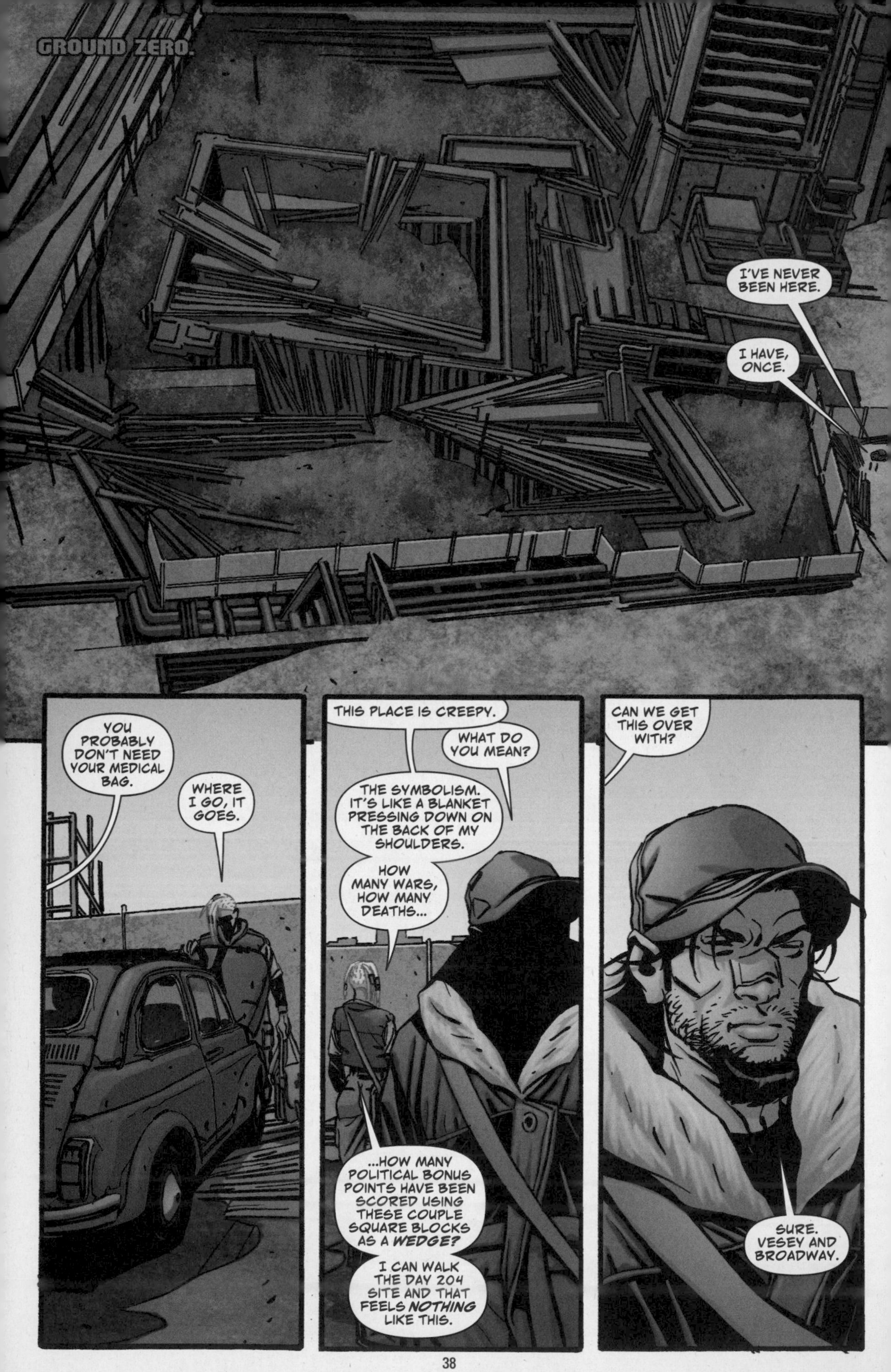
GROUND ZERO.
I'VE NEVER BEEN HERE.
I HAVE, ONCE.
YOU PROBABLY DON'T NEED YOUR MEDICAL BAG.
WHERE I GO, IT GOES.
THIS PLACE IS CREEPY.
WHAT DO YOU MEAN?
THE SYMBOLISM. IT'S LIKE A BLANKET PRESSING DOWN ON THE BACK OF MY SHOULDERS.
HOW MANY WARS, HOW MANY DEATHS...
...HOW MANY POLITICAL BONUS POINTS HAVE BEEN SCORED USING THESE COUPLE SQUARE BLOCKS AS A *WEDGE?*
I CAN WALK THE DAY 204 SITE AND THAT FEELS *NOTHING* LIKE THIS.
CAN WE GET THIS OVER WITH?
SURE. VESEY AND BROADWAY.

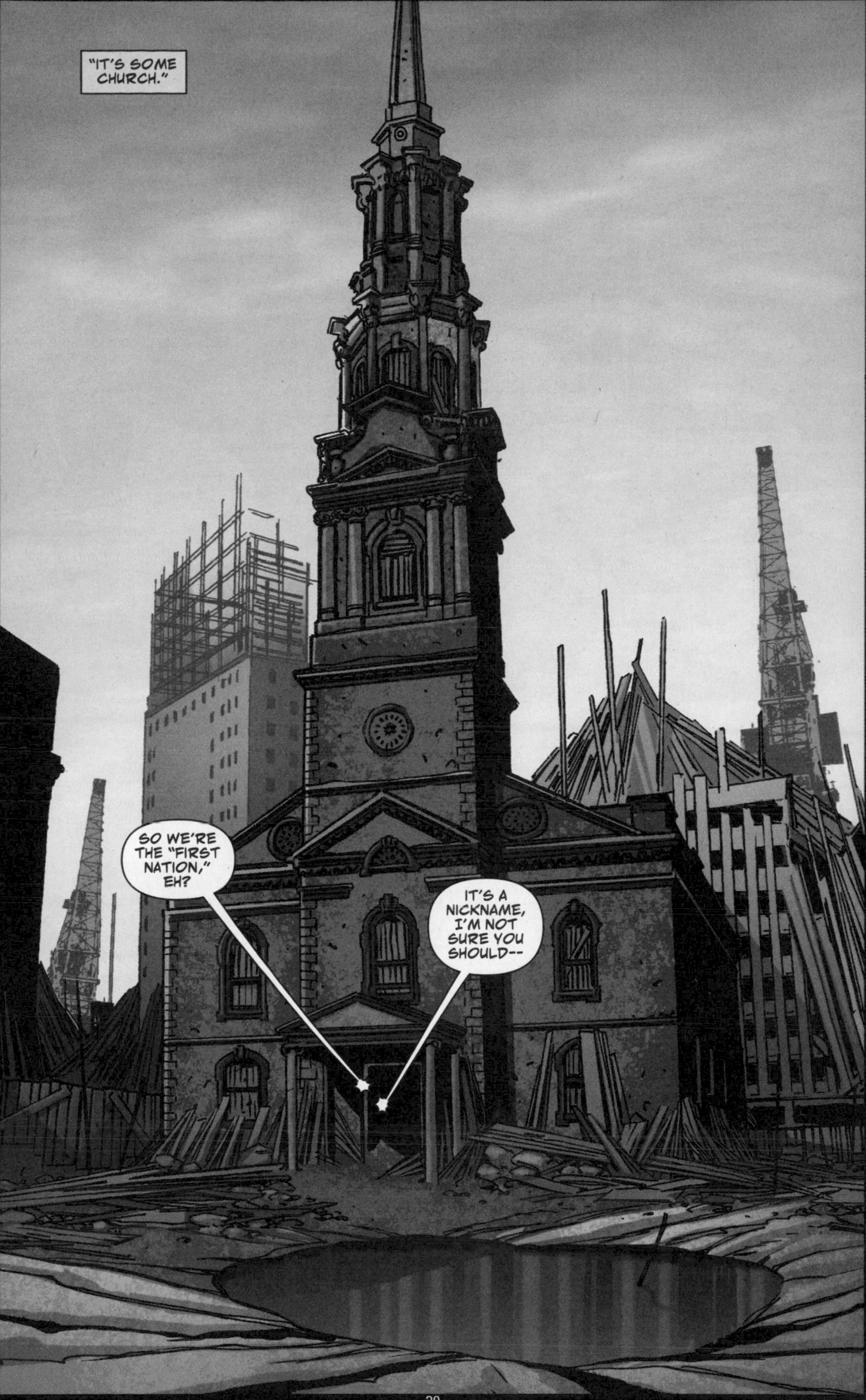
"IT'S SOME CHURCH."
SO WE'RE THE "FIRST NATION," EH?
IT'S A NICKNAME, I'M NOT SURE YOU SHOULD--

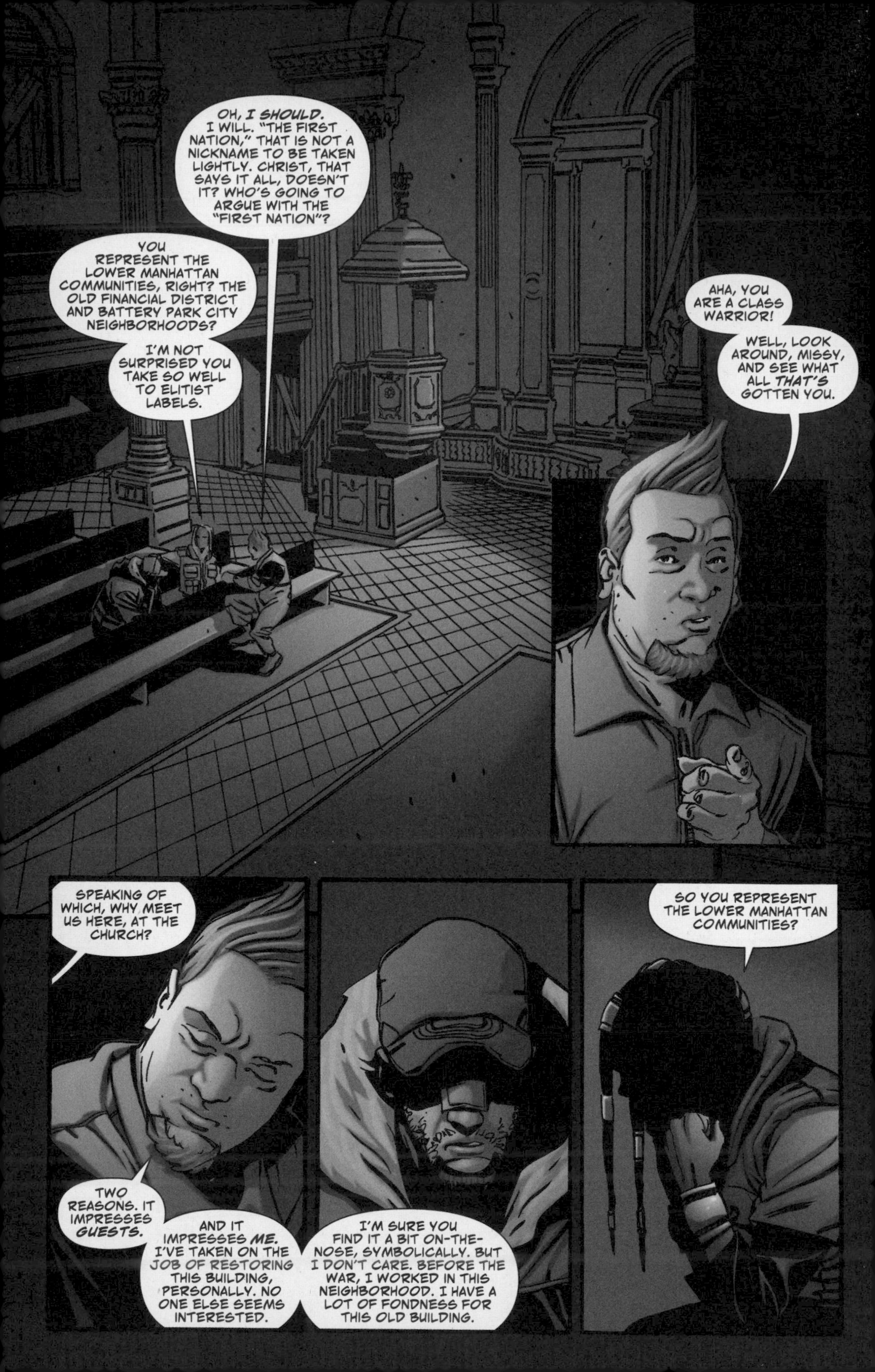
YOU REPRESENT THE LOWER MANHATTAN COMMUNITIES, RIGHT? THE OLD FINANCIAL DISTRICT AND BATTERY PARK CITY NEIGHBORHOODS?
I'M NOT SURPRISED YOU TAKE SO WELL TO ELITIST LABELS.
OH, I SHOULD. I WILL. "THE FIRST NATION," THAT IS NOT A NICKNAME TO BE TAKEN LIGHTLY. CHRIST, THAT SAYS IT ALL, DOESN'T IT? WHO'S GOING TO ARGUE WITH THE "FIRST NATION"?
AHA, YOU ARE A CLASS WARRIOR!
WELL, LOOK AROUND, MISSY, AND SEE WHAT ALL THAT'S GOTTEN YOU.
SPEAKING OF WHICH, WHY MEET US HERE, AT THE CHURCH?
TWO REASONS. IT IMPRESSES GUESTS.
AND IT IMPRESSES ME. I'VE TAKEN ON THE JOB OF RESTORING THIS BUILDING, PERSONALLY. NO ONE ELSE SEEMS INTERESTED.
I'M SURE YOU FIND IT A BIT ON-THE-NOSE, SYMBOLICALLY. BUT I DON'T CARE. BEFORE THE WAR, I WORKED IN THIS NEIGHBORHOOD. I HAVE A LOT OF FONDNESS FOR THIS OLD BUILDING.
SO YOU REPRESENT THE LOWER MANHATTAN COMMUNITIES?

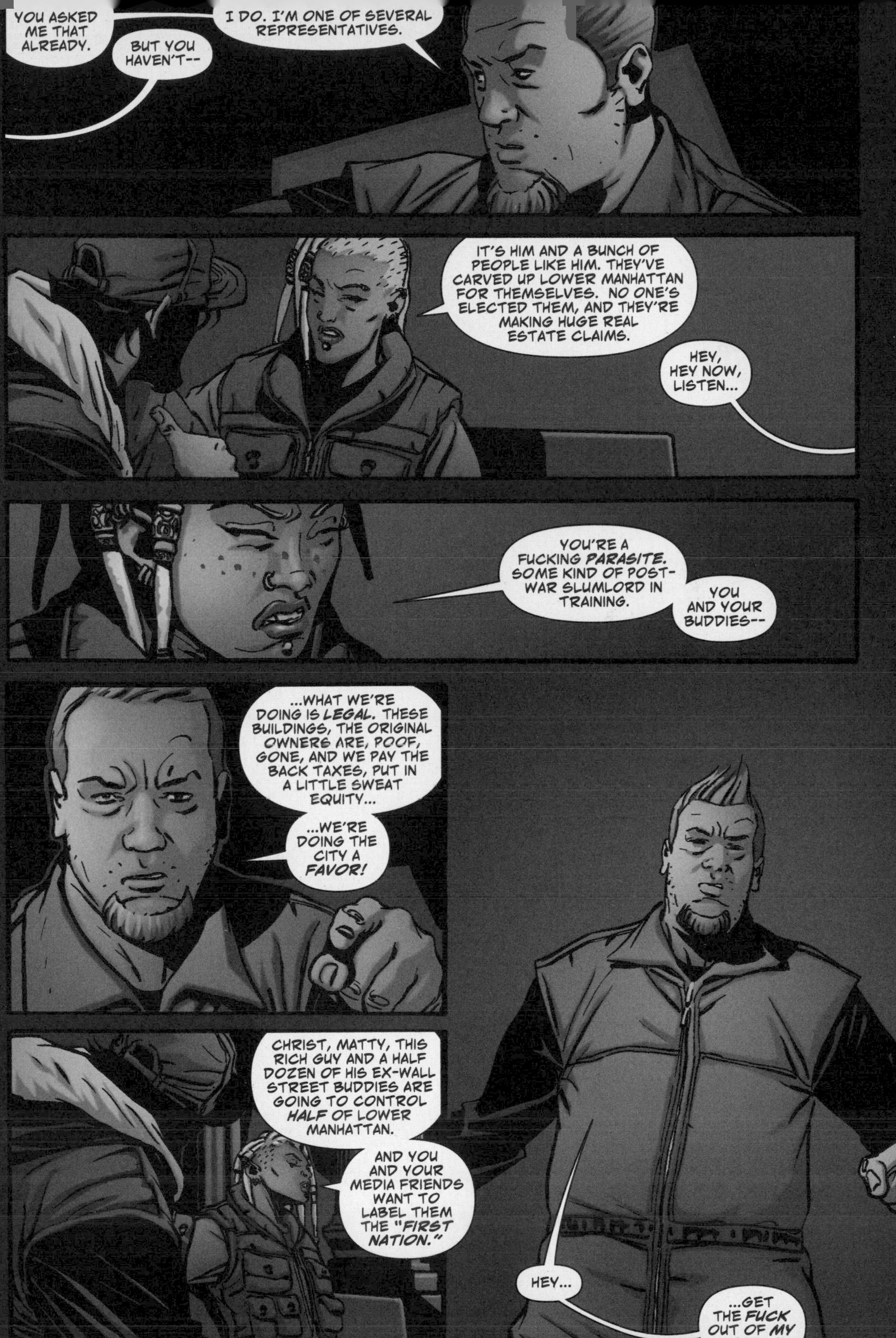
YOU ASKED ME THAT ALREADY.
I DO. I'M ONE OF SEVERAL REPRESENTATIVES.
BUT YOU HAVEN'T--
IT'S HIM AND A BUNCH OF PEOPLE LIKE HIM. THEY'VE CARVED UP LOWER MANHATTAN FOR THEMSELVES. NO ONE'S ELECTED THEM, AND THEY'RE MAKING HUGE REAL ESTATE CLAIMS.
HEY, HEY NOW, LISTEN...
YOU'RE A FUCKING PARASITE. SOME KIND OF POST-WAR SLUMLORD IN TRAINING.
YOU AND YOUR BUDDIES--
...WHAT WE'RE DOING IS LEGAL. THESE BUILDINGS, THE ORIGINAL OWNERS ARE, POOF, GONE, AND WE PAY THE BACK TAXES, PUT IN A LITTLE SWEAT EQUITY...
...WE'RE DOING THE CITY A FAVOR!
CHRIST, MATTY, THIS RICH GUY AND A HALF DOZEN OF HIS EX-WALL STREET BUDDIES ARE GOING TO CONTROL HALF OF LOWER MANHATTAN.
AND YOU AND YOUR MEDIA FRIENDS WANT TO LABEL THEM THE "FIRST NATION."
HEY...
...GET THE FUCK OUT OF MY CHURCH.

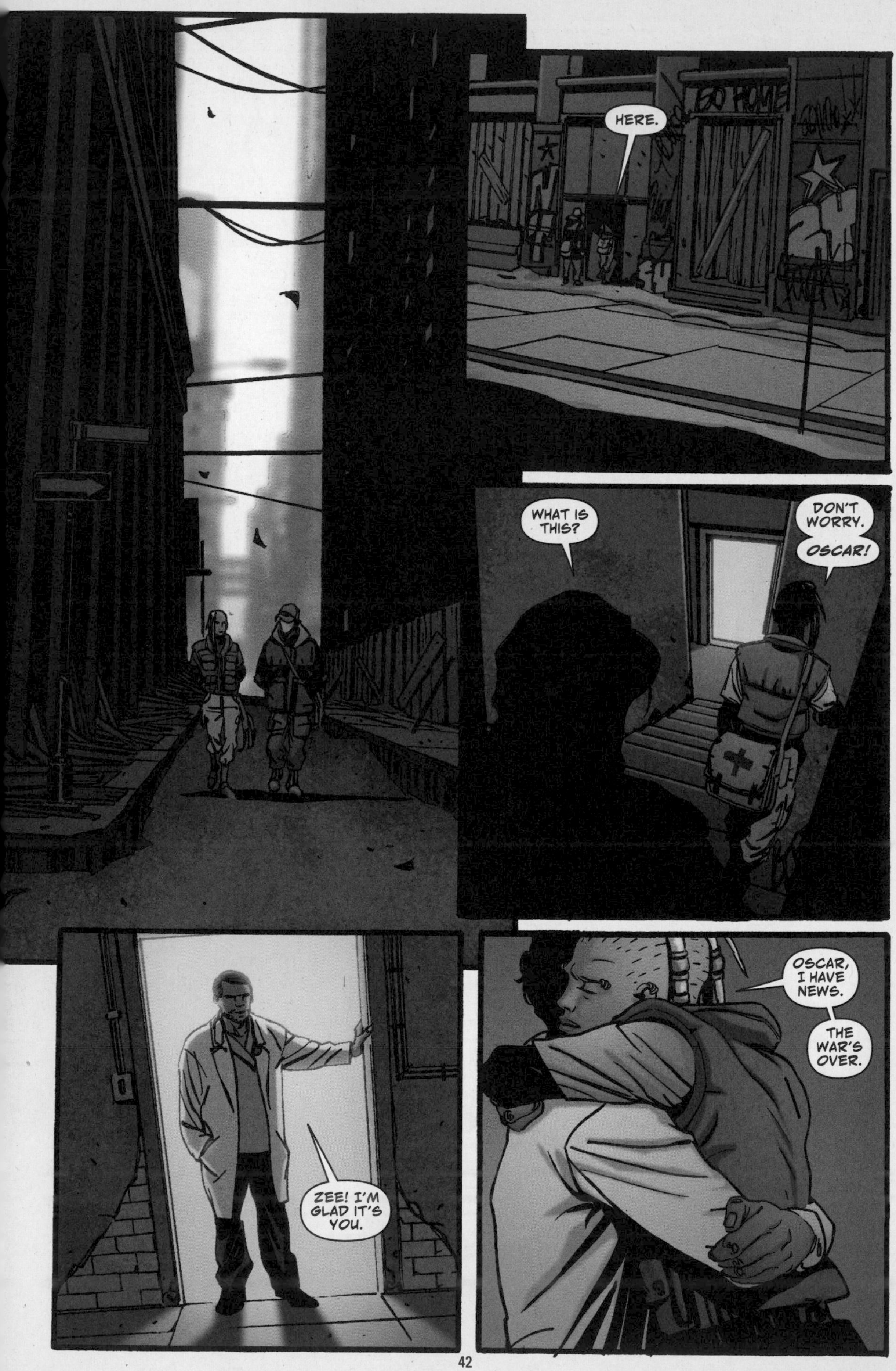
HERE.
GO HOME
WHAT IS THIS?
DON'T WORRY.
OSCAR!
ZEE! I'M GLAD IT'S YOU.
OSCAR, I HAVE NEWS.
THE WAR'S OVER.

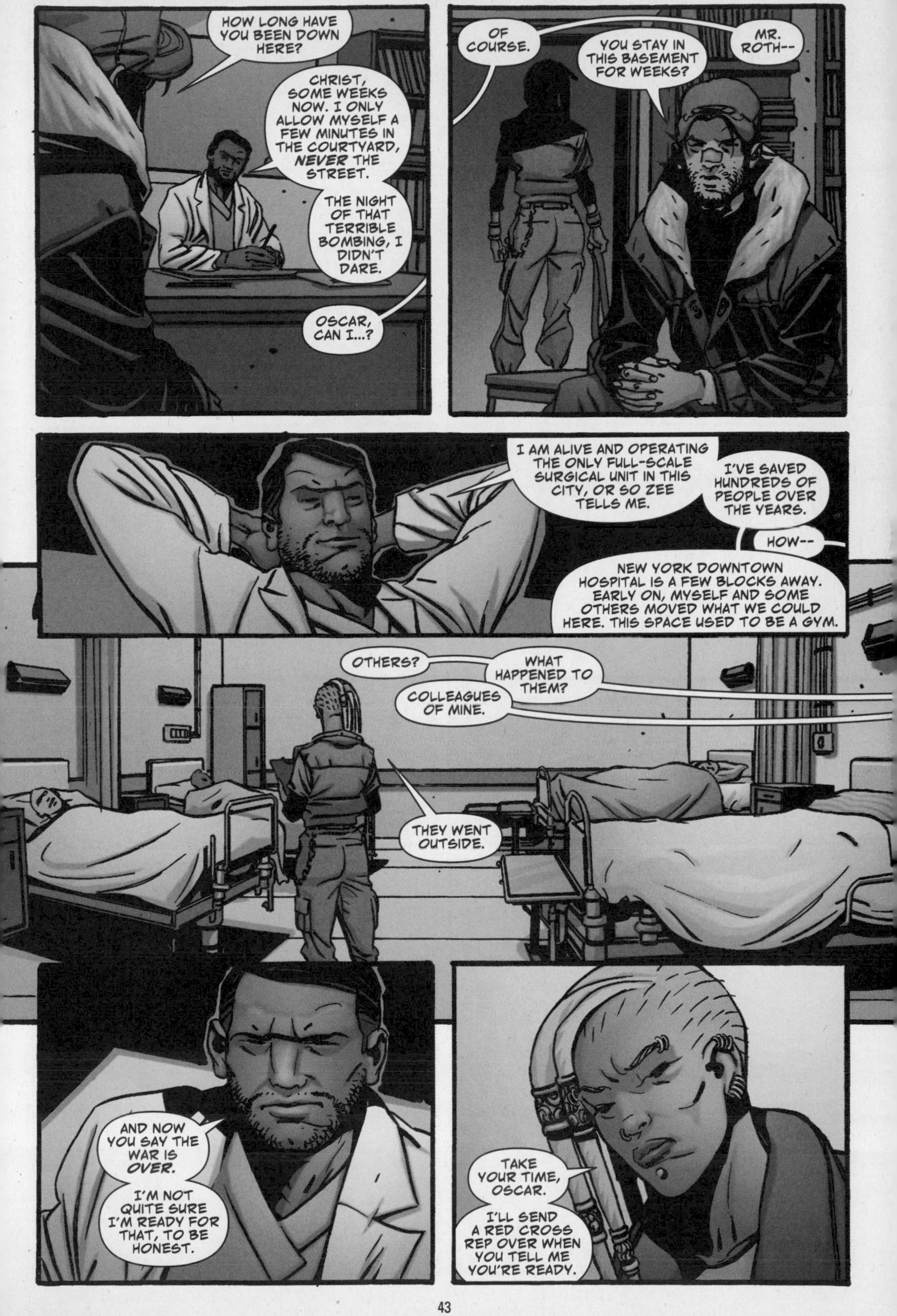
HOW LONG HAVE YOU BEEN DOWN HERE?
CHRIST, SOME WEEKS NOW. I ONLY ALLOW MYSELF A FEW MINUTES IN THE COURTYARD, *NEVER* THE STREET.
THE NIGHT OF THAT TERRIBLE BOMBING, I DIDN'T DARE.
OSCAR, CAN I...?
OF COURSE.
MR. ROTH--
YOU STAY IN THIS BASEMENT FOR WEEKS?
I AM ALIVE AND OPERATING THE ONLY FULL-SCALE SURGICAL UNIT IN THIS CITY, OR SO ZEE TELLS ME.
I'VE SAVED HUNDREDS OF PEOPLE OVER THE YEARS.
HOW--
NEW YORK DOWNTOWN HOSPITAL IS A FEW BLOCKS AWAY. EARLY ON, MYSELF AND SOME OTHERS MOVED WHAT WE COULD HERE. THIS SPACE USED TO BE A GYM.
OTHERS?
WHAT HAPPENED TO THEM?
COLLEAGUES OF MINE.
THEY WENT OUTSIDE.
AND NOW YOU SAY THE WAR IS *OVER*.
I'M NOT QUITE SURE I'M READY FOR THAT, TO BE HONEST.
TAKE YOUR TIME, OSCAR.
I'LL SEND A RED CROSS REP OVER WHEN YOU TELL ME YOU'RE READY.

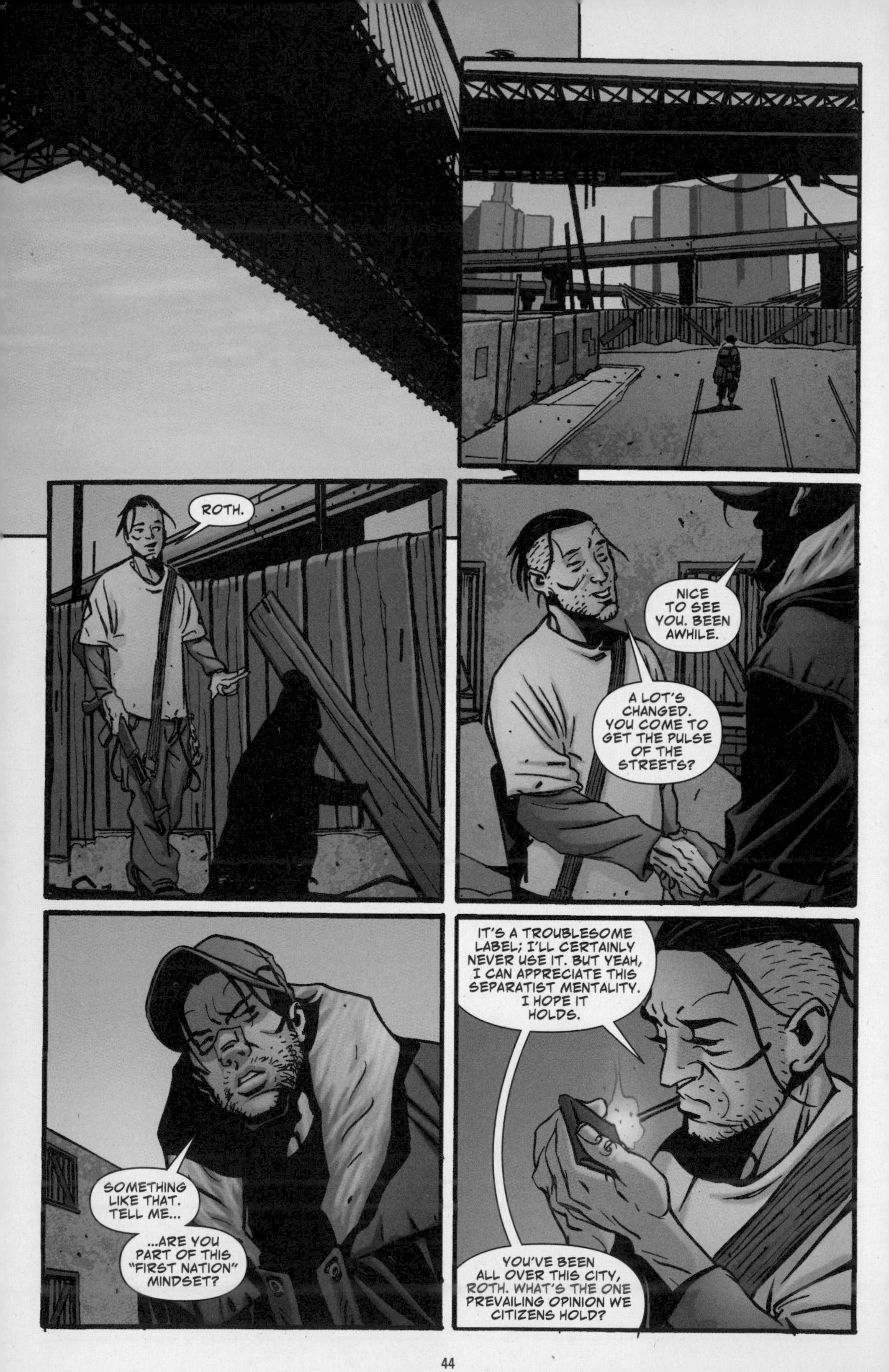
ROTH.
NICE TO SEE YOU. BEEN AWHILE.
A LOT'S CHANGED. YOU COME TO GET THE PULSE OF THE STREETS?
SOMETHING LIKE THAT. TELL ME...
...ARE YOU PART OF THIS "FIRST NATION" MINDSET?
IT'S A TROUBLESOME LABEL; I'LL CERTAINLY NEVER USE IT. BUT YEAH, I CAN APPRECIATE THIS SEPARATIST MENTALITY. I HOPE IT HOLDS.
YOU'VE BEEN ALL OVER THIS CITY, ROTH. WHAT'S THE ONE PREVAILING OPINION WE CITIZENS HOLD?

"GET OUT AND LEAVE US ALONE."

BINGO. THIS FRACTURING OF THE CITY, WHO KNOWS HOW LONG IT'LL LAST, BUT YOU GET IT, RIGHT? THERE'S *NO GOING BACK* TO THE WAY IT WAS.

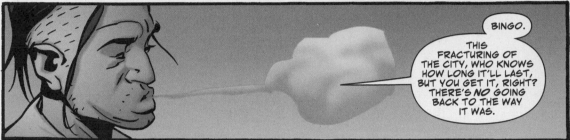

HOW WAS IT? SPECIFICALLY LOWER MANHATTAN.

LOADED WITH SYMBOLISM. YOU KNOW THOSE REAL ESTATE DOUCHEBAGS, OBSESSED WITH A MONEY-DRIVEN CITY THAT I DON'T THINK WILL EVER EXIST AGAIN.

THOSE GUYS HAVE ANOTHER THING COMING IF THEY THINK THEY CAN JUST LAY CLAIM TO BILLIONS OF DOLLARS IN REAL ESTATE.

BUT THEY ARE BOTH THE WORST AND BEST EXAMPLES OF WHAT I'M TALKING ABOUT.

THIS IS WHAT PEOPLE THINK OF WHEN THEY THINK OF LOWER MANHATTAN. TRADITIONALLY, I MEAN:

MONEY, TERRORISM, FINANCE, REAL ESTATE DOUCHE-BAGS. WE HAVE TO CHANGE THAT.

TO WHAT?

FUCKED IF I KNOW.

"GET OUT AND LEAVE US ALONE," I GUESS. WE'LL FIGURE IT OUT.

YOU'RE STILL CARRYING A WEAPON.

I AM.

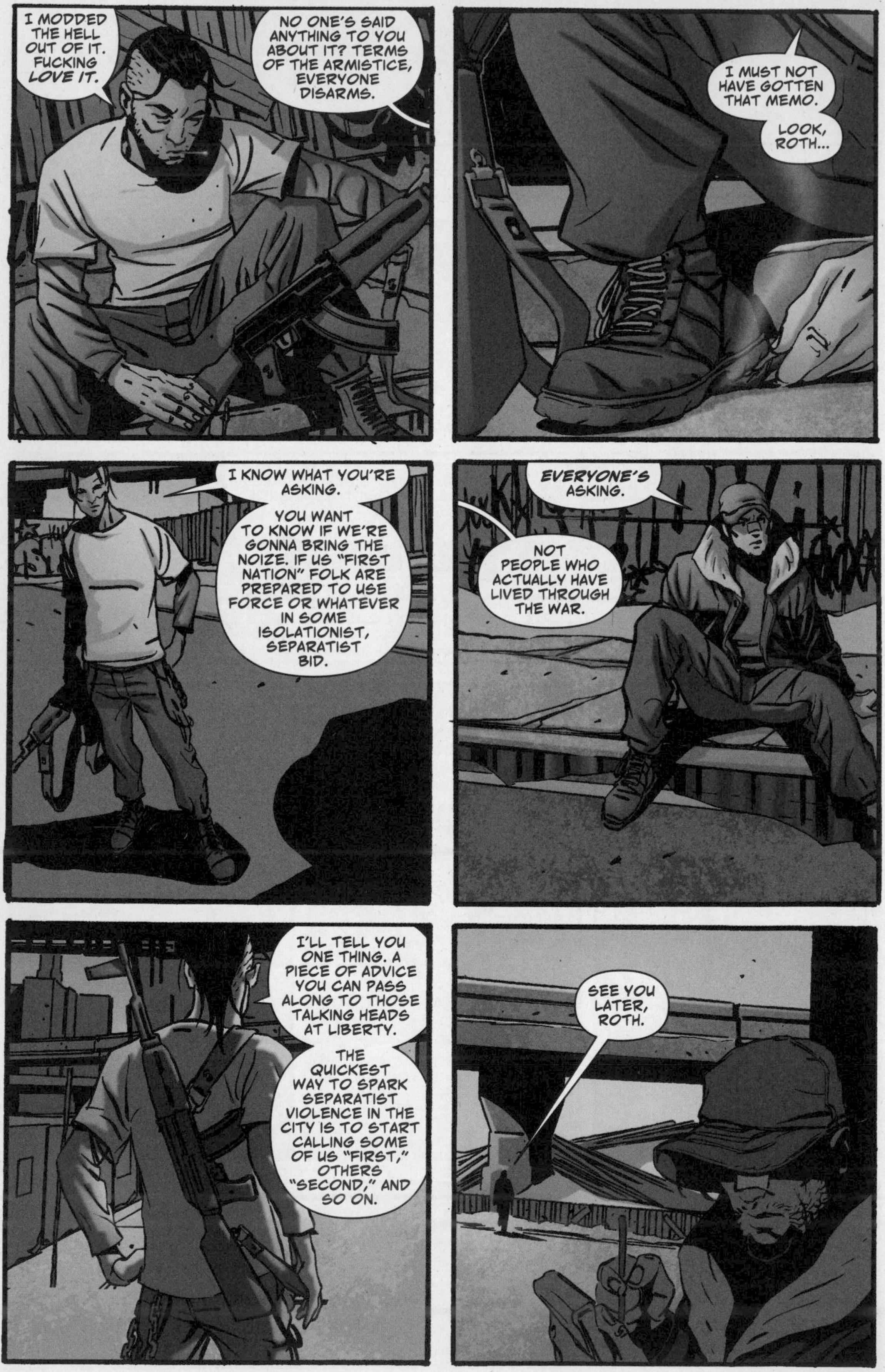
I MODDED THE HELL OUT OF IT. FUCKING *LOVE IT.*
NO ONE'S SAID ANYTHING TO YOU ABOUT IT? TERMS OF THE ARMISTICE, EVERYONE DISARMS.
I MUST NOT HAVE GOTTEN THAT MEMO.
LOOK, ROTH...
I KNOW WHAT YOU'RE ASKING.
YOU WANT TO KNOW IF WE'RE GONNA BRING THE NOIZE. IF US "FIRST NATION" FOLK ARE PREPARED TO USE FORCE OR WHATEVER IN SOME ISOLATIONIST, SEPARATIST BID.
EVERYONE'S ASKING.
NOT PEOPLE WHO ACTUALLY HAVE LIVED THROUGH THE WAR.
I'LL TELL YOU ONE THING. A PIECE OF ADVICE YOU CAN PASS ALONG TO THOSE TALKING HEADS AT LIBERTY.
THE QUICKEST WAY TO SPARK SEPARATIST VIOLENCE IN THE CITY IS TO START CALLING SOME OF US "FIRST," OTHERS "SECOND," AND SO ON.
SEE YOU LATER, ROTH.

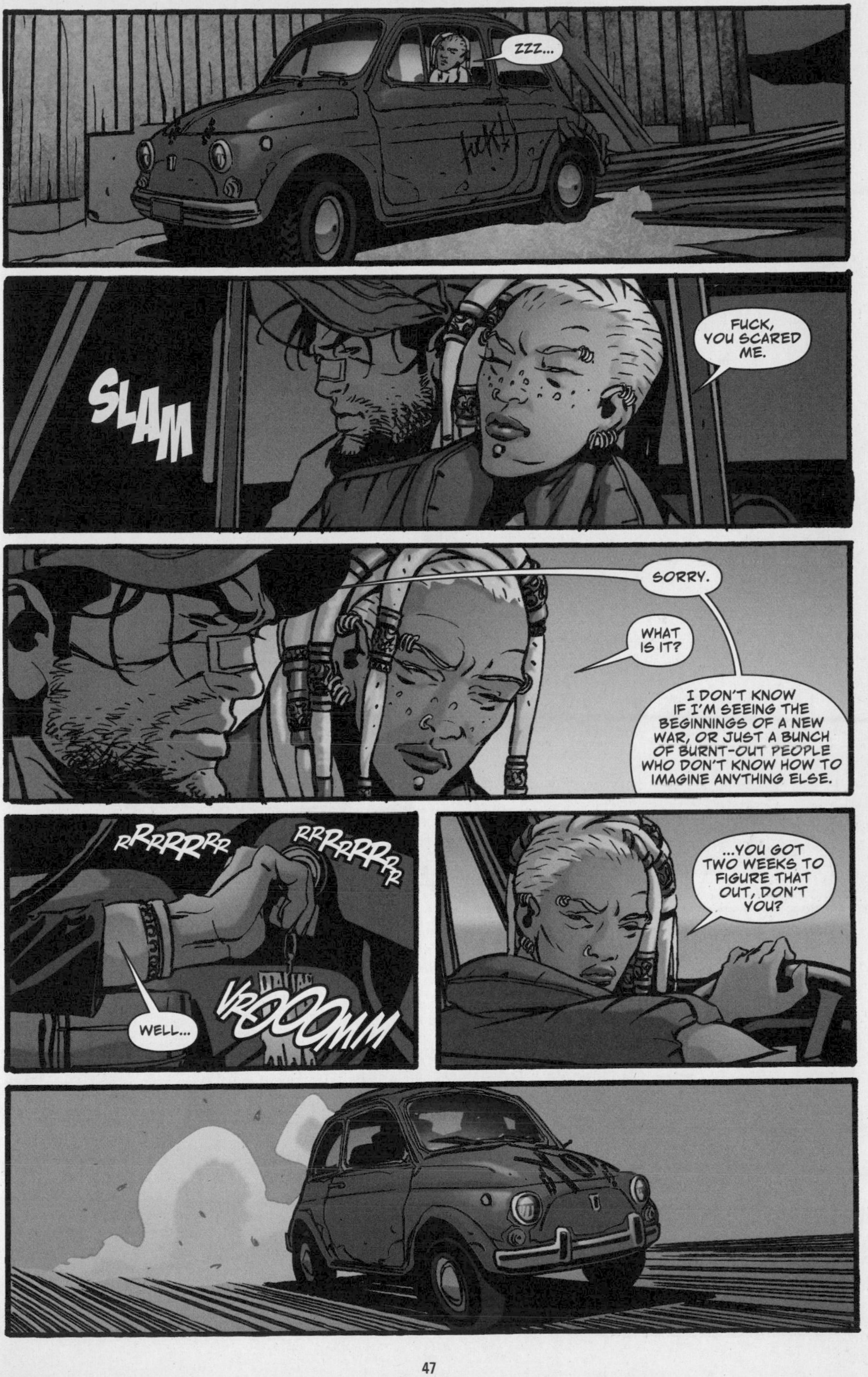
ZZZ...
FUCK!
SLAM
FUCK, YOU SCARED ME.
SORRY.
WHAT IS IT?
I DON'T KNOW IF I'M SEEING THE BEGINNINGS OF A NEW WAR, OR JUST A BUNCH OF BURNT-OUT PEOPLE WHO DON'T KNOW HOW TO IMAGINE ANYTHING ELSE.
RRRRRRRR
RRRRRRRRR
WELL...
VROOOOMM
...YOU GOT TWO WEEKS TO FIGURE THAT OUT, DON'T YOU?

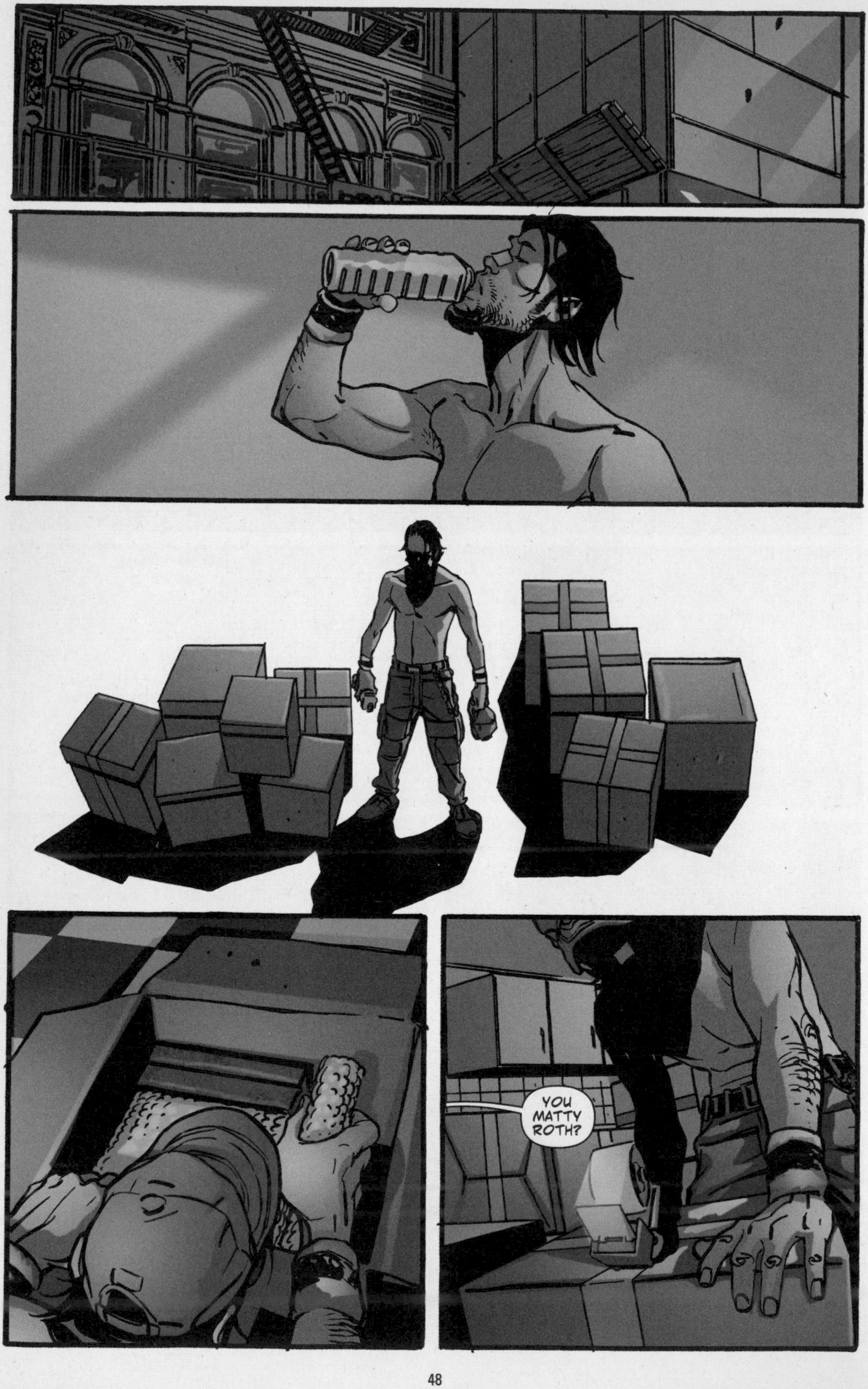
YOU MATTY ROTH?

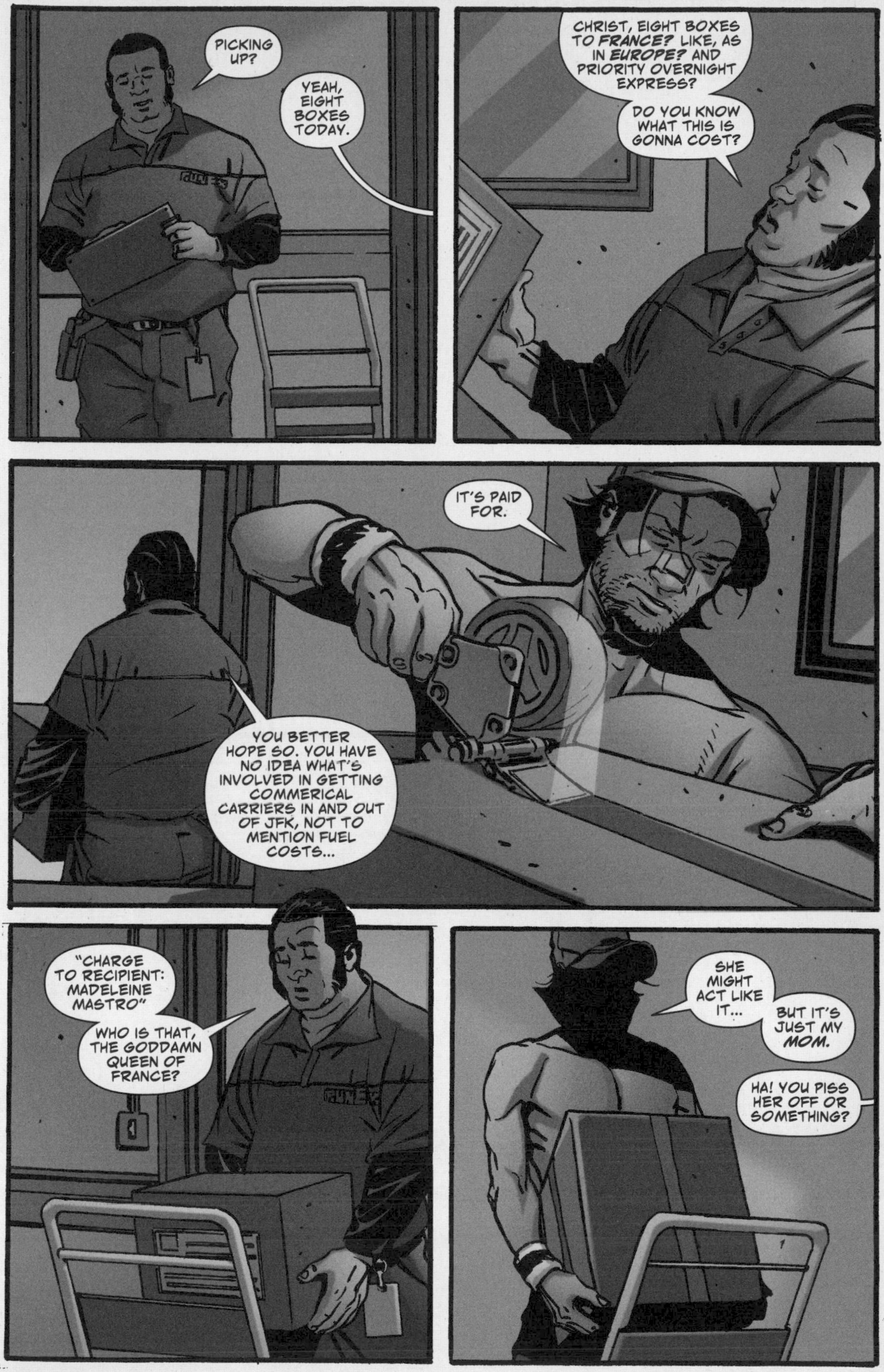
PICKING UP?
YEAH, EIGHT BOXES TODAY.
CHRIST, EIGHT BOXES TO FRANCE? LIKE, AS IN EUROPE? AND PRIORITY OVERNIGHT EXPRESS?
DO YOU KNOW WHAT THIS IS GONNA COST?
IT'S PAID FOR.
YOU BETTER HOPE SO. YOU HAVE NO IDEA WHAT'S INVOLVED IN GETTING COMMERICAL CARRIERS IN AND OUT OF JFK, NOT TO MENTION FUEL COSTS...
"CHARGE TO RECIPIENT: MADELEINE MASTRO"
WHO IS THAT, THE GODDAMN QUEEN OF FRANCE?
SHE MIGHT ACT LIKE IT...
BUT IT'S JUST MY MOM.
HA! YOU PISS HER OFF OR SOMETHING?

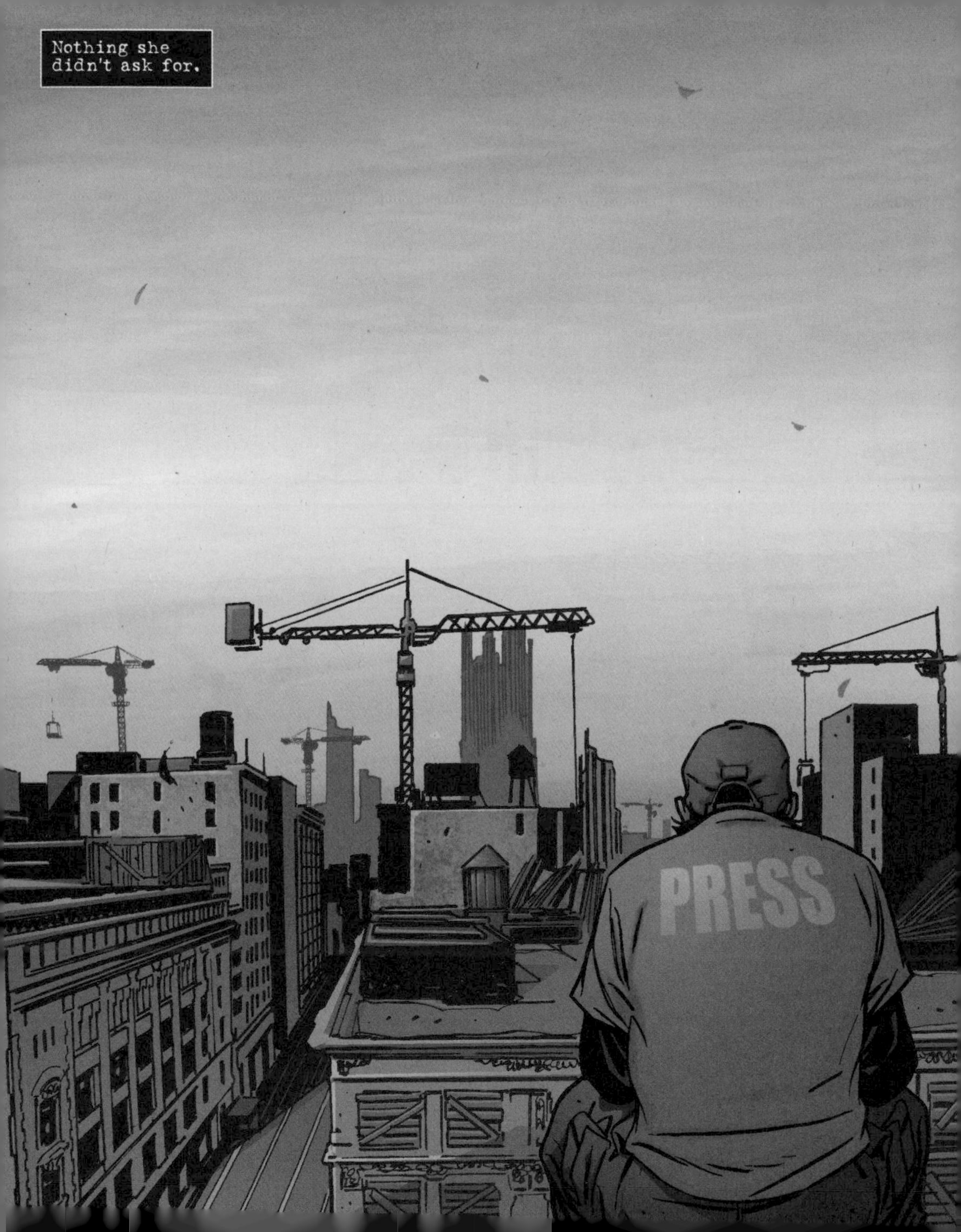
Nothing she didn't ask for.
PRESS

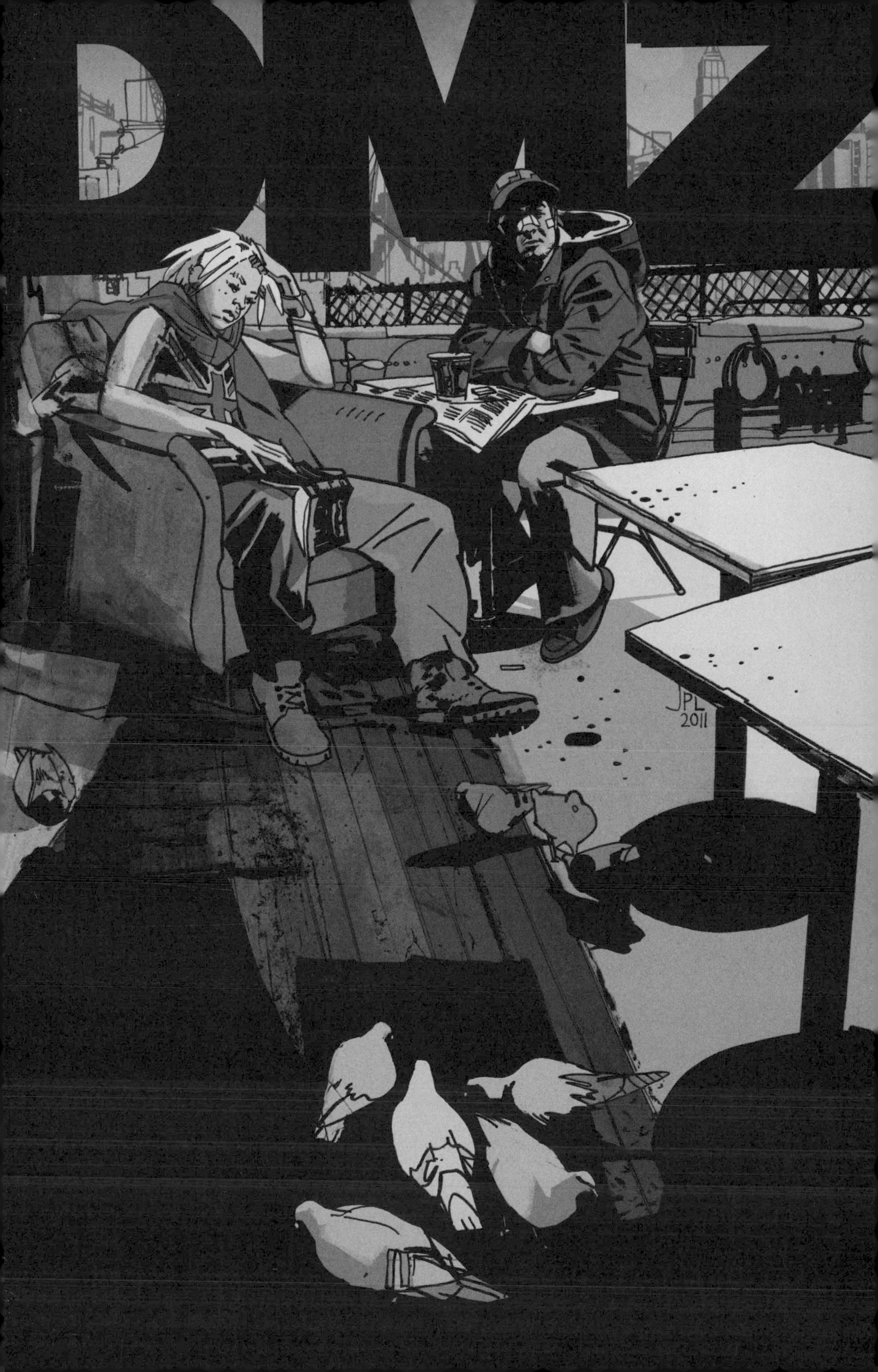
DMZ
JPL
2011

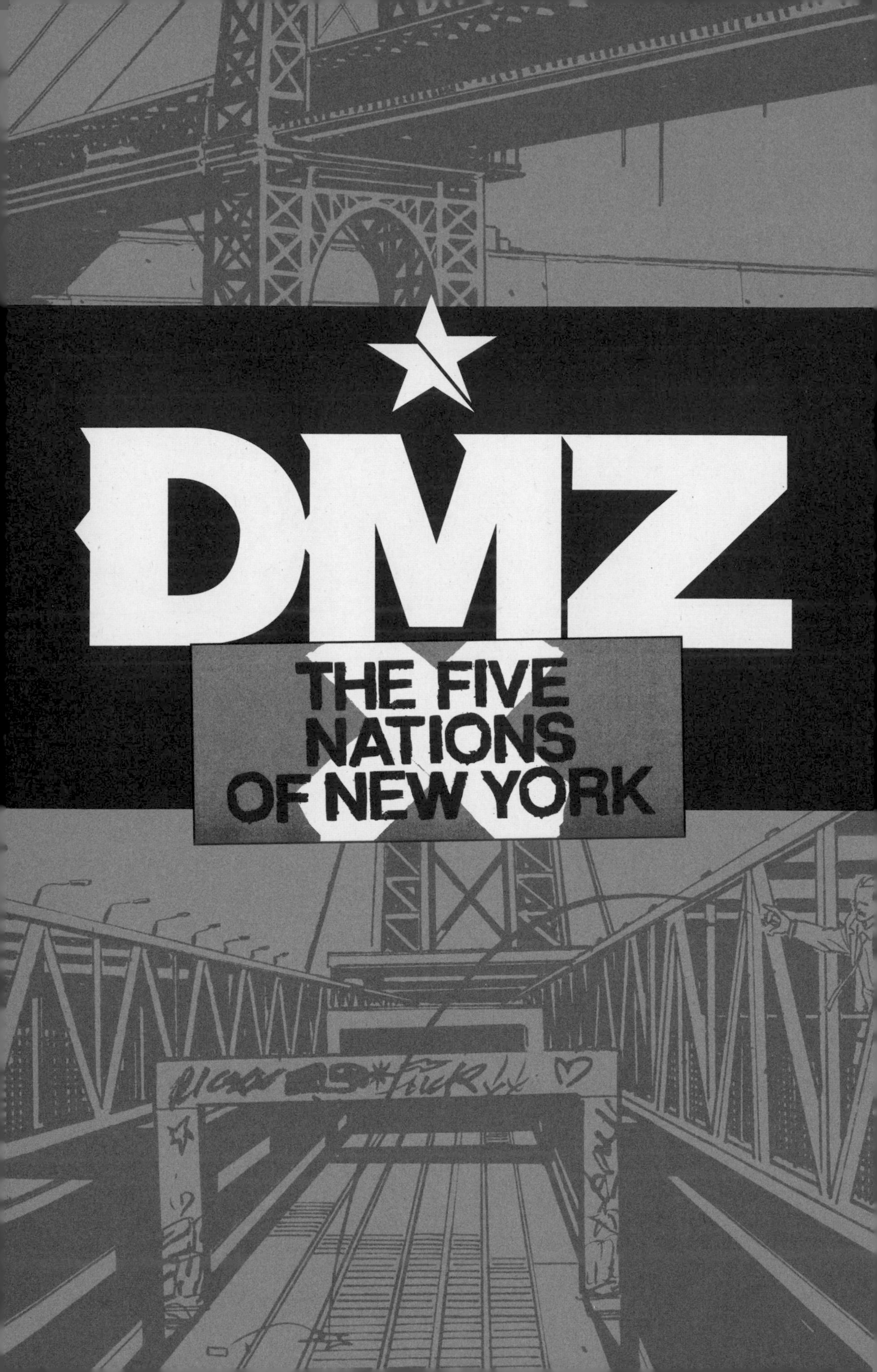
DMZ
THE FIVE NATIONS OF NEW YORK

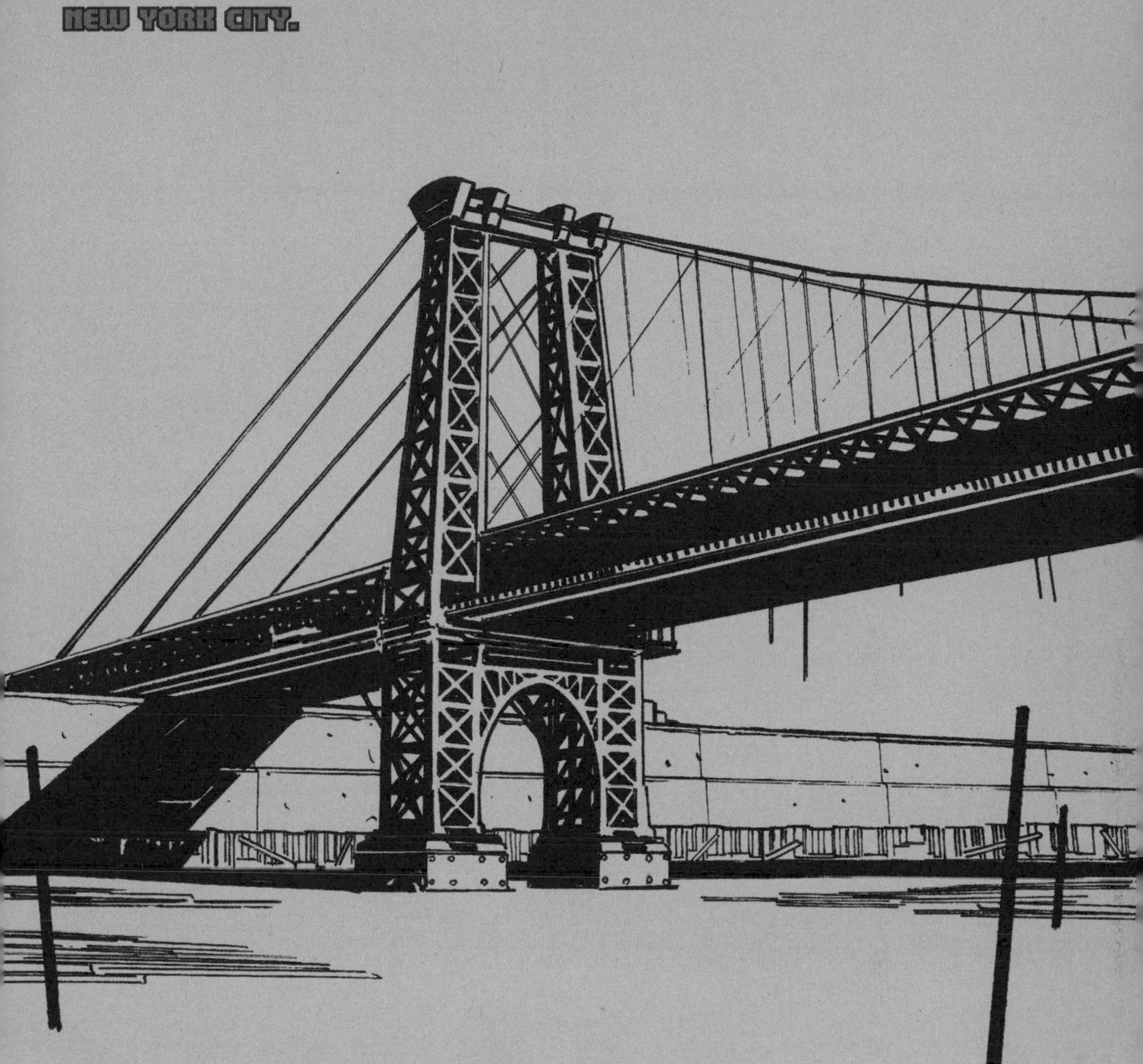
NEW YORK CITY.

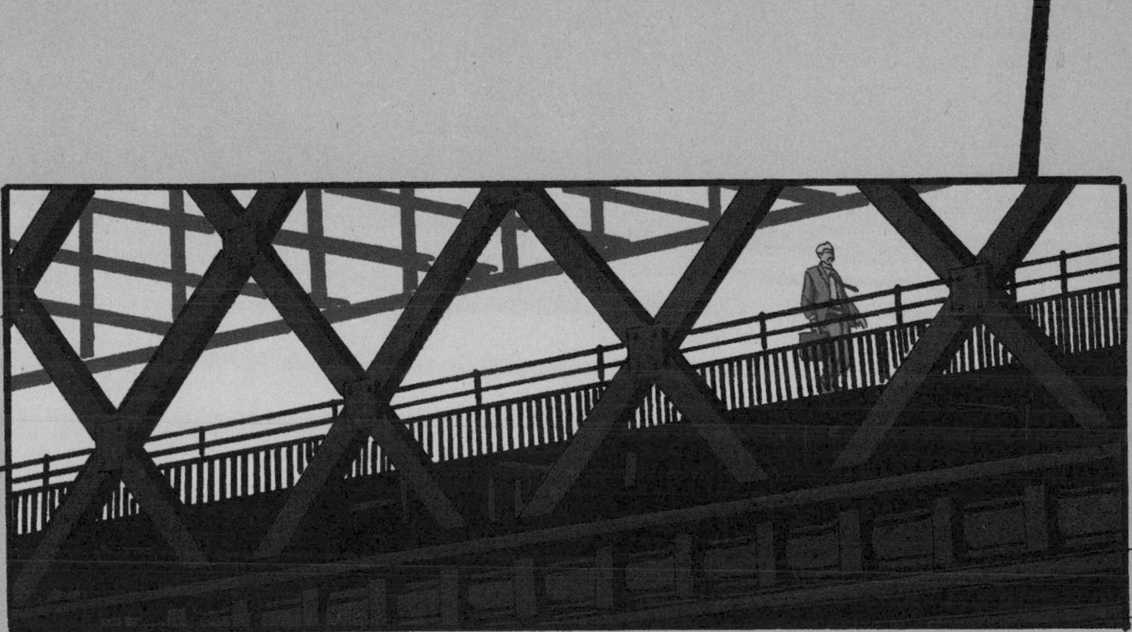

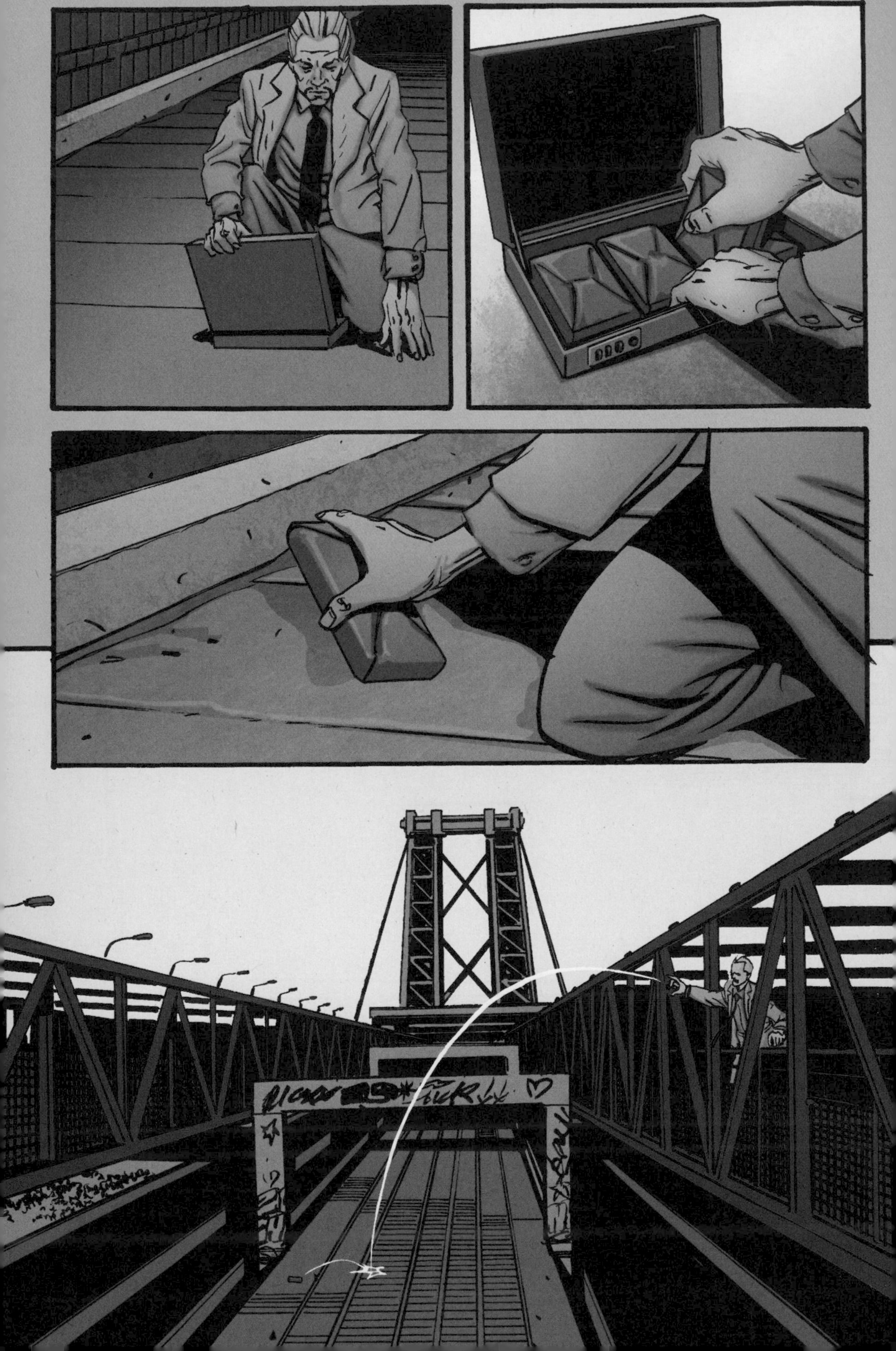

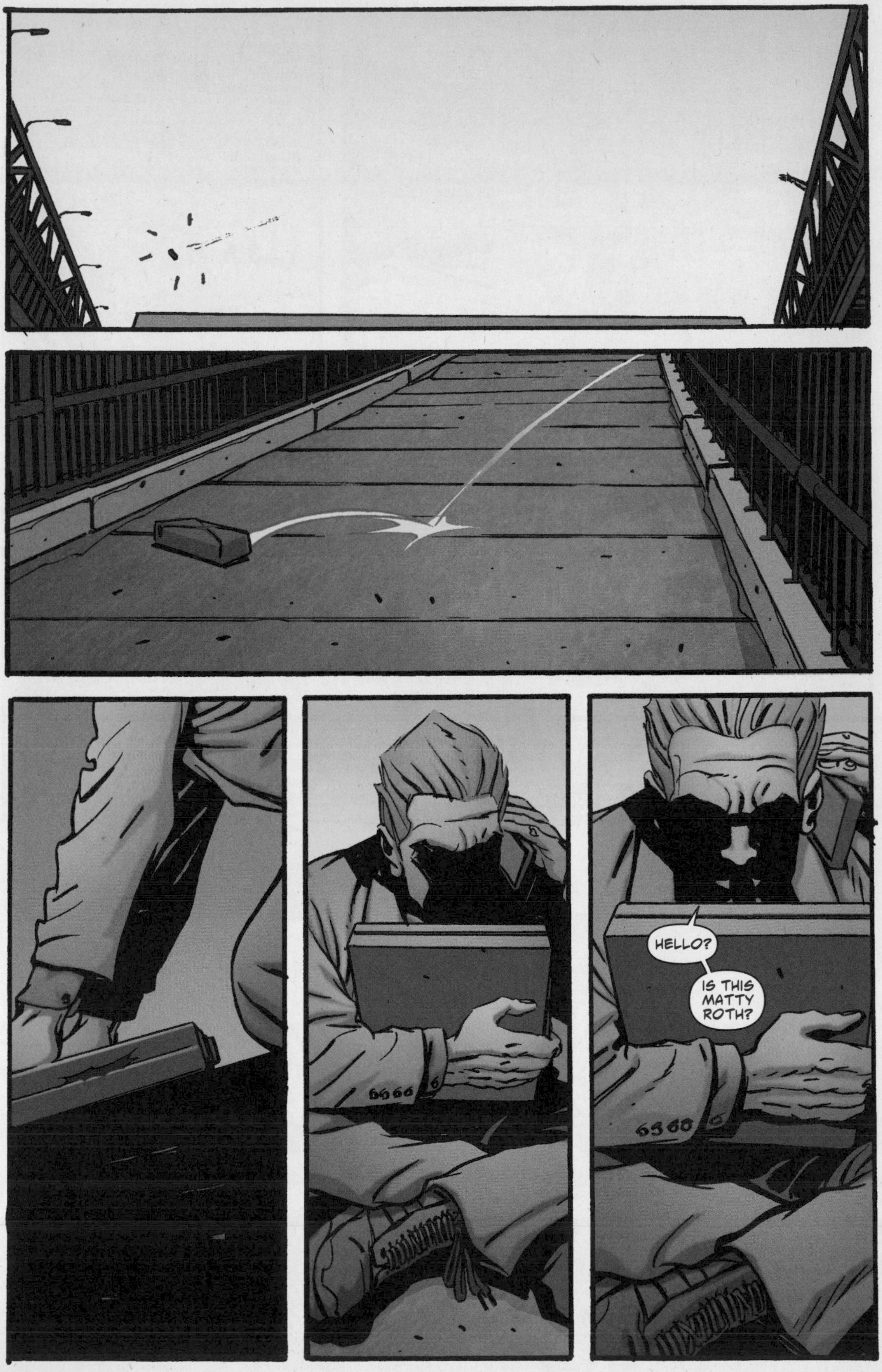
HELLO?
IS THIS MATTY ROTH?

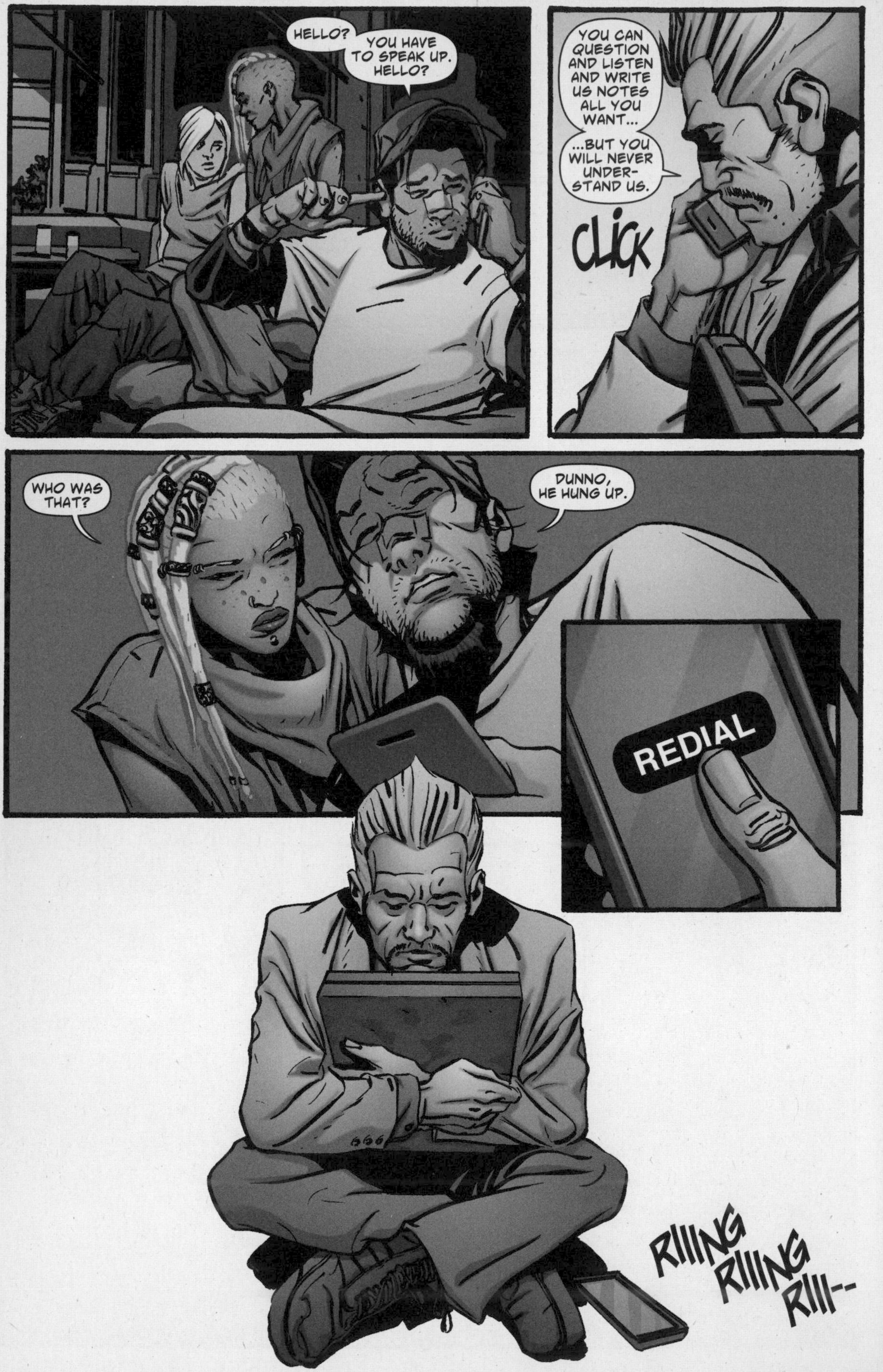
HELLO?
YOU HAVE TO SPEAK UP. HELLO?
YOU CAN QUESTION AND LISTEN AND WRITE US NOTES ALL YOU WANT...
...BUT YOU WILL NEVER UNDER-STAND US.
CLICK
WHO WAS THAT?
DUNNO, HE HUNG UP.
REDIAL
RIIING RIIING RIII--

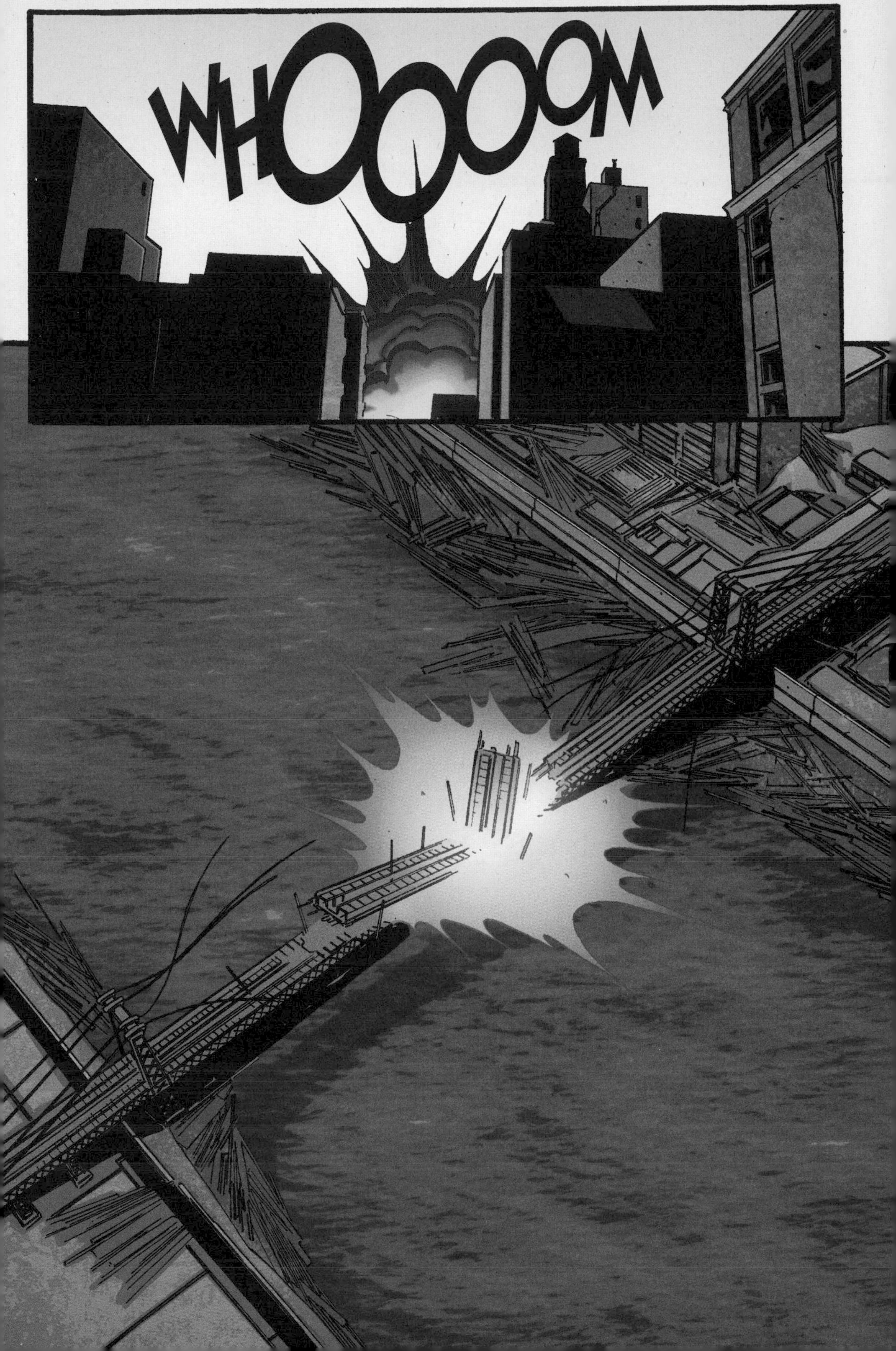
WHOOOOM

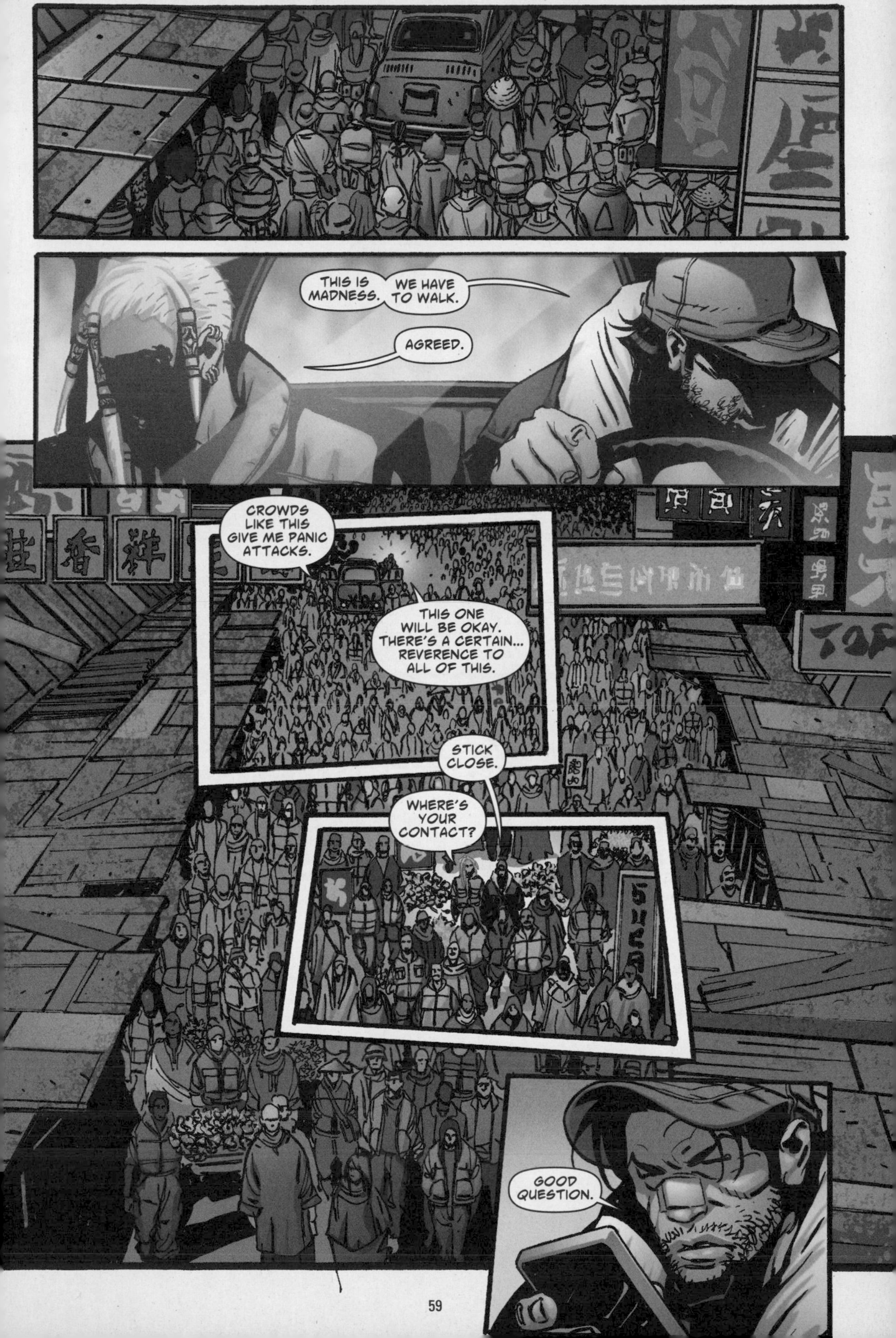

THIS IS MADNESS.
WE HAVE TO WALK.
AGREED.
CROWDS LIKE THIS GIVE ME PANIC ATTACKS.
THIS ONE WILL BE OKAY. THERE'S A CERTAIN... REVERENCE TO ALL OF THIS.
STICK CLOSE.
WHERE'S YOUR CONTACT?
GOOD QUESTION.

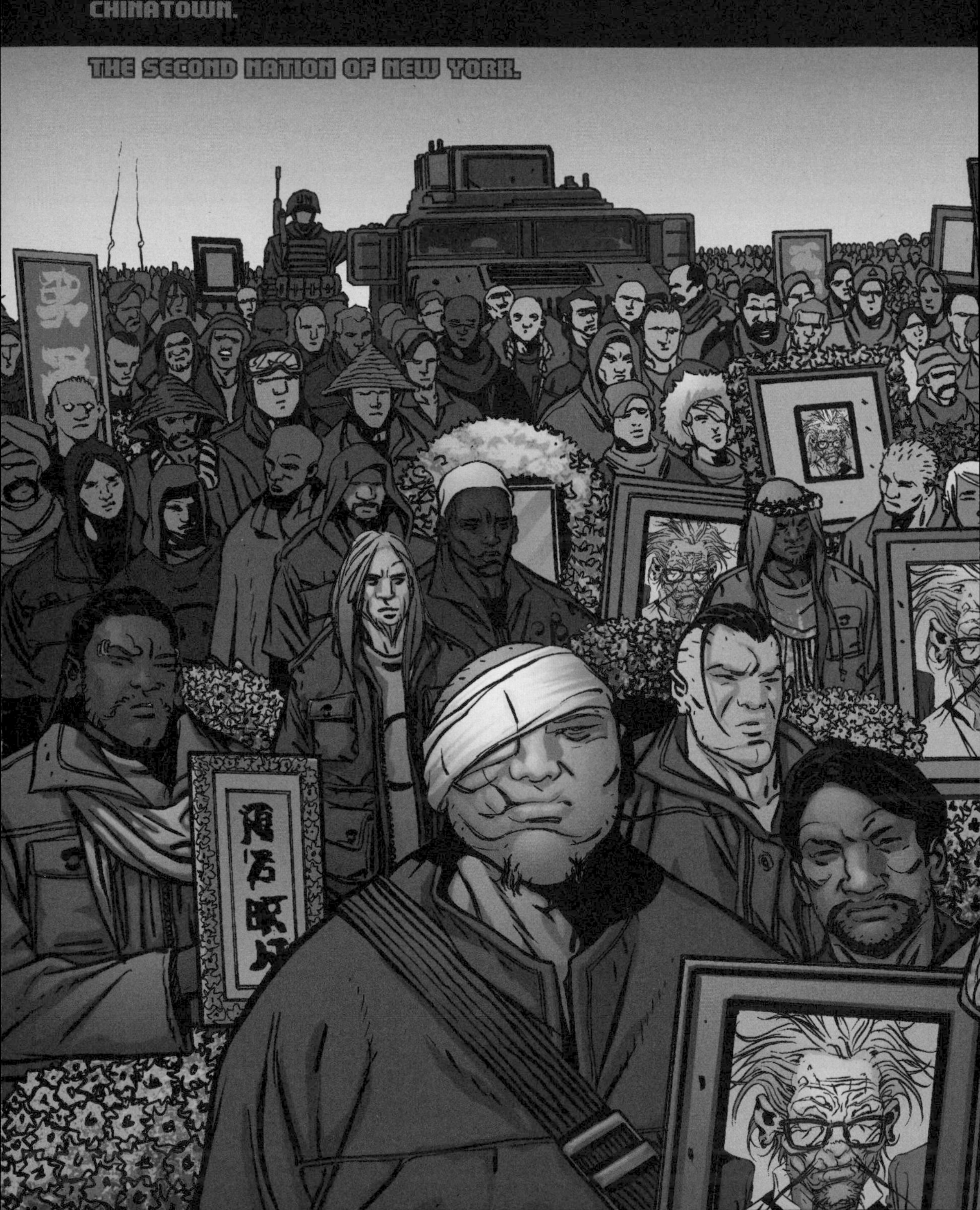
CHINATOWN.
THE SECOND NATION OF NEW YORK.

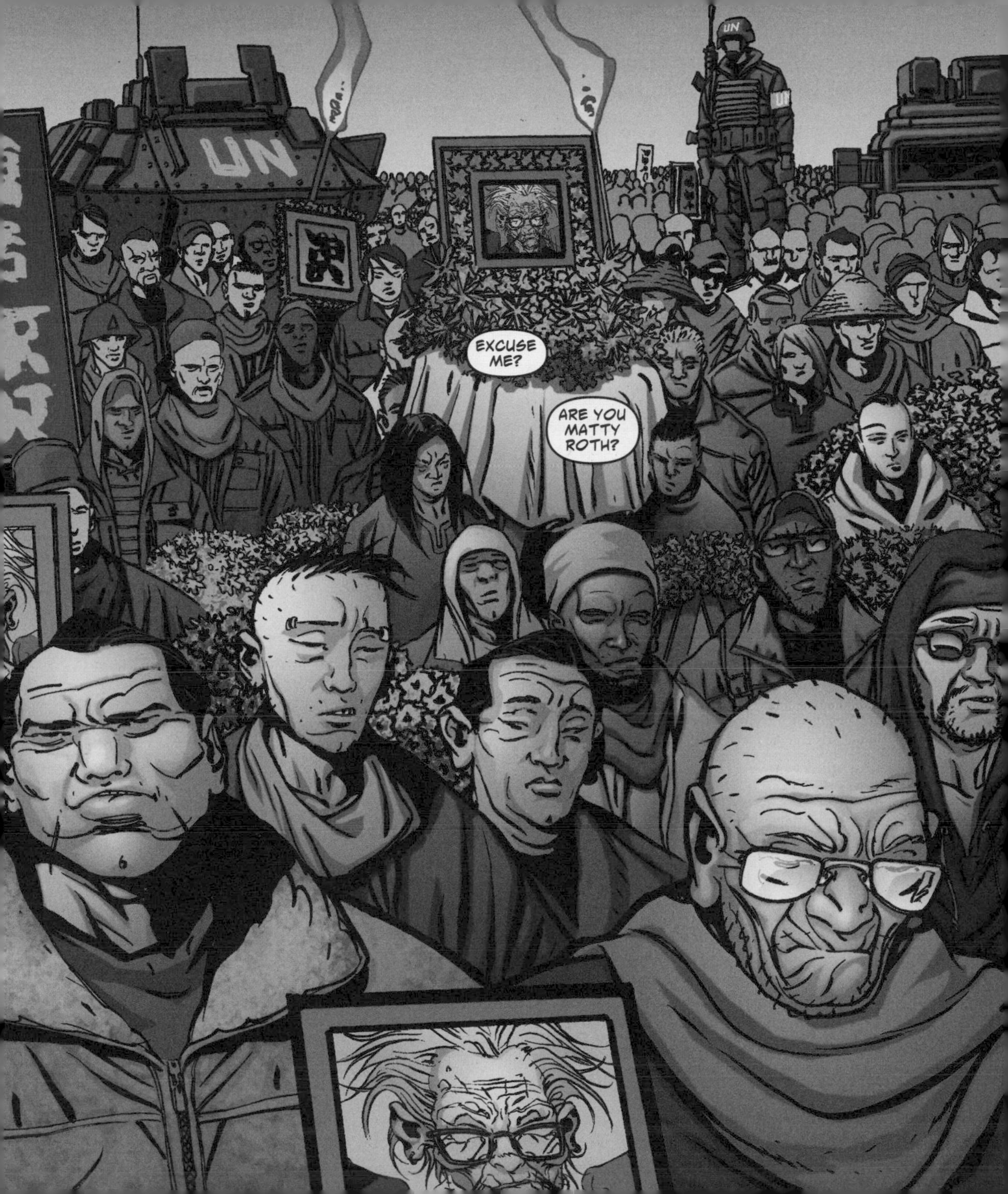
EXCUSE ME?
ARE YOU MATTY ROTH?

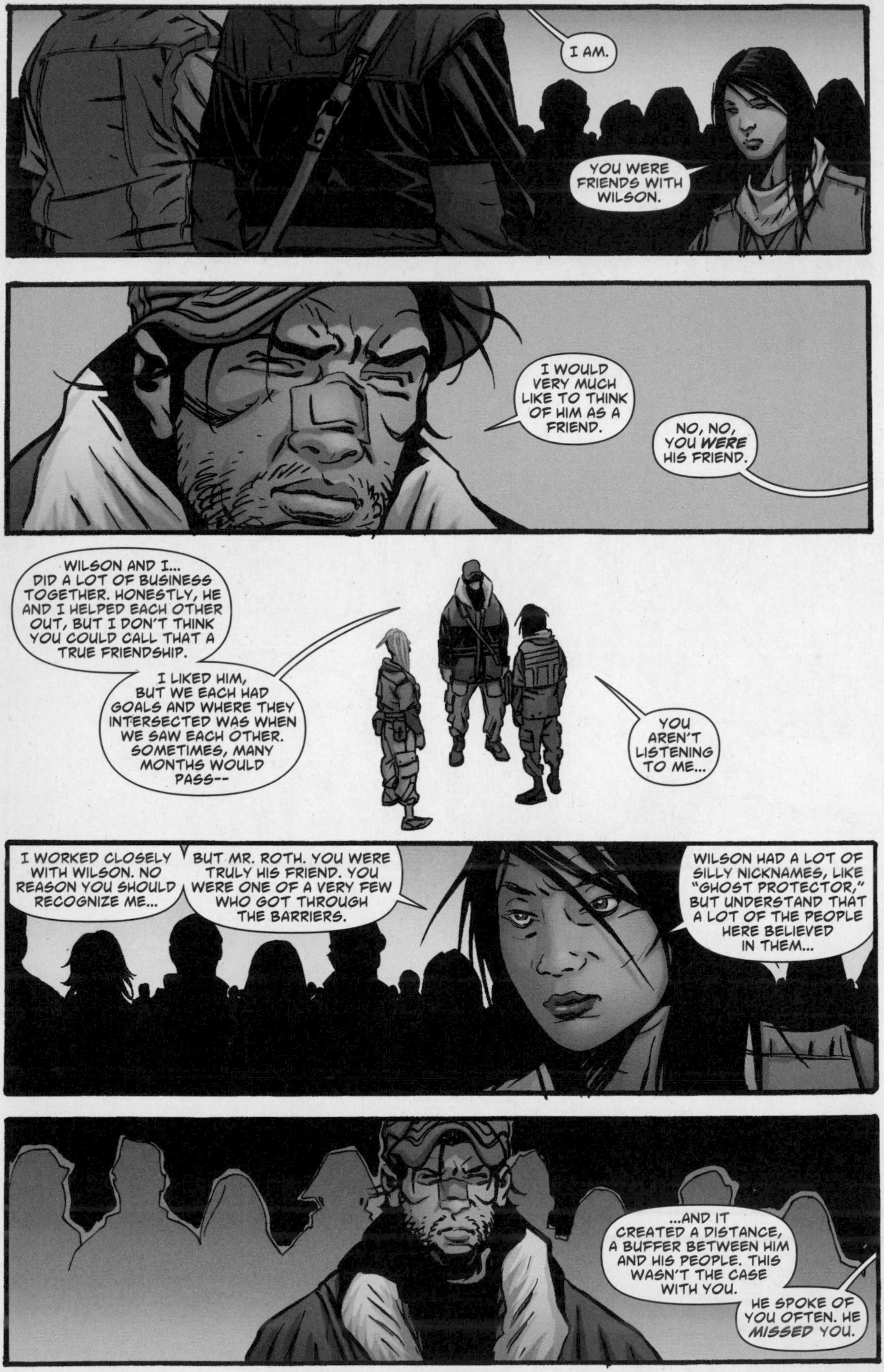
I AM.
YOU WERE FRIENDS WITH WILSON.
I WOULD VERY MUCH LIKE TO THINK OF HIM AS A FRIEND.
NO, NO, YOU WERE HIS FRIEND.
WILSON AND I... DID A LOT OF BUSINESS TOGETHER. HONESTLY, HE AND I HELPED EACH OTHER OUT, BUT I DON'T THINK YOU COULD CALL THAT A TRUE FRIENDSHIP.
I LIKED HIM, BUT WE EACH HAD GOALS AND WHERE THEY INTERSECTED WAS WHEN WE SAW EACH OTHER. SOMETIMES, MANY MONTHS WOULD PASS--
YOU AREN'T LISTENING TO ME...
I WORKED CLOSELY WITH WILSON. NO REASON YOU SHOULD RECOGNIZE ME...
BUT MR. ROTH. YOU WERE TRULY HIS FRIEND. YOU WERE ONE OF A VERY FEW WHO GOT THROUGH THE BARRIERS.
WILSON HAD A LOT OF SILLY NICKNAMES, LIKE "GHOST PROTECTOR," BUT UNDERSTAND THAT A LOT OF THE PEOPLE HERE BELIEVED IN THEM...
...AND IT CREATED A DISTANCE, A BUFFER BETWEEN HIM AND HIS PEOPLE. THIS WASN'T THE CASE WITH YOU.
HE SPOKE OF YOU OFTEN. HE MISSED YOU.

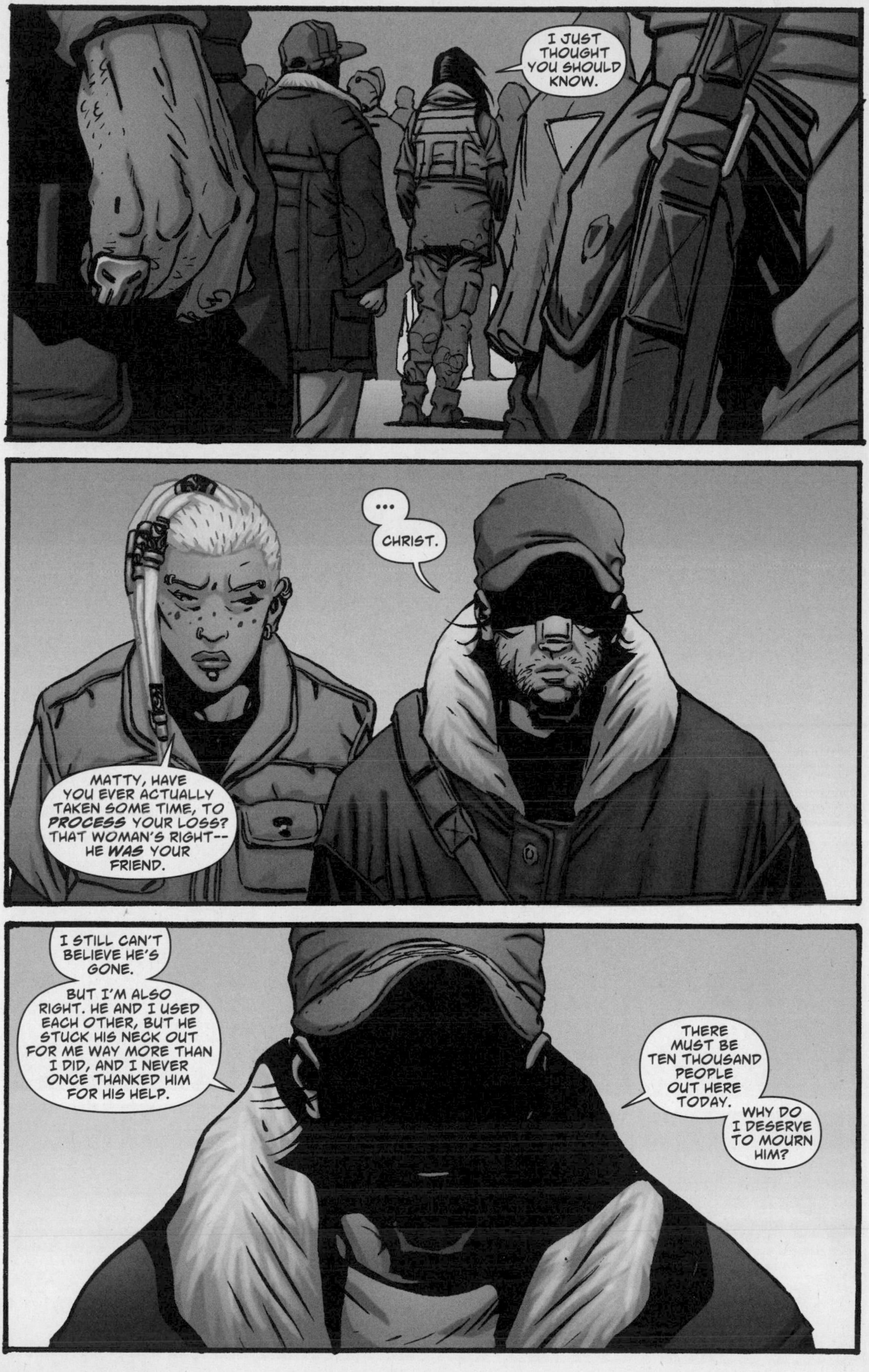
I JUST THOUGHT YOU SHOULD KNOW.
...
CHRIST.
MATTY, HAVE YOU EVER ACTUALLY TAKEN SOME TIME, TO PROCESS YOUR LOSS? THAT WOMAN'S RIGHT-- HE WAS YOUR FRIEND.
I STILL CAN'T BELIEVE HE'S GONE.
BUT I'M ALSO RIGHT. HE AND I USED EACH OTHER, BUT HE STUCK HIS NECK OUT FOR ME WAY MORE THAN I DID, AND I NEVER ONCE THANKED HIM FOR HIS HELP.
THERE MUST BE TEN THOUSAND PEOPLE OUT HERE TODAY.
WHY DO I DESERVE TO MOURN HIM?

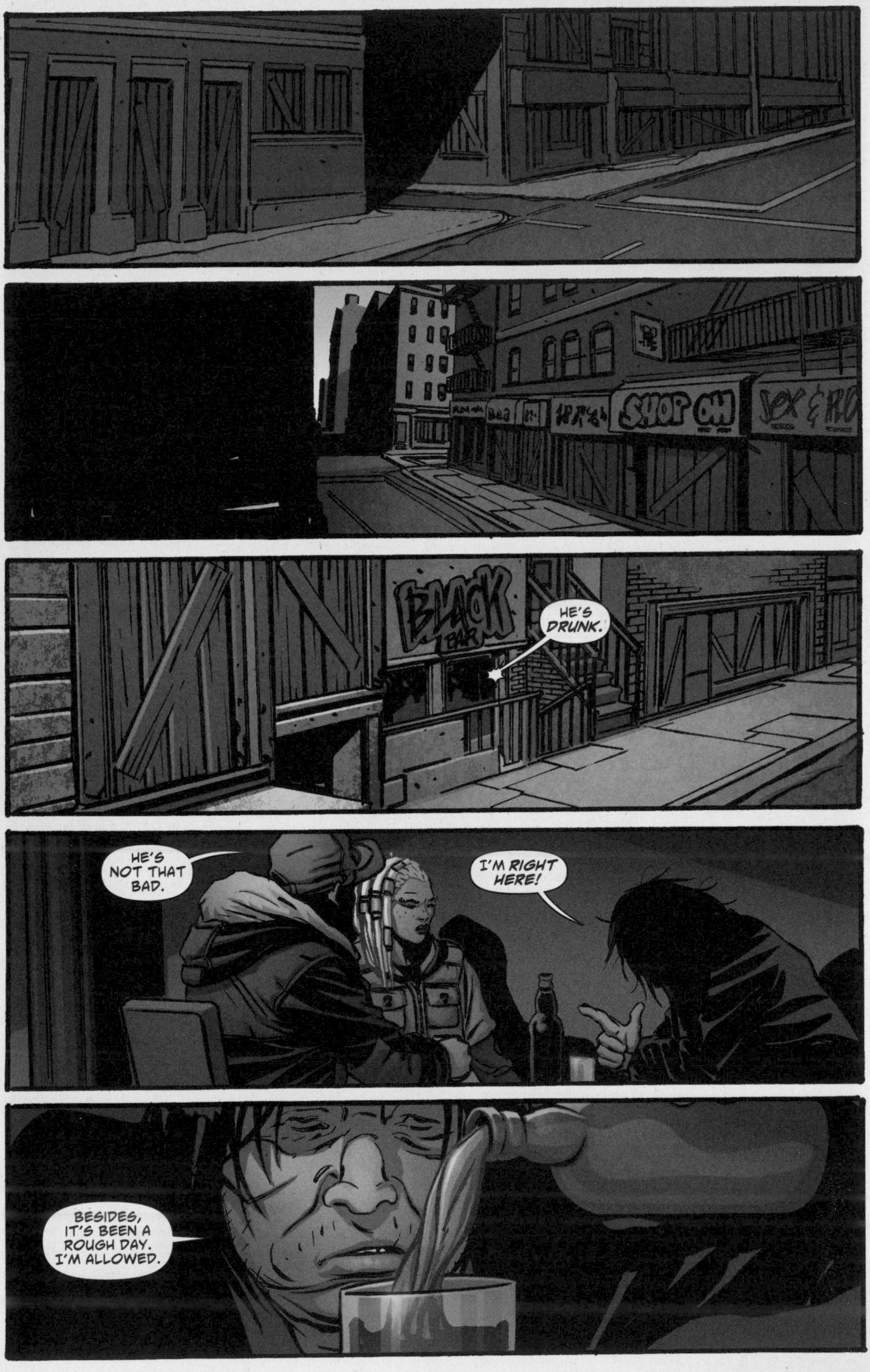
SHOP OH
BLACK BAR
HE'S DRUNK.
HE'S NOT THAT BAD.
I'M RIGHT HERE!
BESIDES, IT'S BEEN A ROUGH DAY. I'M ALLOWED.

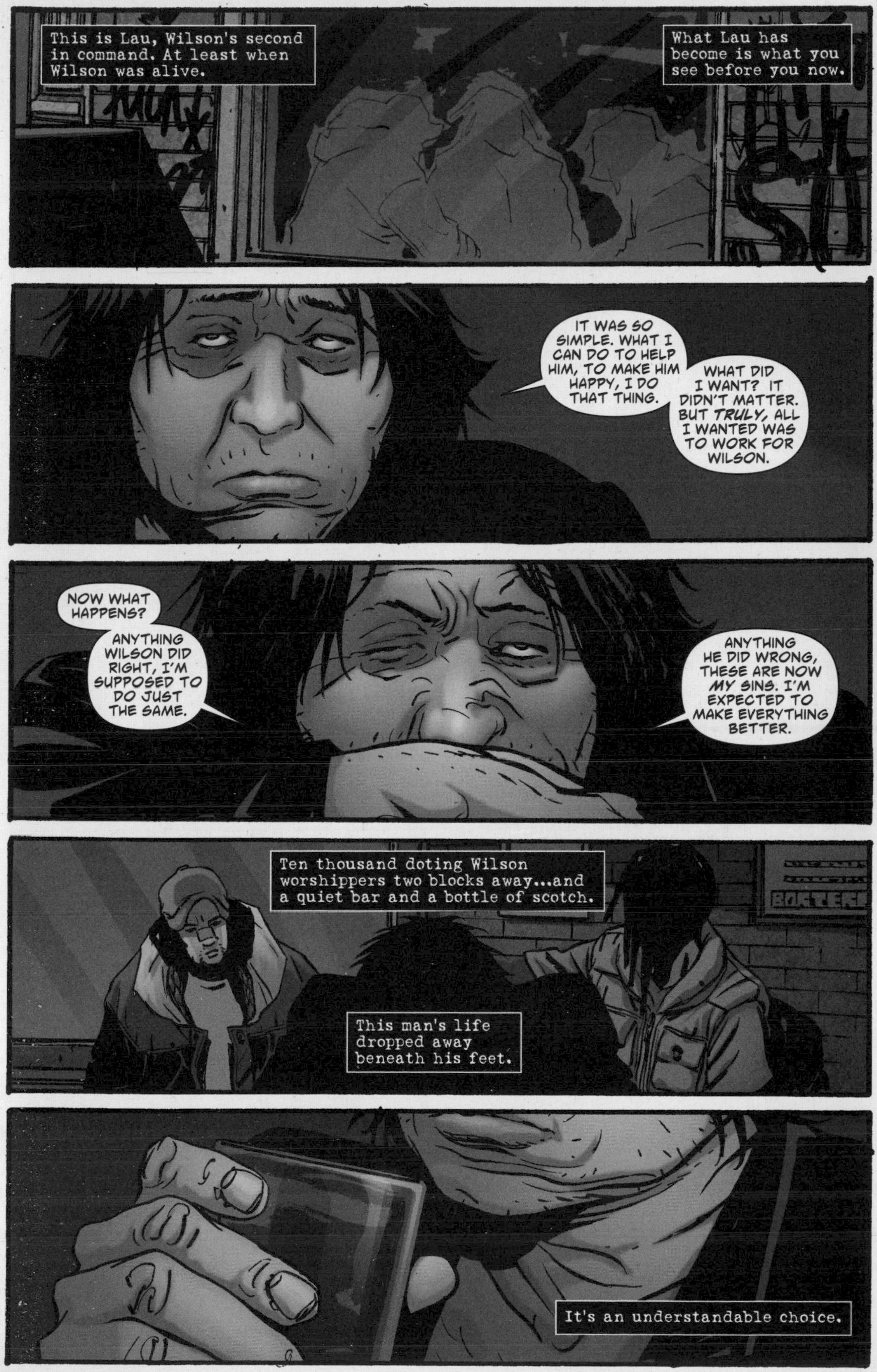
This is Lau, Wilson's second in command. At least when Wilson was alive.
What Lau has become is what you see before you now.
IT WAS SO SIMPLE. WHAT I CAN DO TO HELP HIM, TO MAKE HIM HAPPY, I DO THAT THING.
WHAT DID I WANT? IT DIDN'T MATTER. BUT TRULY, ALL I WANTED WAS TO WORK FOR WILSON.
NOW WHAT HAPPENS?
ANYTHING WILSON DID RIGHT, I'M SUPPOSED TO DO JUST THE SAME.
ANYTHING HE DID WRONG, THESE ARE NOW MY SINS. I'M EXPECTED TO MAKE EVERYTHING BETTER.
Ten thousand doting Wilson worshippers two blocks away...and a quiet bar and a bottle of scotch.
This man's life dropped away beneath his feet.
It's an understandable choice.

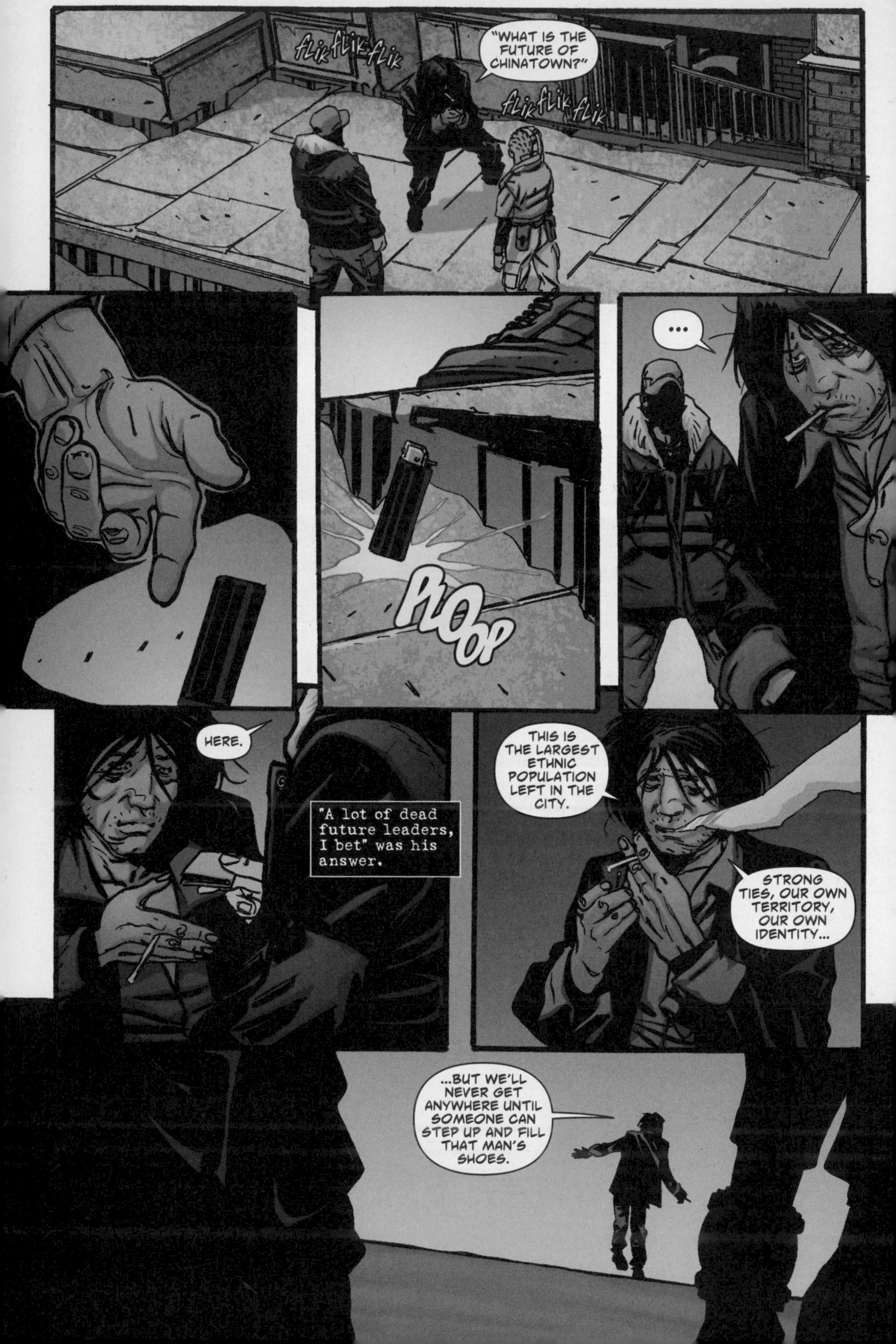
"WHAT IS THE FUTURE OF CHINATOWN?"
FLIK FLIK FLIK
FLIK FLIK FLIK
PLOOP
...
HERE.
"A lot of dead future leaders, I bet" was his answer.
THIS IS THE LARGEST ETHNIC POPULATION LEFT IN THE CITY.
STRONG TIES, OUR OWN TERRITORY, OUR OWN IDENTITY...
...BUT WE'LL NEVER GET ANYWHERE UNTIL SOMEONE CAN STEP UP AND FILL THAT MAN'S SHOES.

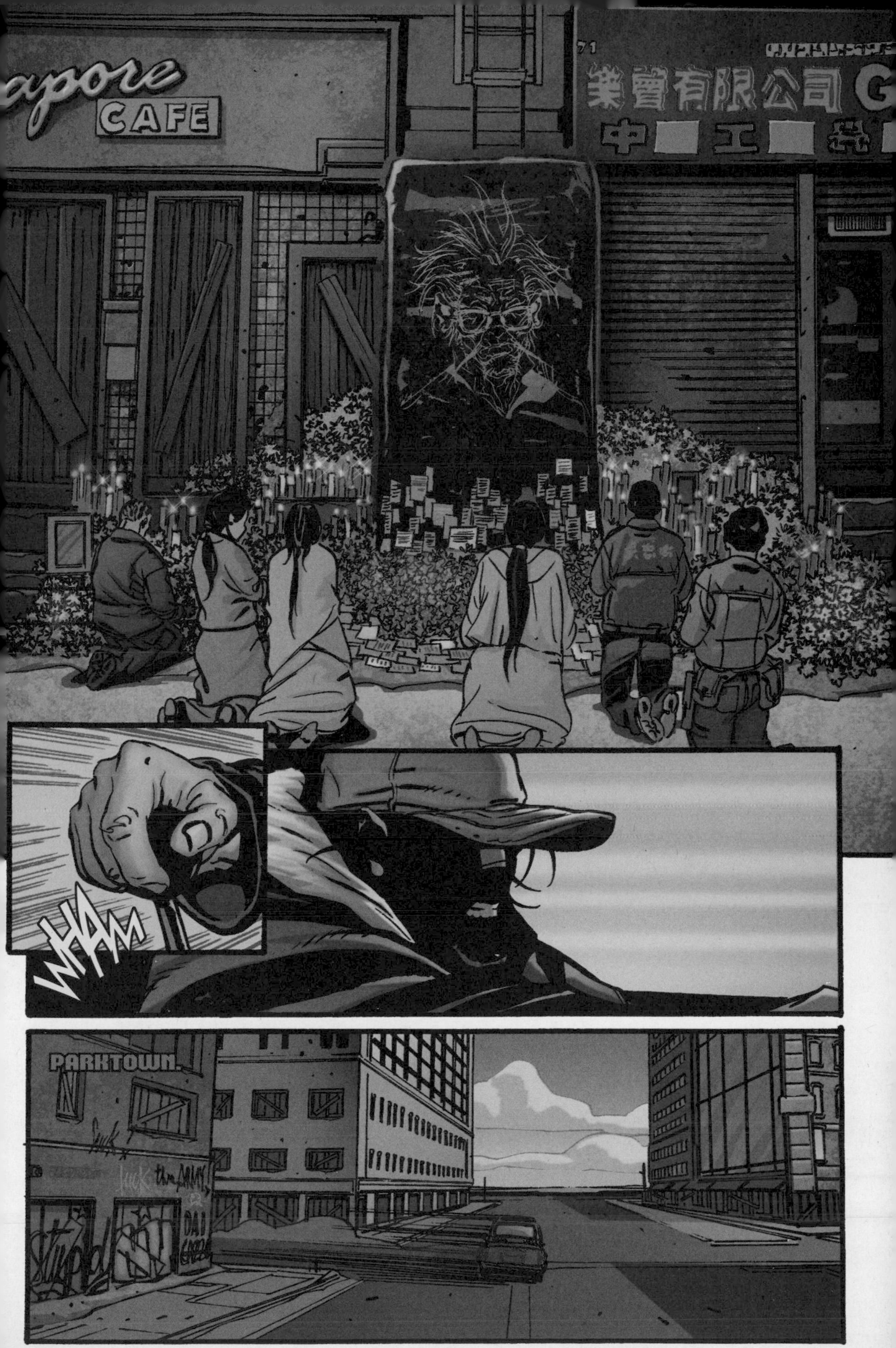
apore
CAFE
71
有限公司
WHAM
PARKTOWN.

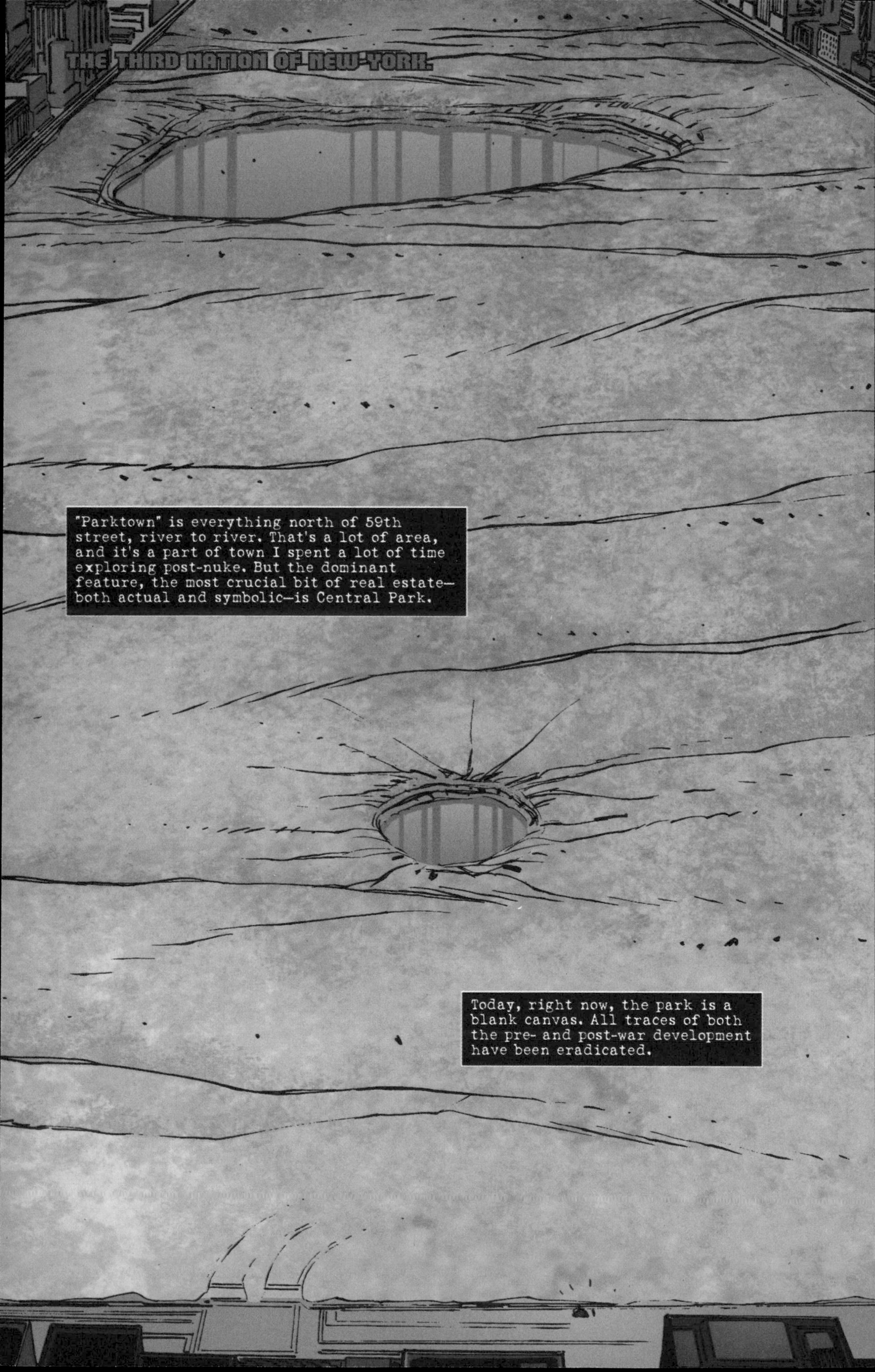
THE THIRD NATION OF NEW YORK.
"Parktown" is everything north of 59th street, river to river. That's a lot of area, and it's a part of town I spent a lot of time exploring post-nuke. But the dominant feature, the most crucial bit of real estate—both actual and symbolic—is Central Park.
Today, right now, the park is a blank canvas. All traces of both the pre- and post-war development have been eradicated.

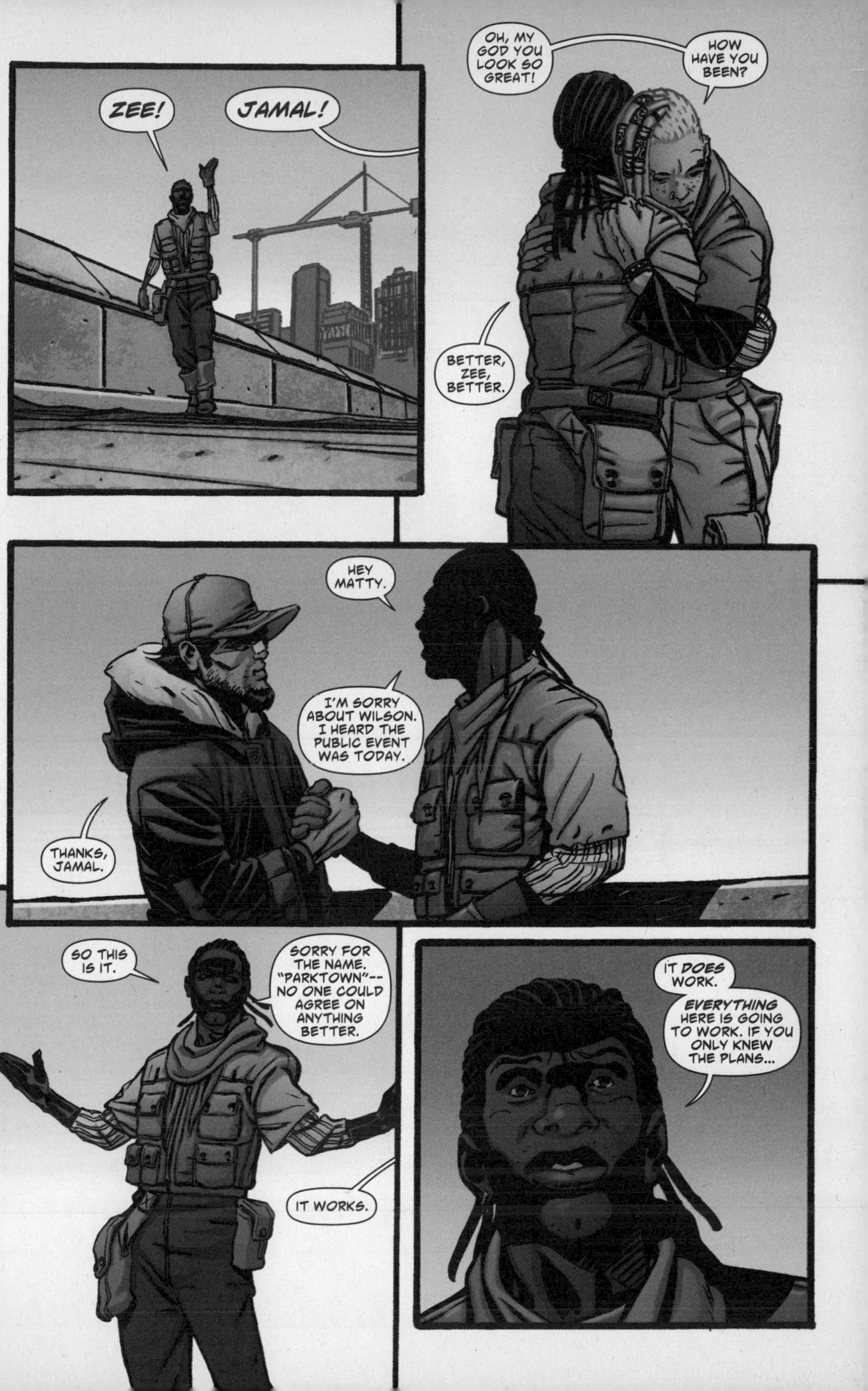
ZEE!
JAMAL!
OH, MY GOD YOU LOOK SO GREAT!
HOW HAVE YOU BEEN?
BETTER, ZEE, BETTER.
HEY MATTY.
I'M SORRY ABOUT WILSON. I HEARD THE PUBLIC EVENT WAS TODAY.
THANKS, JAMAL.
SO THIS IS IT.
SORRY FOR THE NAME. "PARKTOWN"-- NO ONE COULD AGREE ON ANYTHING BETTER.
IT WORKS.
IT DOES WORK.
EVERYTHING HERE IS GOING TO WORK. IF YOU ONLY KNEW THE PLANS...

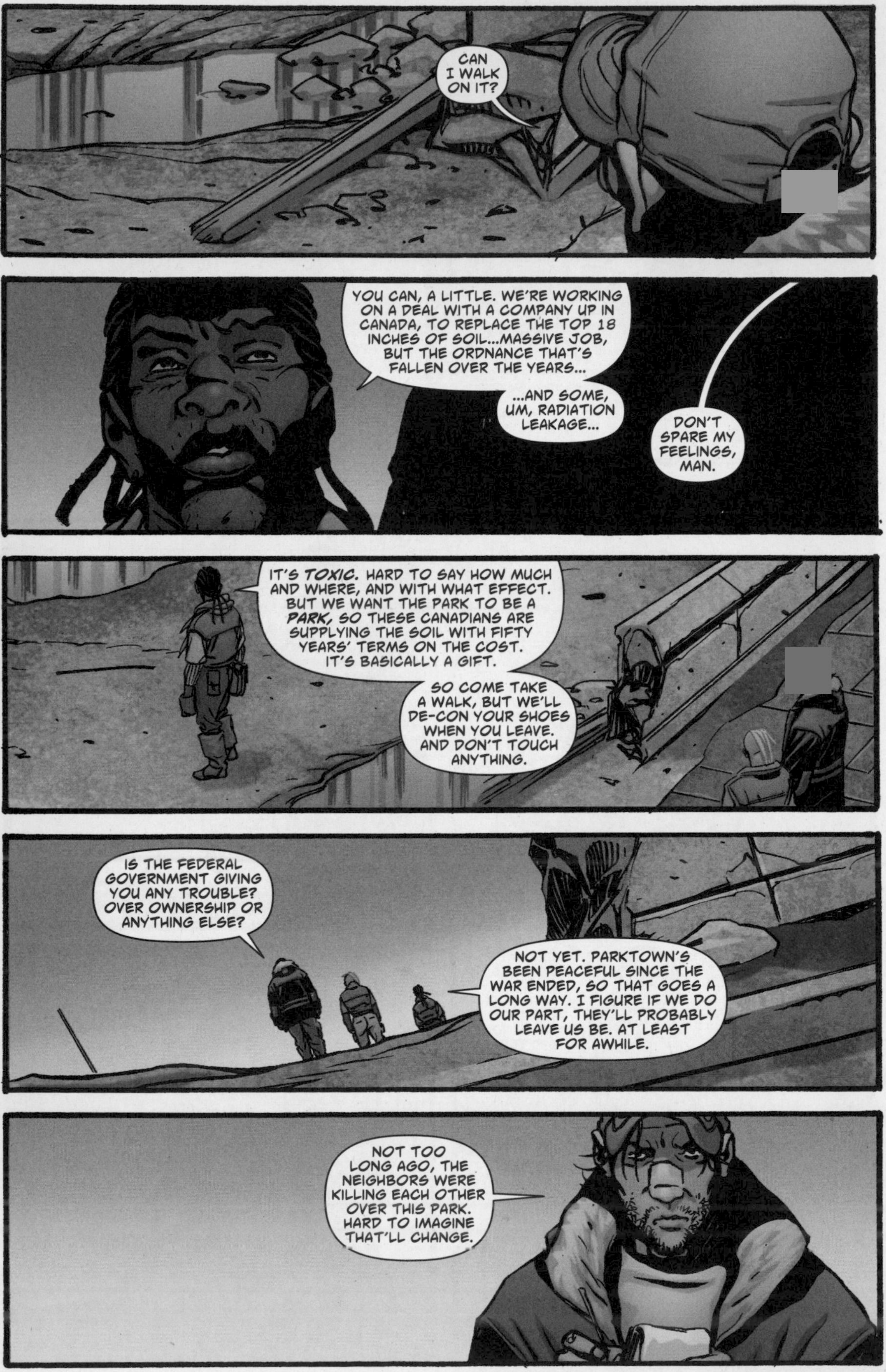
CAN I WALK ON IT?
YOU CAN, A LITTLE. WE'RE WORKING ON A DEAL WITH A COMPANY UP IN CANADA, TO REPLACE THE TOP 18 INCHES OF SOIL...MASSIVE JOB, BUT THE ORDNANCE THAT'S FALLEN OVER THE YEARS...
...AND SOME, UM, RADIATION LEAKAGE...
DON'T SPARE MY FEELINGS, MAN.
IT'S *TOXIC*. HARD TO SAY HOW MUCH AND WHERE, AND WITH WHAT EFFECT. BUT WE WANT THE PARK TO BE A *PARK,* SO THESE CANADIANS ARE SUPPLYING THE SOIL WITH FIFTY YEARS' TERMS ON THE COST. IT'S BASICALLY A GIFT.
SO COME TAKE A WALK, BUT WE'LL DE-CON YOUR SHOES WHEN YOU LEAVE. AND DON'T TOUCH ANYTHING.
IS THE FEDERAL GOVERNMENT GIVING YOU ANY TROUBLE? OVER OWNERSHIP OR ANYTHING ELSE?
NOT YET. PARKTOWN'S BEEN PEACEFUL SINCE THE WAR ENDED, SO THAT GOES A LONG WAY. I FIGURE IF WE DO OUR PART, THEY'LL PROBABLY LEAVE US BE. AT LEAST FOR AWHILE.
NOT TOO LONG AGO, THE NEIGHBORS WERE KILLING EACH OTHER OVER THIS PARK. HARD TO IMAGINE THAT'LL CHANGE.

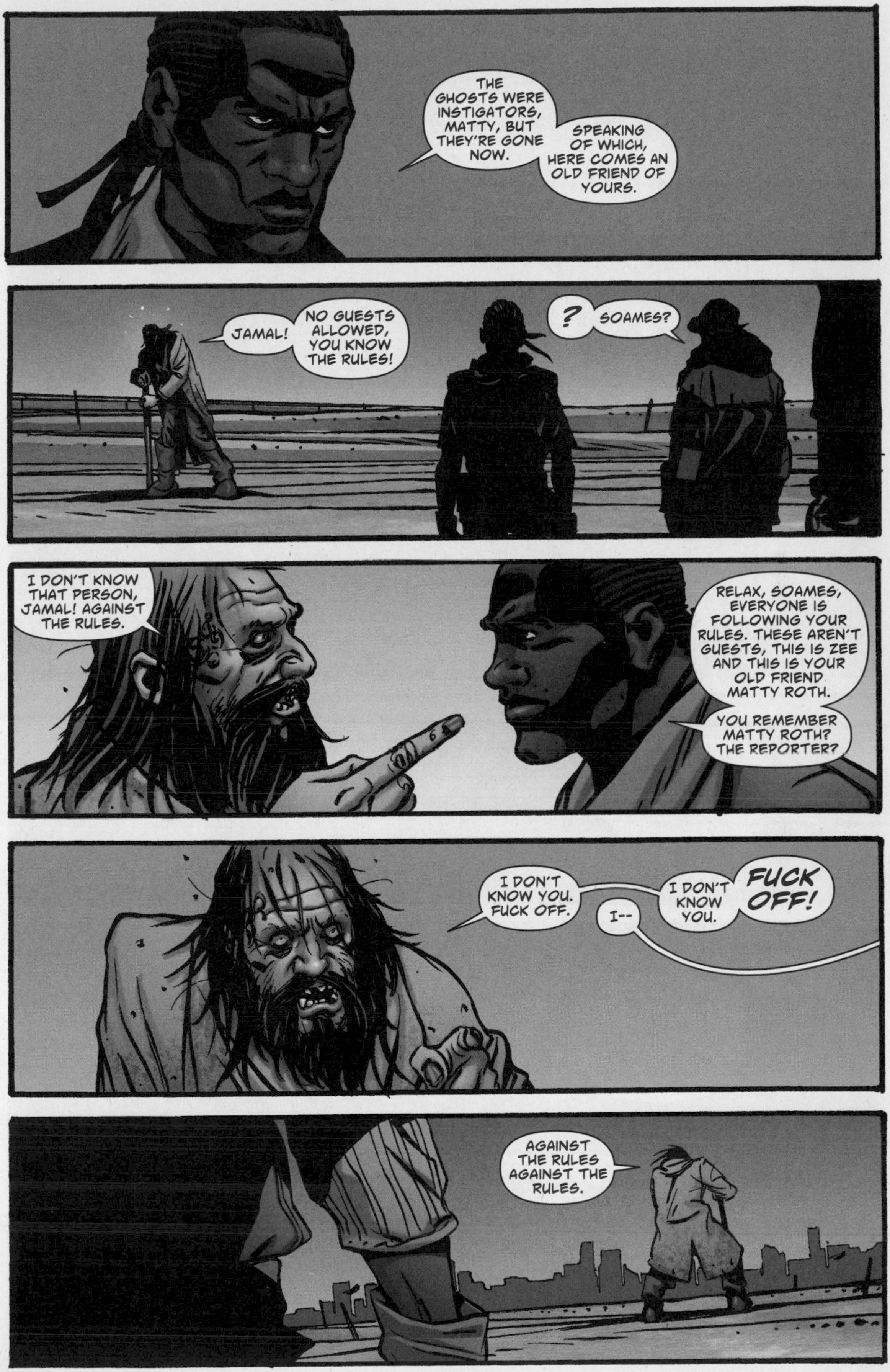
THE GHOSTS WERE INSTIGATORS, MATTY, BUT THEY'RE GONE NOW.
SPEAKING OF WHICH, HERE COMES AN OLD FRIEND OF YOURS.
JAMAL!
NO GUESTS ALLOWED, YOU KNOW THE RULES!
?
SOAMES?
I DON'T KNOW THAT PERSON, JAMAL! AGAINST THE RULES.
RELAX, SOAMES, EVERYONE IS FOLLOWING YOUR RULES. THESE AREN'T GUESTS, THIS IS ZEE AND THIS IS YOUR OLD FRIEND MATTY ROTH.
YOU REMEMBER MATTY ROTH? THE REPORTER?
I DON'T KNOW YOU. FUCK OFF.
I--
I DON'T KNOW YOU.
FUCK OFF!
AGAINST THE RULES AGAINST THE RULES.

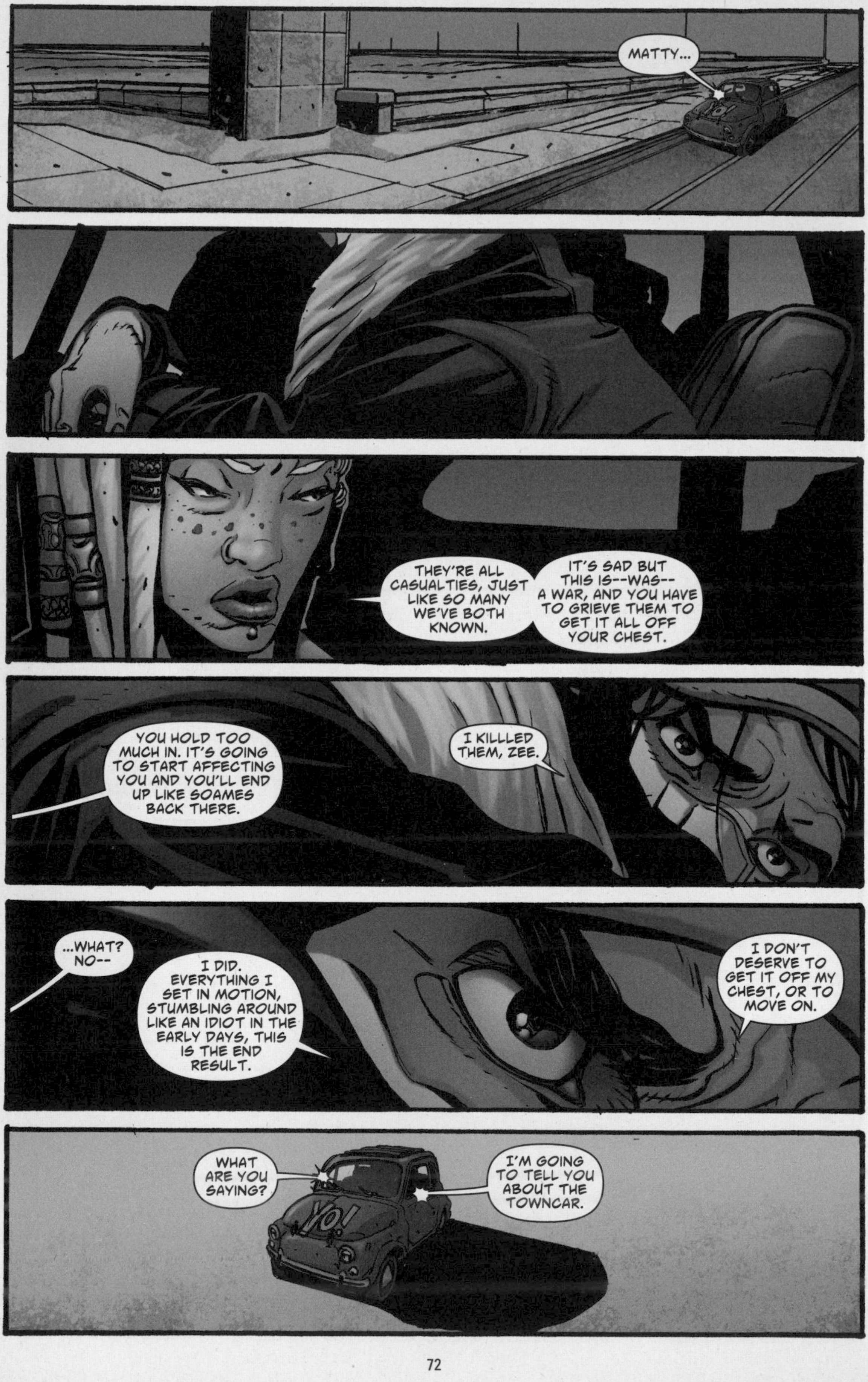
MATTY...
THEY'RE ALL CASUALTIES, JUST LIKE SO MANY WE'VE BOTH KNOWN.
IT'S SAD BUT THIS IS--WAS--A WAR, AND YOU HAVE TO GRIEVE THEM TO GET IT ALL OFF YOUR CHEST.
YOU HOLD TOO MUCH IN. IT'S GOING TO START AFFECTING YOU AND YOU'LL END UP LIKE SOAMES BACK THERE.
I KILLLED THEM, ZEE.
...WHAT? NO--
I DID. EVERYTHING I SET IN MOTION, STUMBLING AROUND LIKE AN IDIOT IN THE EARLY DAYS, THIS IS THE END RESULT.
I DON'T DESERVE TO GET IT OFF MY CHEST, OR TO MOVE ON.
WHAT ARE YOU SAYING?
YO!
I'M GOING TO TELL YOU ABOUT THE TOWNCAR.

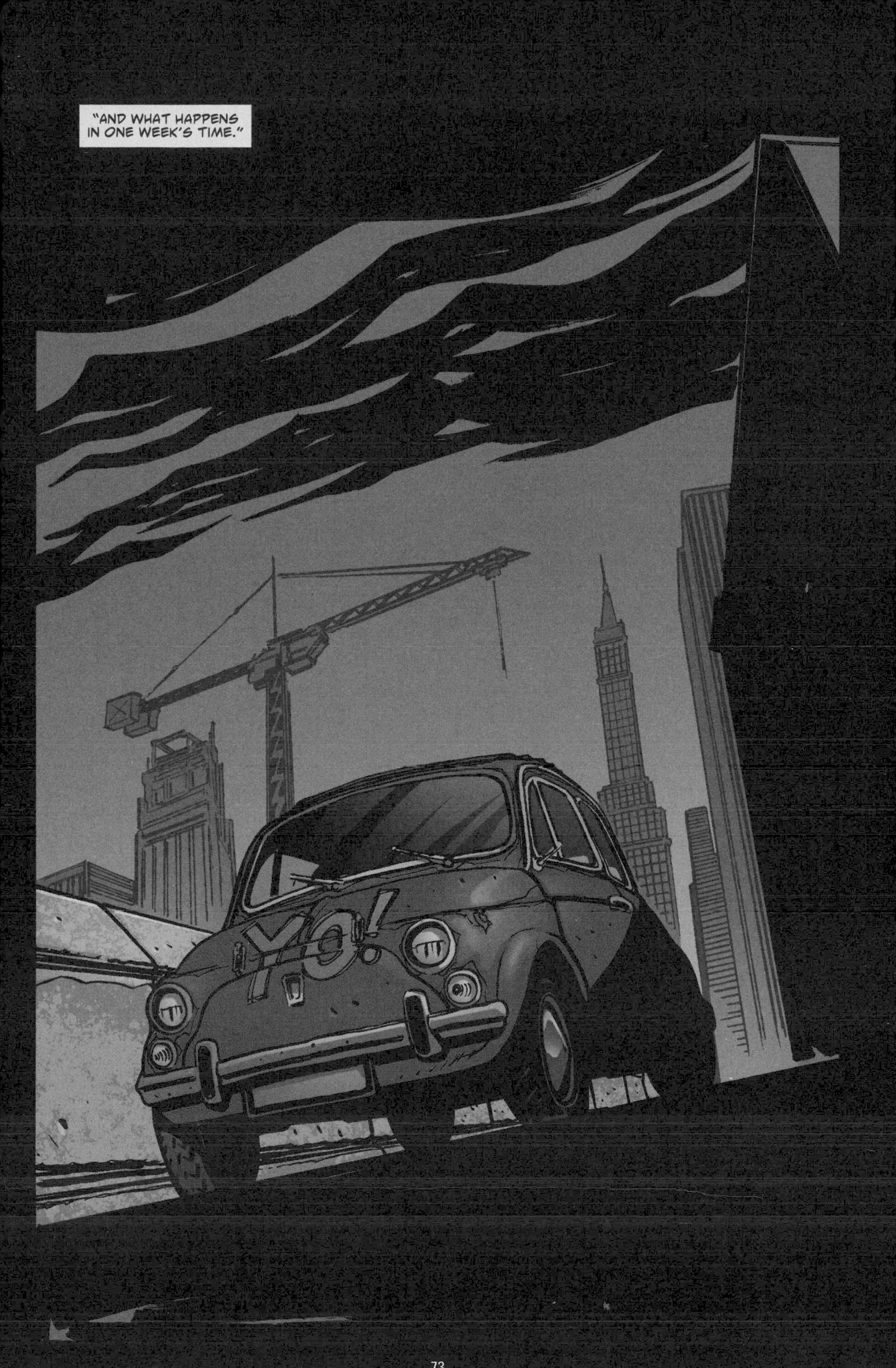
"AND WHAT HAPPENS IN ONE WEEK'S TIME."
YO!

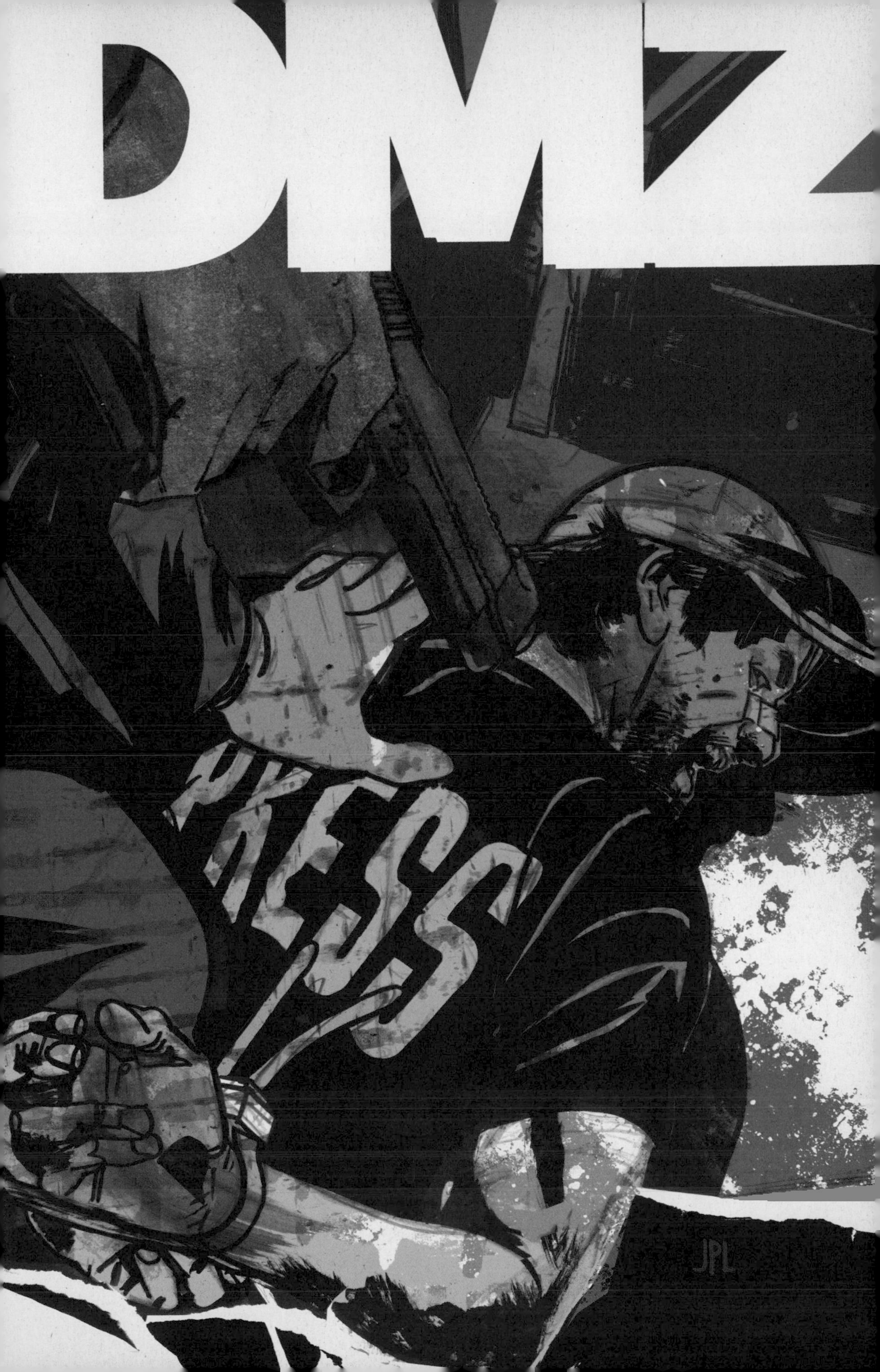
DMZ
PRESS
JPL

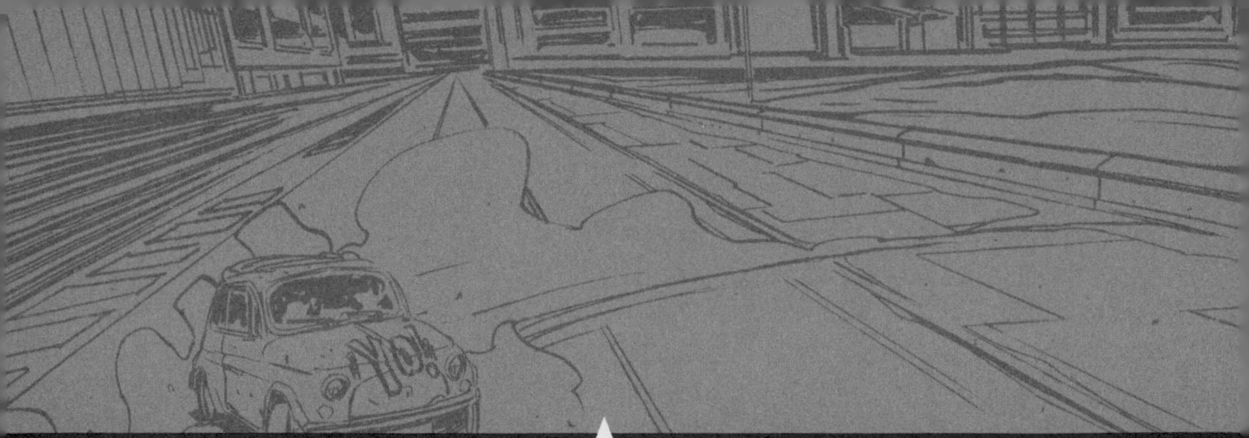
YO!

DMZ

THE FIVE NATIONS OF NEW YORK

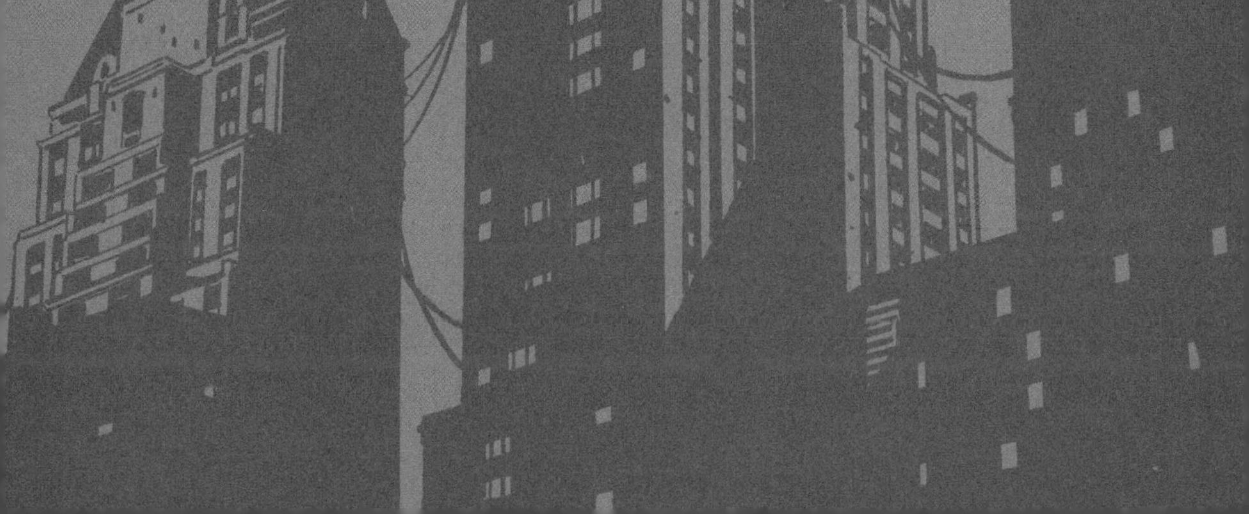

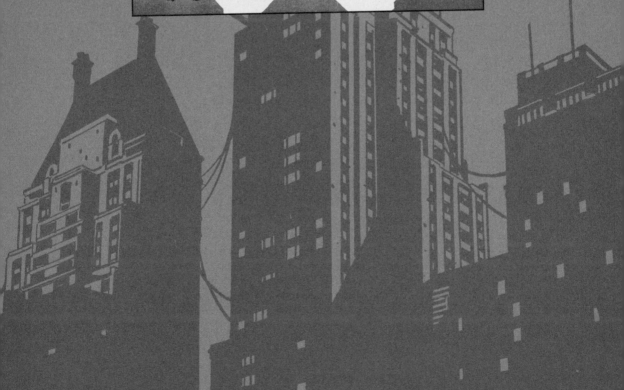

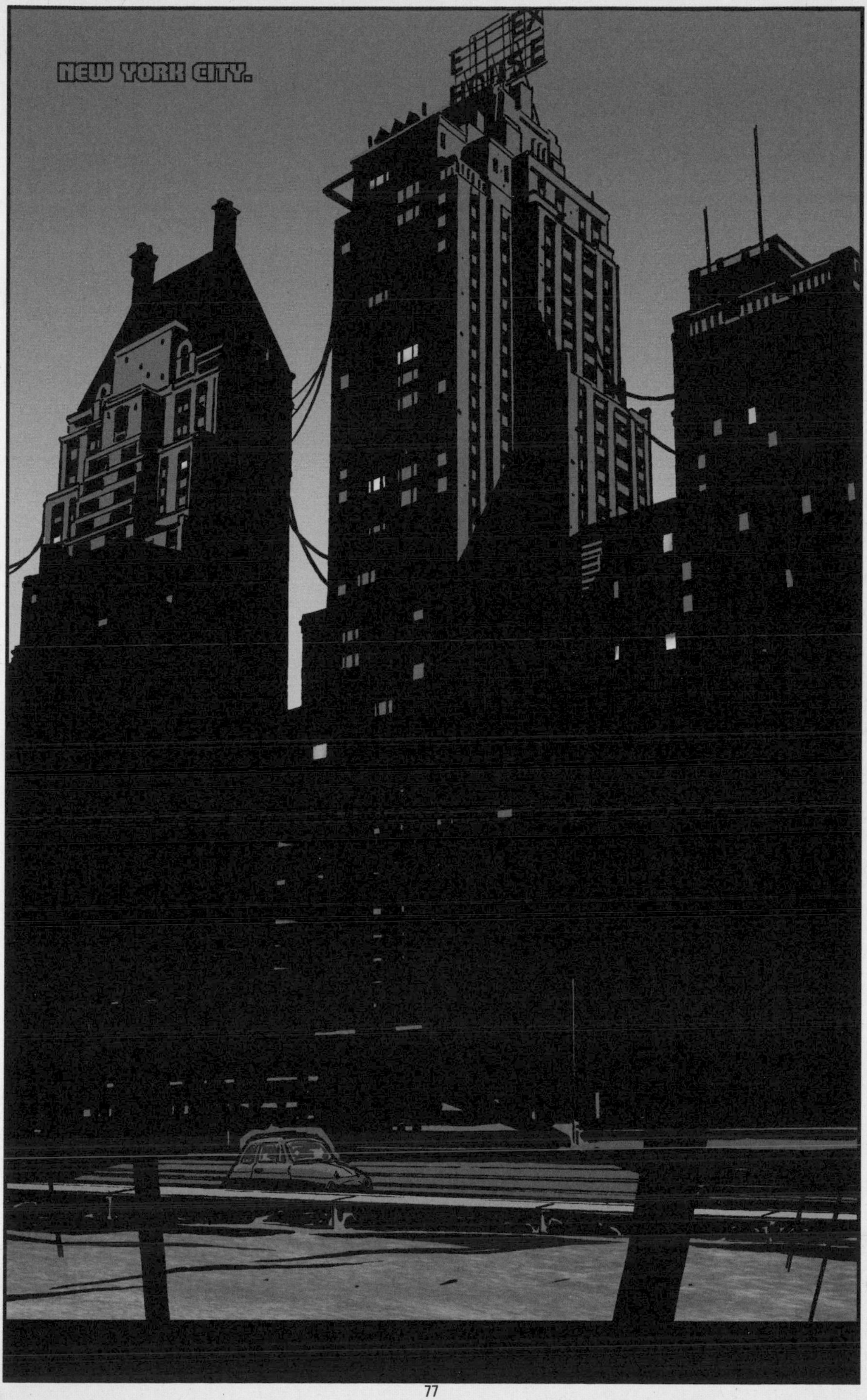
NEW YORK CITY.

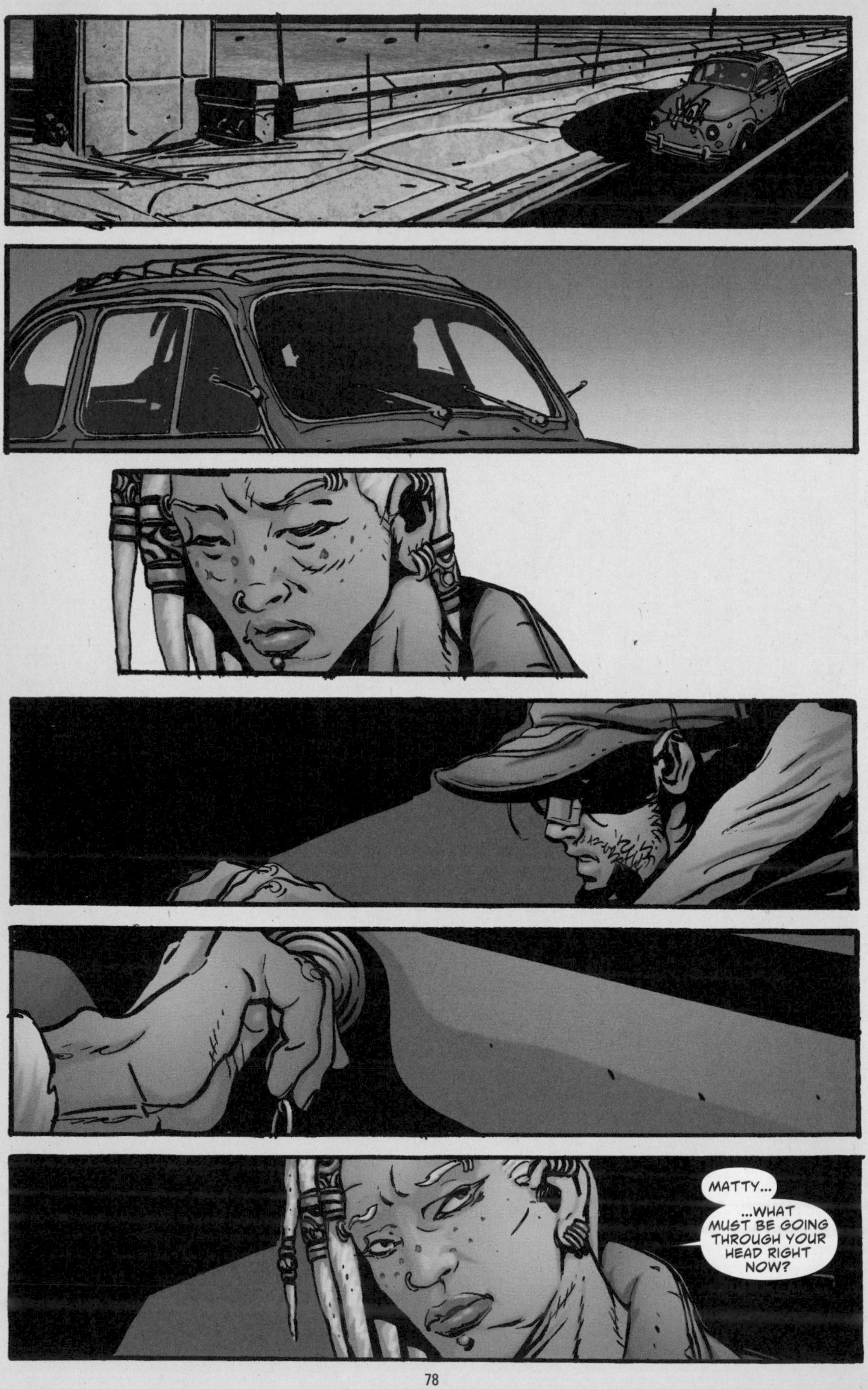
MATTY...
...WHAT MUST BE GOING THROUGH YOUR HEAD RIGHT NOW?

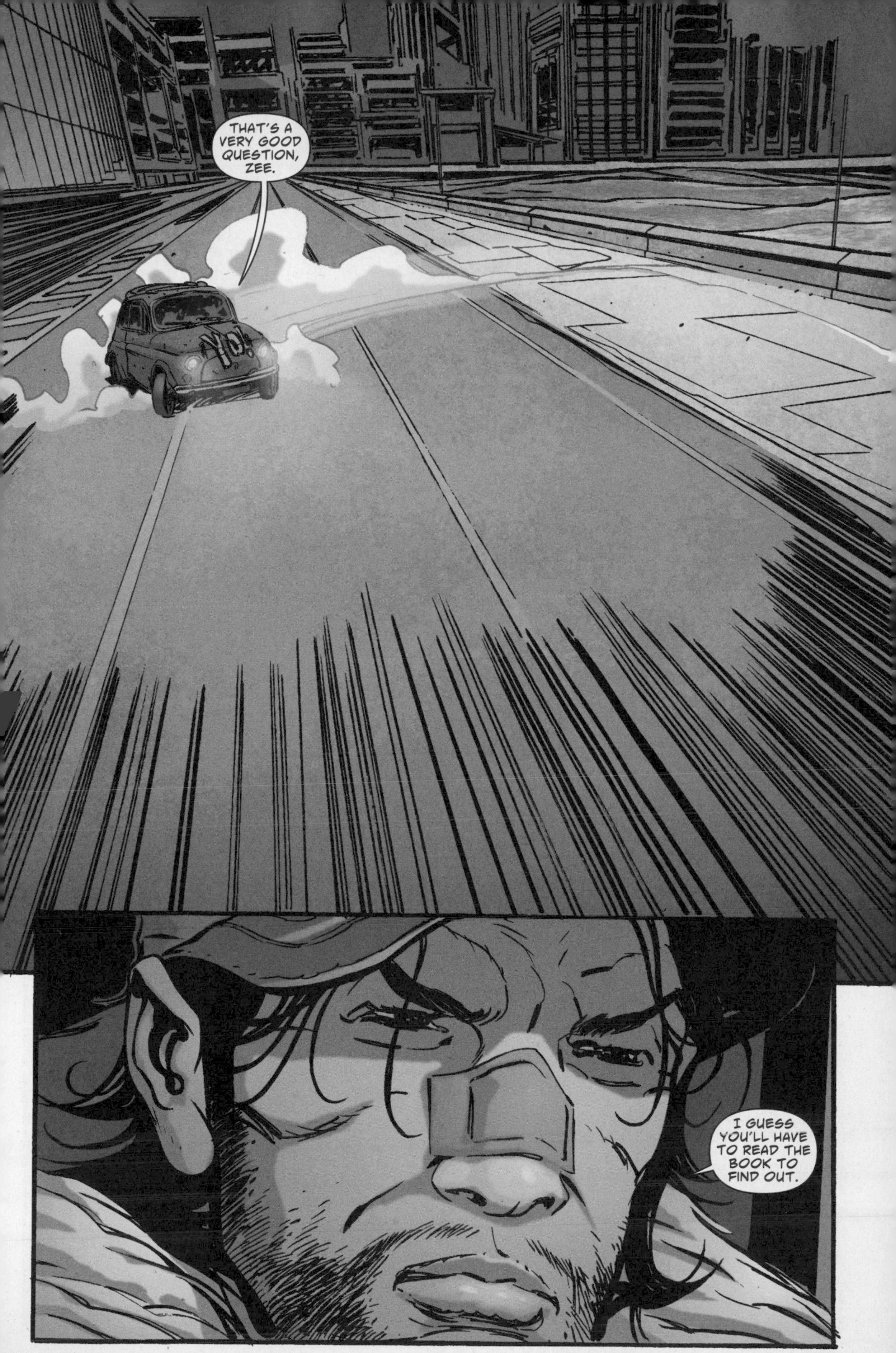
THAT'S A VERY GOOD QUESTION, ZEE.
YO!
I GUESS YOU'LL HAVE TO READ THE BOOK TO FIND OUT.

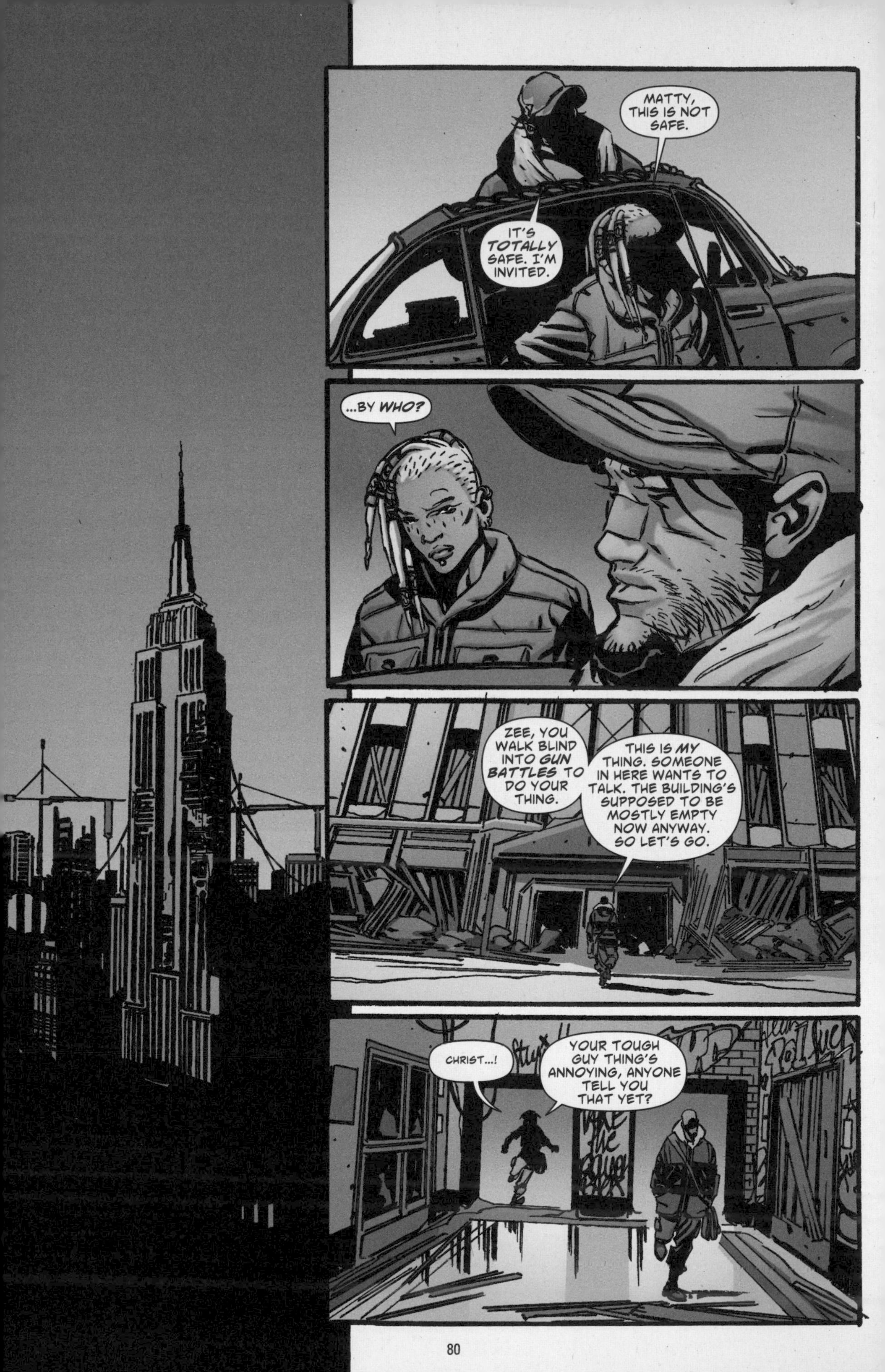
MATTY, THIS IS NOT SAFE.
IT'S TOTALLY SAFE. I'M INVITED.
...BY WHO?
ZEE, YOU WALK BLIND INTO GUN BATTLES TO DO YOUR THING.
THIS IS MY THING. SOMEONE IN HERE WANTS TO TALK. THE BUILDING'S SUPPOSED TO BE MOSTLY EMPTY NOW ANYWAY. SO LET'S GO.
CHRIST...!
YOUR TOUGH GUY THING'S ANNOYING, ANYONE TELL YOU THAT YET?

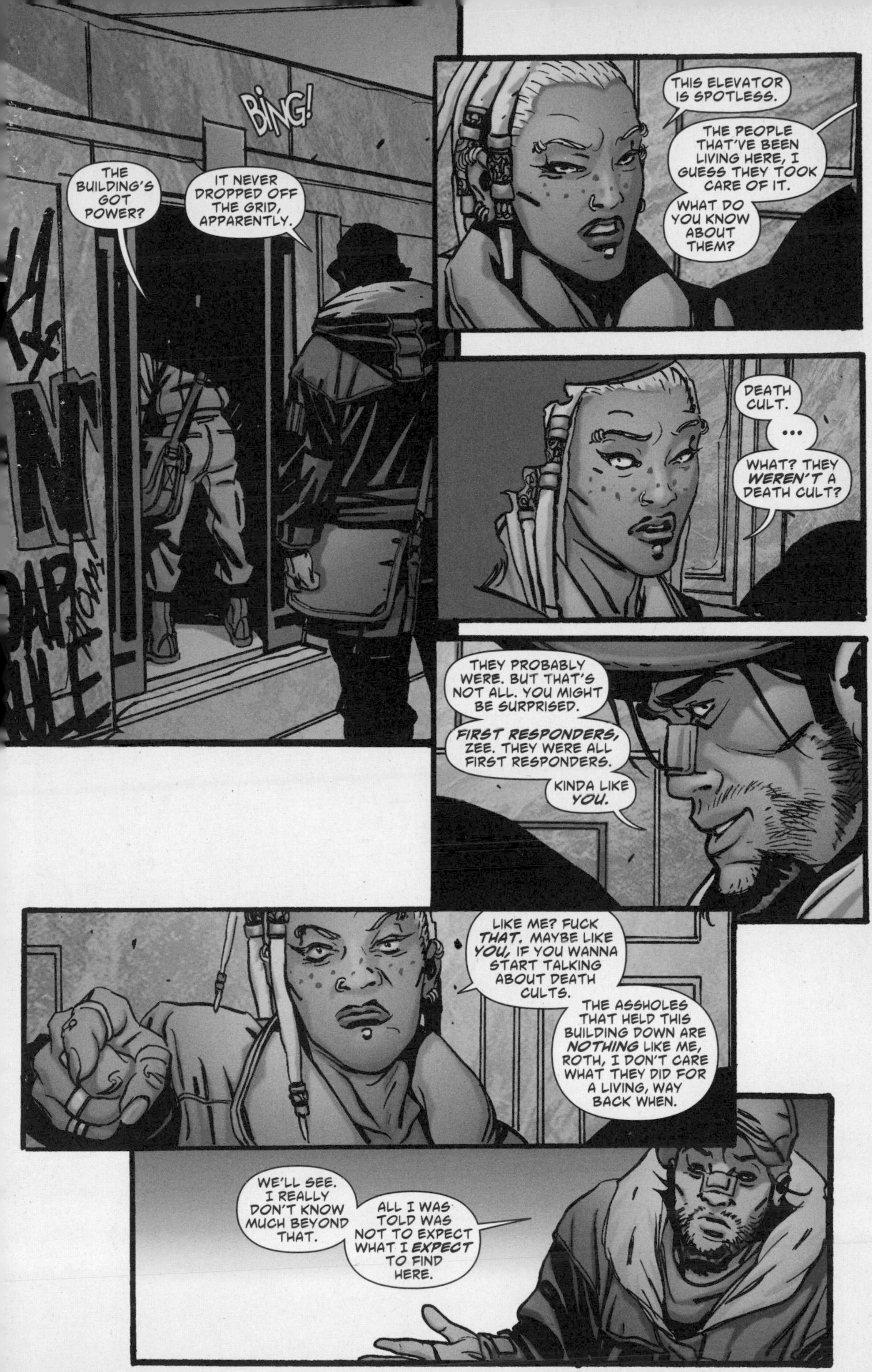
BING!
THE BUILDING'S GOT POWER?
IT NEVER DROPPED OFF THE GRID, APPARENTLY.
THIS ELEVATOR IS SPOTLESS.
THE PEOPLE THAT'VE BEEN LIVING HERE, I GUESS THEY TOOK CARE OF IT.
WHAT DO YOU KNOW ABOUT THEM?
DEATH CULT.
...
WHAT? THEY WEREN'T A DEATH CULT?
THEY PROBABLY WERE. BUT THAT'S NOT ALL. YOU MIGHT BE SURPRISED.
FIRST RESPONDERS, ZEE. THEY WERE ALL FIRST RESPONDERS.
KINDA LIKE YOU.
LIKE ME? FUCK THAT. MAYBE LIKE YOU, IF YOU WANNA START TALKING ABOUT DEATH CULTS.
THE ASSHOLES THAT HELD THIS BUILDING DOWN ARE NOTHING LIKE ME, ROTH, I DON'T CARE WHAT THEY DID FOR A LIVING, WAY BACK WHEN.
WE'LL SEE. I REALLY DON'T KNOW MUCH BEYOND THAT.
ALL I WAS TOLD WAS NOT TO EXPECT WHAT I EXPECT TO FIND HERE.

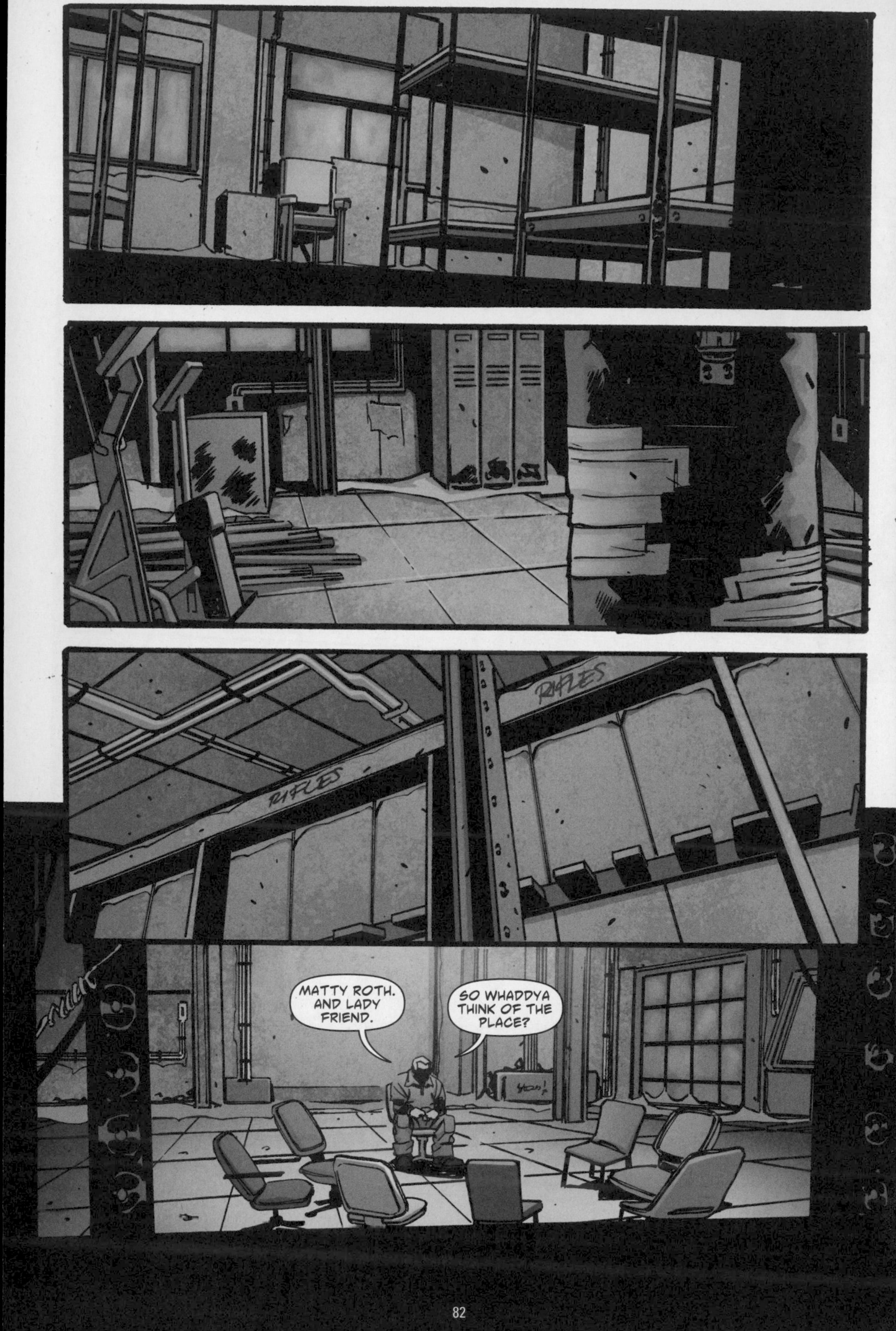
RIFLES
RIFLES
MATTY ROTH. AND LADY FRIEND.
SO WHADDYA THINK OF THE PLACE?

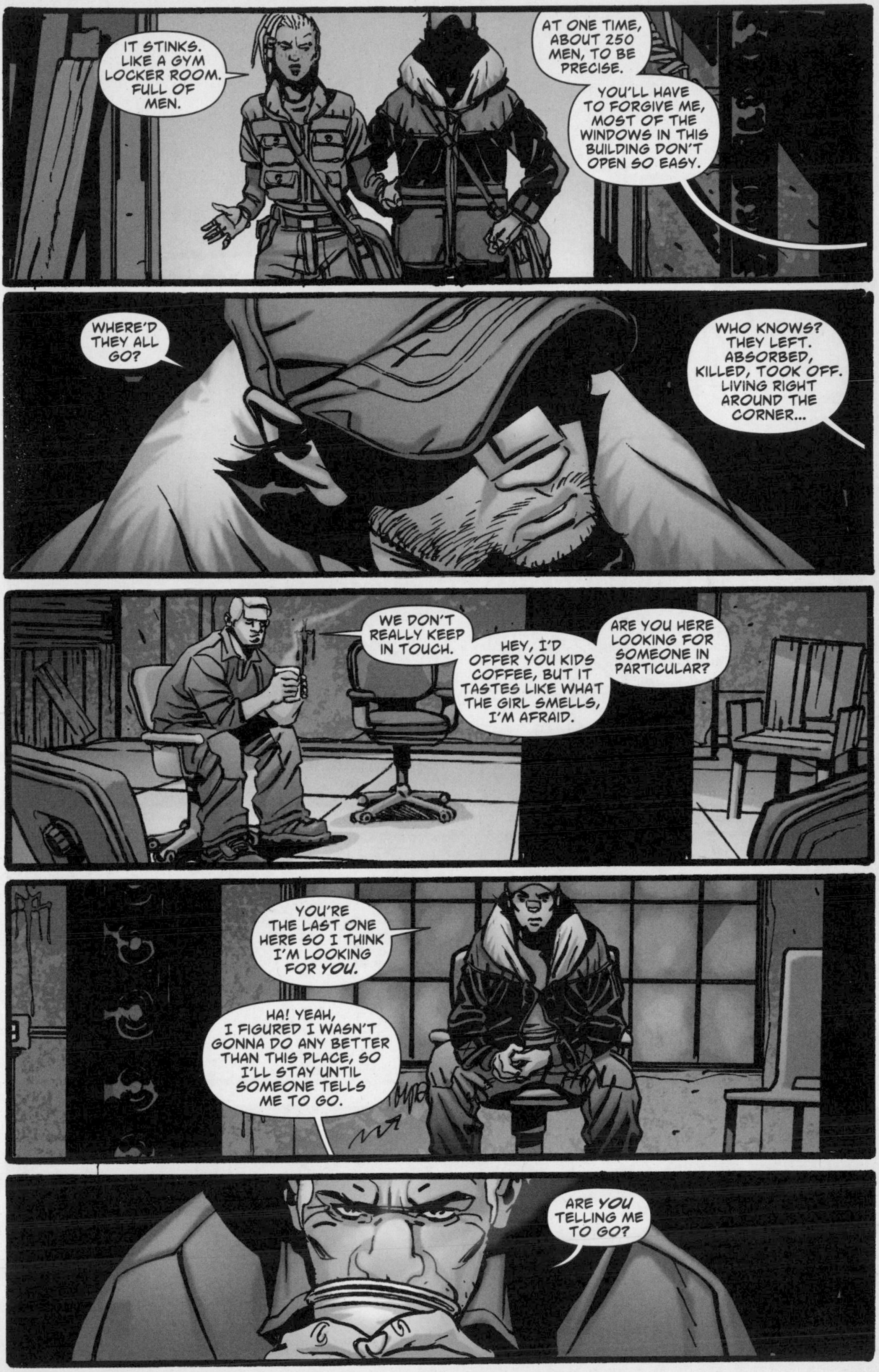
IT STINKS. LIKE A GYM LOCKER ROOM. FULL OF MEN.
AT ONE TIME, ABOUT 250 MEN, TO BE PRECISE.
YOU'LL HAVE TO FORGIVE ME, MOST OF THE WINDOWS IN THIS BUILDING DON'T OPEN SO EASY.
WHERE'D THEY ALL GO?
WHO KNOWS? THEY LEFT. ABSORBED, KILLED, TOOK OFF. LIVING RIGHT AROUND THE CORNER...
WE DON'T REALLY KEEP IN TOUCH.
HEY, I'D OFFER YOU KIDS COFFEE, BUT IT TASTES LIKE WHAT THE GIRL SMELLS, I'M AFRAID.
ARE YOU HERE LOOKING FOR SOMEONE IN PARTICULAR?
YOU'RE THE LAST ONE HERE SO I THINK I'M LOOKING FOR YOU.
HA! YEAH, I FIGURED I WASN'T GONNA DO ANY BETTER THAN THIS PLACE, SO I'LL STAY UNTIL SOMEONE TELLS ME TO GO.
ARE YOU TELLING ME TO GO?

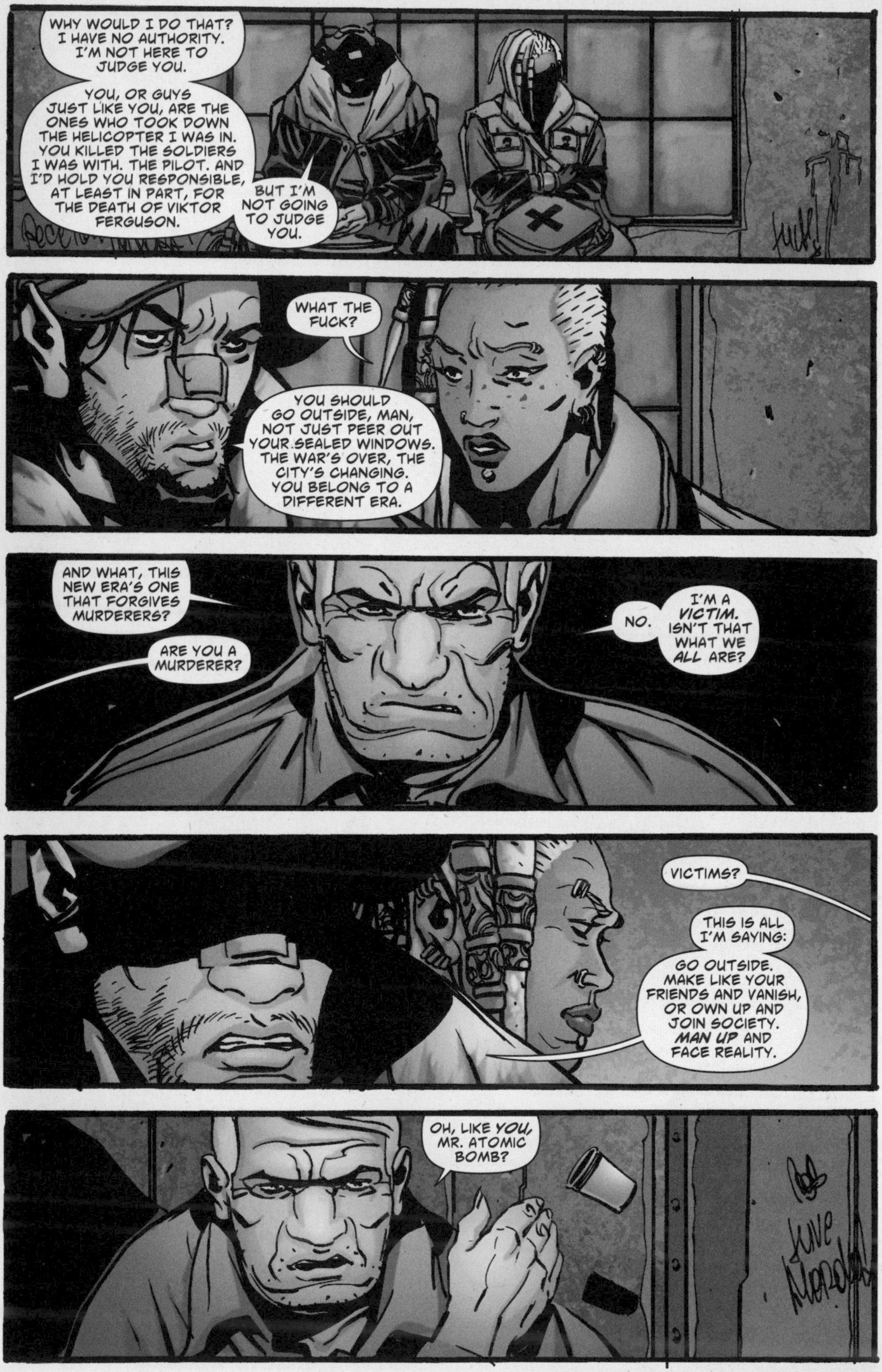
WHY WOULD I DO THAT? I HAVE NO AUTHORITY. I'M NOT HERE TO JUDGE YOU.
YOU, OR GUYS JUST LIKE YOU, ARE THE ONES WHO TOOK DOWN THE HELICOPTER I WAS IN. YOU KILLED THE SOLDIERS I WAS WITH. THE PILOT. AND I'D HOLD YOU RESPONSIBLE, AT LEAST IN PART, FOR THE DEATH OF VIKTOR FERGUSON.
BUT I'M NOT GOING TO JUDGE YOU.
FUCK!
WHAT THE FUCK?
YOU SHOULD GO OUTSIDE, MAN, NOT JUST PEER OUT YOUR SEALED WINDOWS. THE WAR'S OVER, THE CITY'S CHANGING. YOU BELONG TO A DIFFERENT ERA.
AND WHAT, THIS NEW ERA'S ONE THAT FORGIVES MURDERERS?
ARE YOU A MURDERER?
NO.
I'M A *VICTIM.* ISN'T THAT WHAT WE *ALL* ARE?
VICTIMS?
THIS IS ALL I'M SAYING:
GO OUTSIDE. MAKE LIKE YOUR FRIENDS AND VANISH, OR OWN UP AND JOIN SOCIETY. *MAN UP* AND FACE REALITY.
OH, LIKE *YOU,* MR. ATOMIC BOMB?

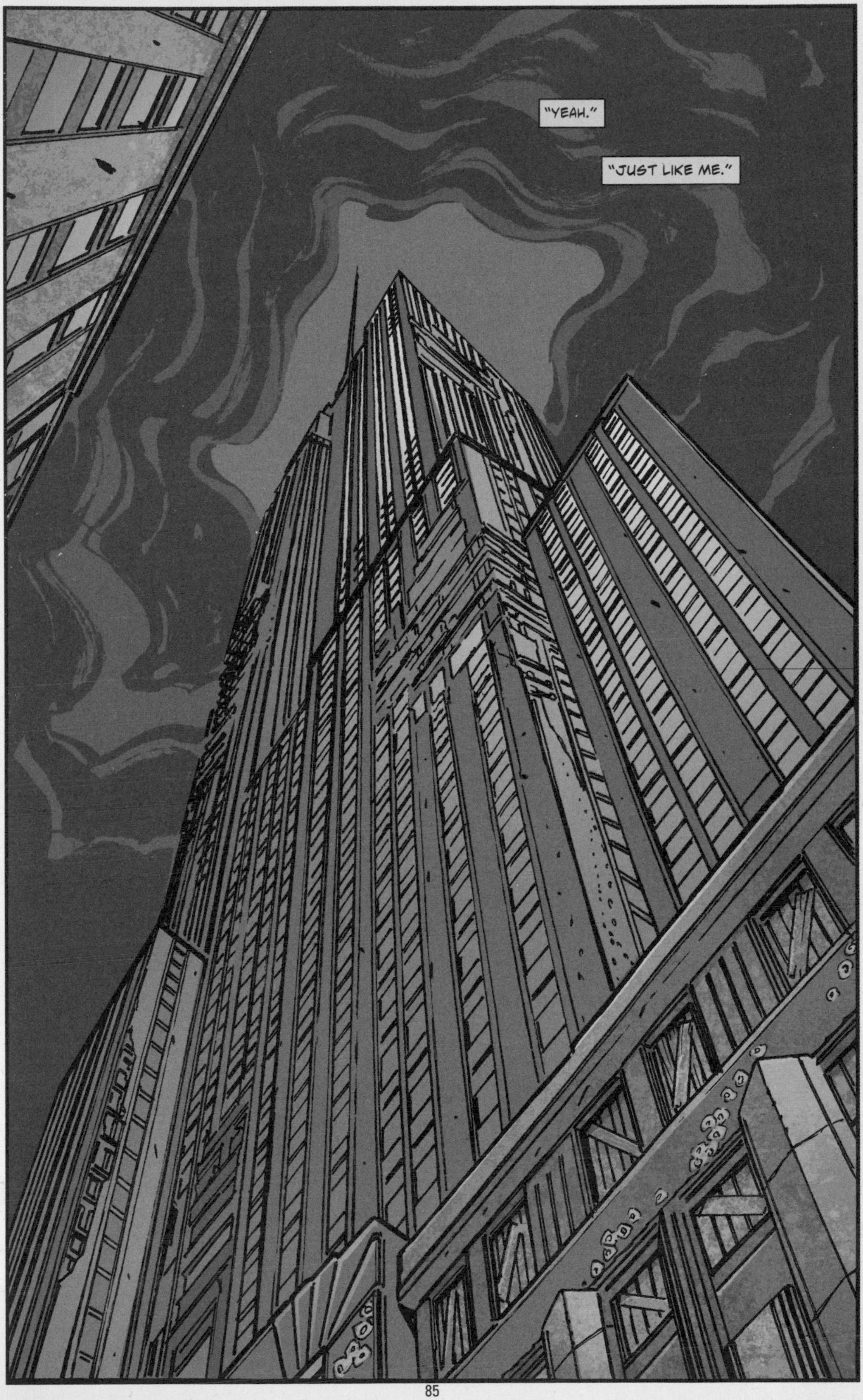
"YEAH."
"JUST LIKE ME."

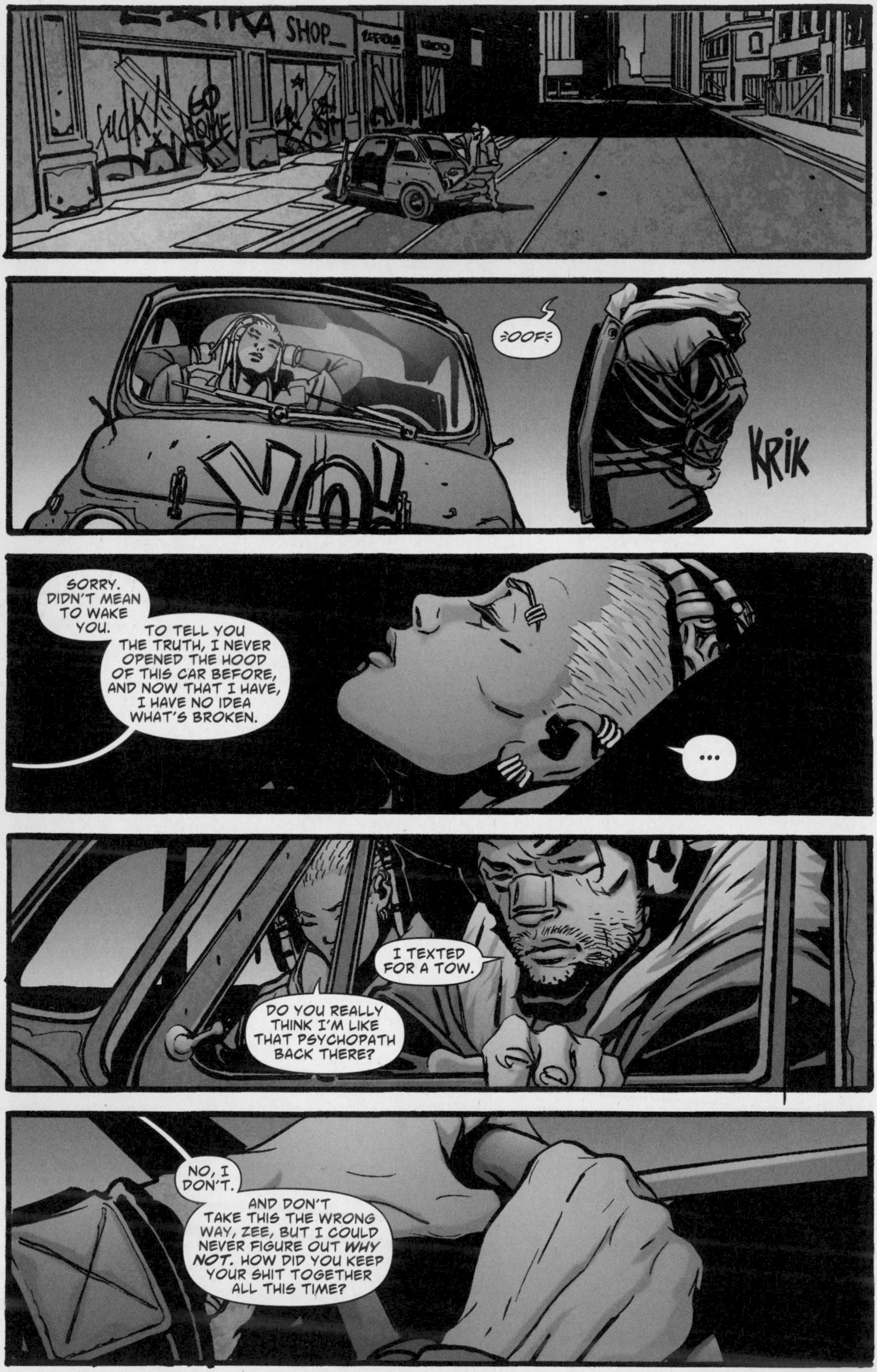
EXTRA SHOP
OOF
KRIK
SORRY. DIDN'T MEAN TO WAKE YOU.
TO TELL YOU THE TRUTH, I NEVER OPENED THE HOOD OF THIS CAR BEFORE, AND NOW THAT I HAVE, I HAVE NO IDEA WHAT'S BROKEN.
...
I TEXTED FOR A TOW.
DO YOU REALLY THINK I'M LIKE THAT PSYCHOPATH BACK THERE?
NO, I DON'T.
AND DON'T TAKE THIS THE WRONG WAY, ZEE, BUT I COULD NEVER FIGURE OUT *WHY NOT*. HOW DID YOU KEEP YOUR SHIT TOGETHER ALL THIS TIME?

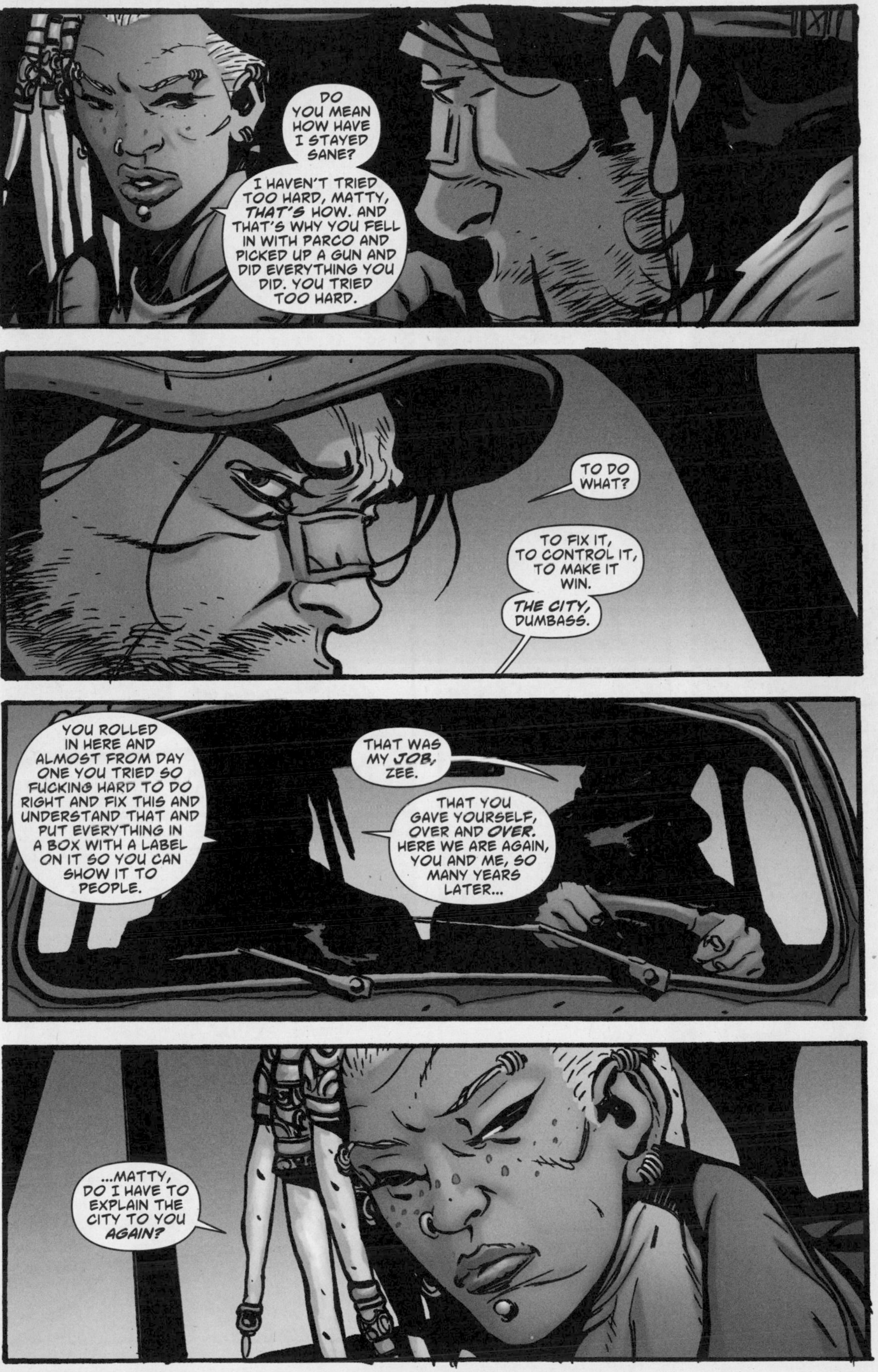
DO YOU MEAN HOW HAVE I STAYED SANE?
I HAVEN'T TRIED TOO HARD, MATTY, THAT'S HOW. AND THAT'S WHY YOU FELL IN WITH PARCO AND PICKED UP A GUN AND DID EVERYTHING YOU DID. YOU TRIED TOO HARD.
TO DO WHAT?
TO FIX IT, TO CONTROL IT, TO MAKE IT WIN.
THE CITY, DUMBASS.
YOU ROLLED IN HERE AND ALMOST FROM DAY ONE YOU TRIED SO FUCKING HARD TO DO RIGHT AND FIX THIS AND UNDERSTAND THAT AND PUT EVERYTHING IN A BOX WITH A LABEL ON IT SO YOU CAN SHOW IT TO PEOPLE.
THAT WAS MY JOB, ZEE.
THAT YOU GAVE YOURSELF, OVER AND OVER. HERE WE ARE AGAIN, YOU AND ME, SO MANY YEARS LATER...
...MATTY, DO I HAVE TO EXPLAIN THE CITY TO YOU AGAIN?

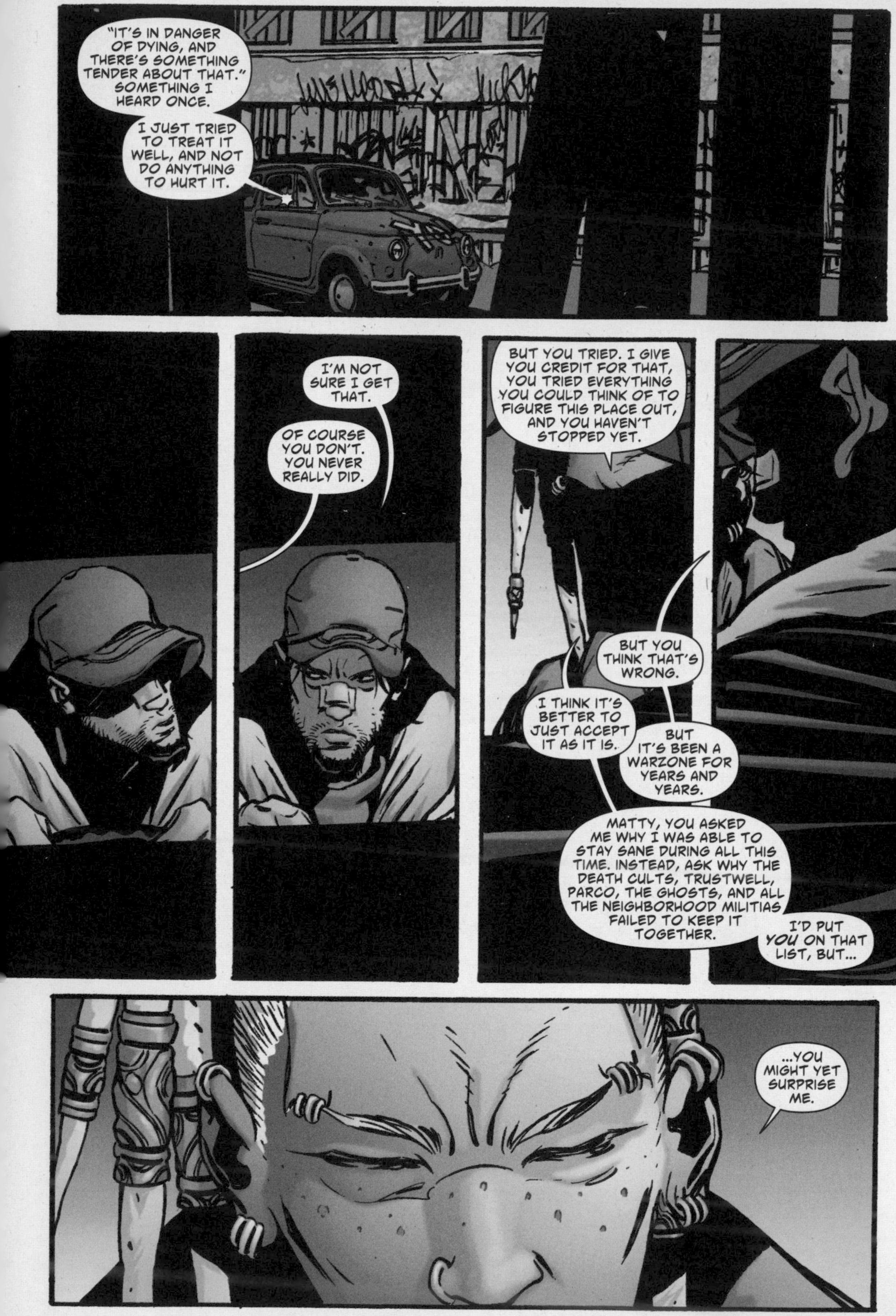
"IT'S IN DANGER OF DYING, AND THERE'S SOMETHING TENDER ABOUT THAT." SOMETHING I HEARD ONCE.
I JUST TRIED TO TREAT IT WELL, AND NOT DO ANYTHING TO HURT IT.
I'M NOT SURE I GET THAT.
OF COURSE YOU DON'T. YOU NEVER REALLY DID.
BUT YOU TRIED. I GIVE YOU CREDIT FOR THAT, YOU TRIED EVERYTHING YOU COULD THINK OF TO FIGURE THIS PLACE OUT, AND YOU HAVEN'T STOPPED YET.
BUT YOU THINK THAT'S WRONG.
I THINK IT'S BETTER TO JUST ACCEPT IT AS IT IS.
BUT IT'S BEEN A WARZONE FOR YEARS AND YEARS.
MATTY, YOU ASKED ME WHY I WAS ABLE TO STAY SANE DURING ALL THIS TIME. INSTEAD, ASK WHY THE DEATH CULTS, TRUSTWELL, PARCO, THE GHOSTS, AND ALL THE NEIGHBORHOOD MILITIAS FAILED TO KEEP IT TOGETHER.
I'D PUT *YOU* ON THAT LIST, BUT...
...YOU MIGHT YET SURPRISE ME.

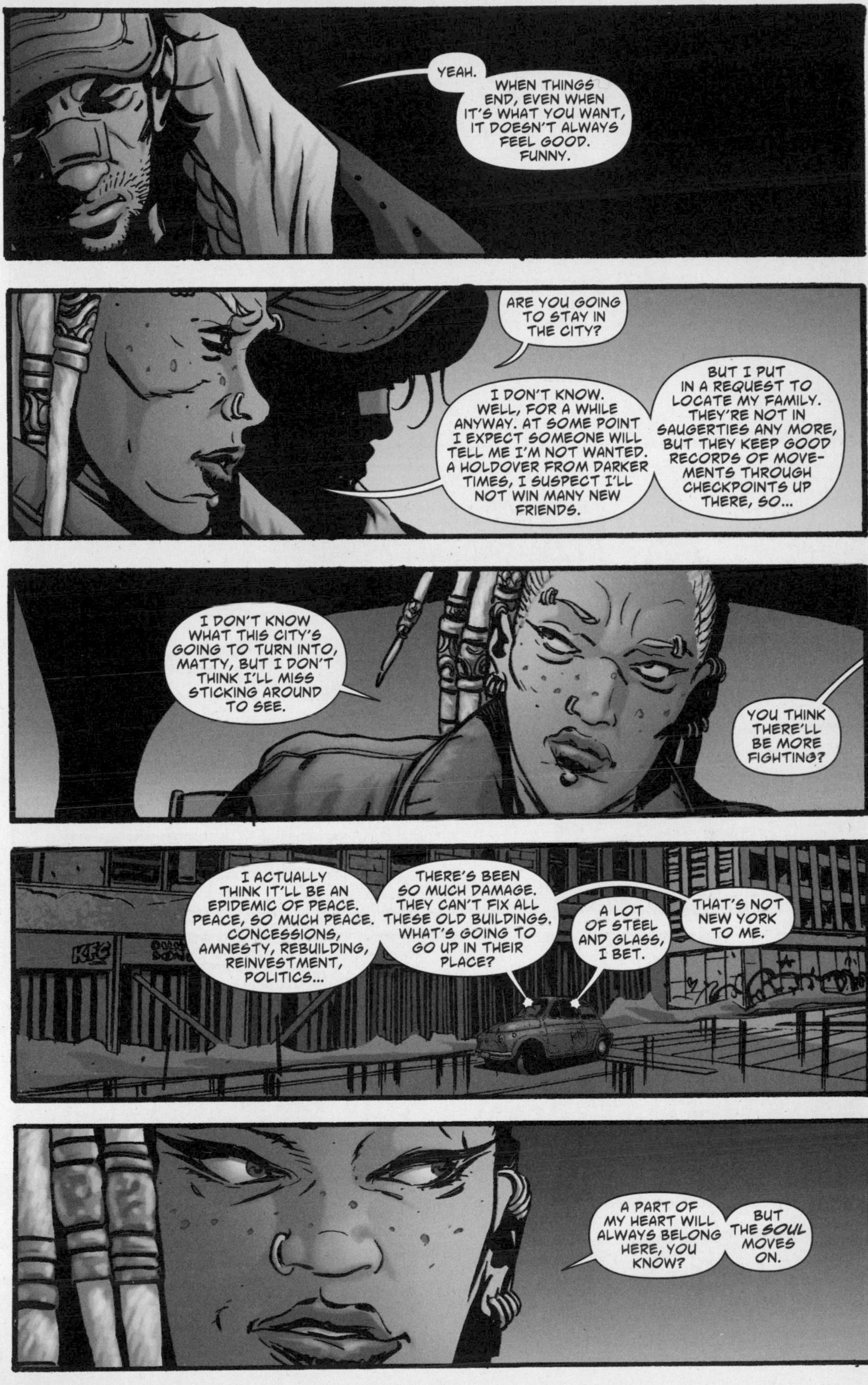
YEAH.
WHEN THINGS END, EVEN WHEN IT'S WHAT YOU WANT, IT DOESN'T ALWAYS FEEL GOOD. FUNNY.
ARE YOU GOING TO STAY IN THE CITY?
I DON'T KNOW. WELL, FOR A WHILE ANYWAY. AT SOME POINT I EXPECT SOMEONE WILL TELL ME I'M NOT WANTED. A HOLDOVER FROM DARKER TIMES, I SUSPECT I'LL NOT WIN MANY NEW FRIENDS.
BUT I PUT IN A REQUEST TO LOCATE MY FAMILY. THEY'RE NOT IN SAUGERTIES ANY MORE, BUT THEY KEEP GOOD RECORDS OF MOVE-MENTS THROUGH CHECKPOINTS UP THERE, SO...
I DON'T KNOW WHAT THIS CITY'S GOING TO TURN INTO, MATTY, BUT I DON'T THINK I'LL MISS STICKING AROUND TO SEE.
YOU THINK THERE'LL BE MORE FIGHTING?
I ACTUALLY THINK IT'LL BE AN EPIDEMIC OF PEACE. PEACE, SO MUCH PEACE. CONCESSIONS, AMNESTY, REBUILDING, REINVESTMENT, POLITICS...
THERE'S BEEN SO MUCH DAMAGE. THEY CAN'T FIX ALL THESE OLD BUILDINGS. WHAT'S GOING TO GO UP IN THEIR PLACE?
A LOT OF STEEL AND GLASS, I BET.
THAT'S NOT NEW YORK TO ME.
KFC
A PART OF MY HEART WILL ALWAYS BELONG HERE, YOU KNOW?
BUT THE *SOUL* MOVES ON.

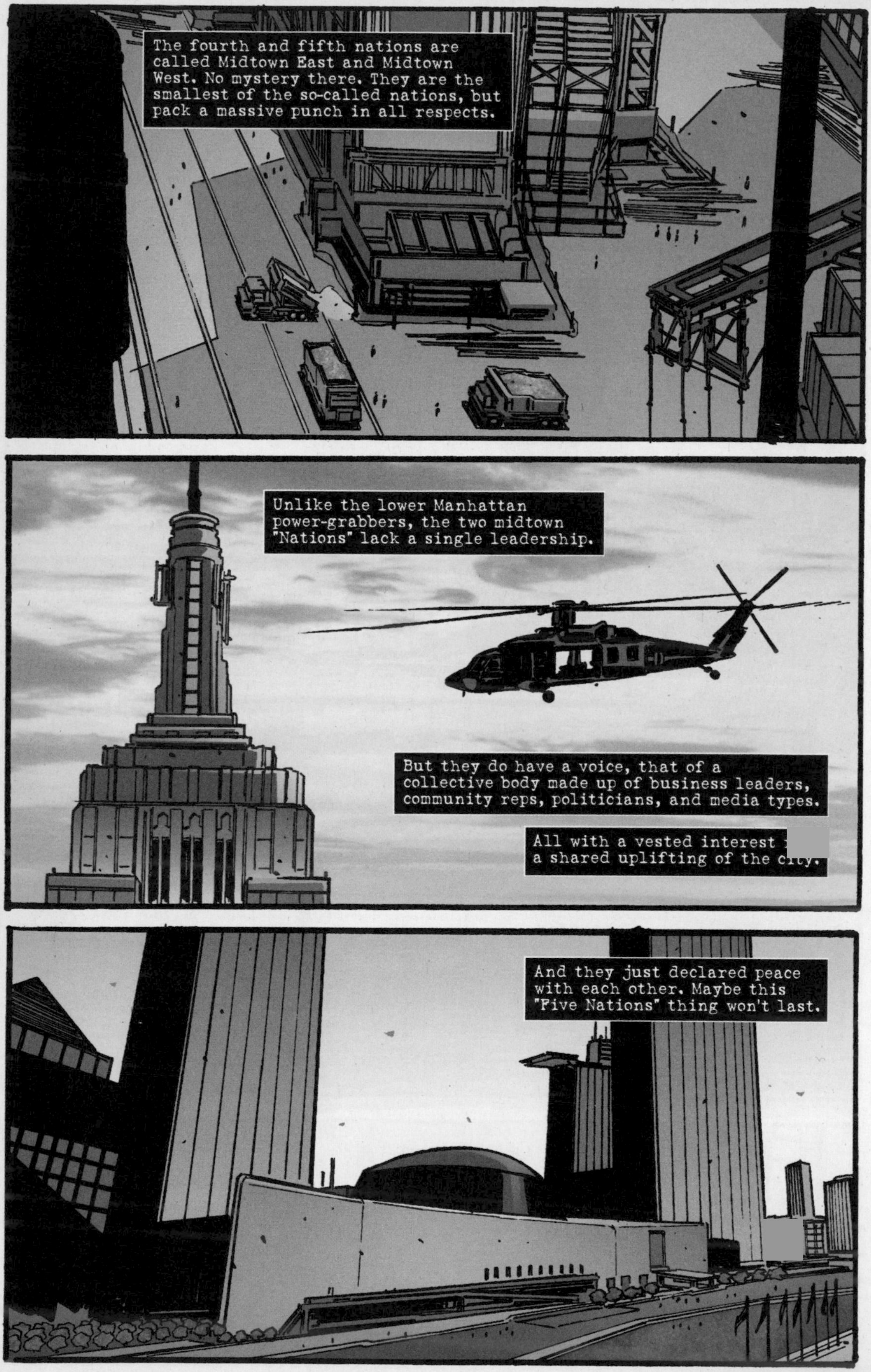
The fourth and fifth nations are called Midtown East and Midtown West. No mystery there. They are the smallest of the so-called nations, but pack a massive punch in all respects.
Unlike the lower Manhattan power-grabbers, the two midtown "Nations" lack a single leadership.
But they do have a voice, that of a collective body made up of business leaders, community reps, politicians, and media types.
All with a vested interest
a shared uplifting of the city.
And they just declared peace with each other. Maybe this "Five Nations" thing won't last.

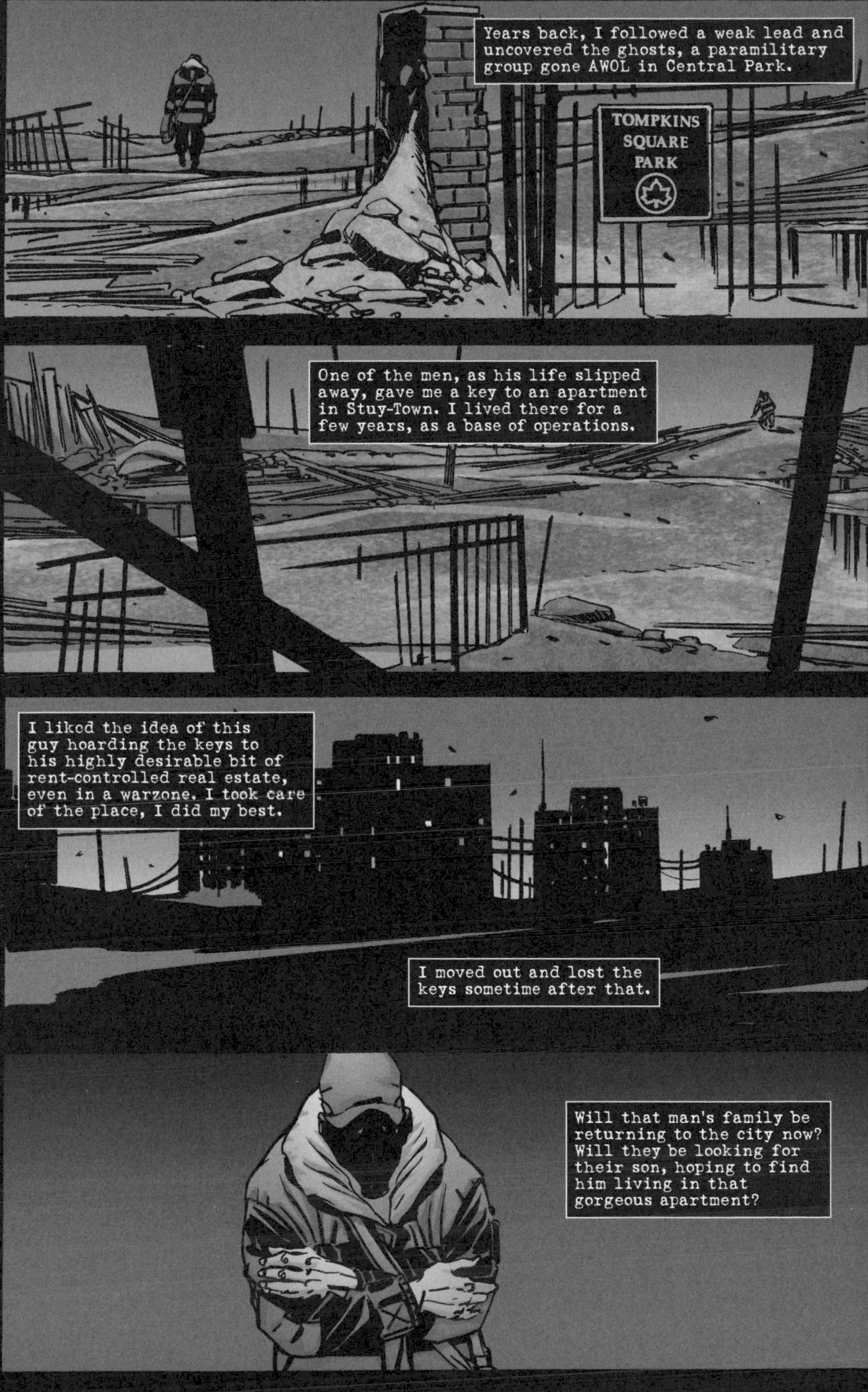
Years back, I followed a weak lead and uncovered the ghosts, a paramilitary group gone AWOL in Central Park.
TOMPKINS SQUARE PARK
One of the men, as his life slipped away, gave me a key to an apartment in Stuy-Town. I lived there for a few years, as a base of operations.
I liked the idea of this guy hoarding the keys to his highly desirable bit of rent-controlled real estate, even in a warzone. I took care of the place, I did my best.
I moved out and lost the keys sometime after that.
Will that man's family be returning to the city now? Will they be looking for their son, hoping to find him living in that gorgeous apartment?

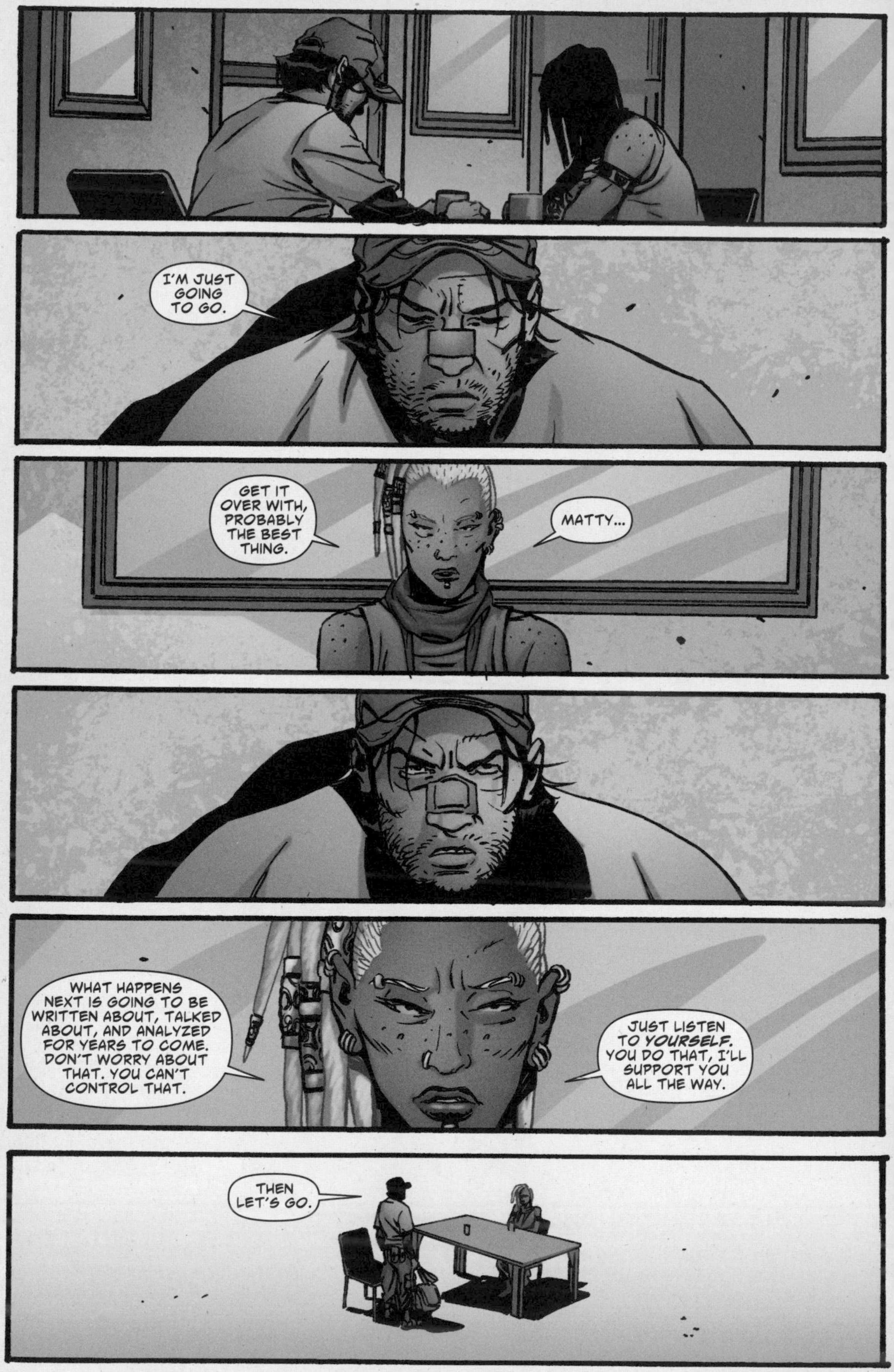
I'M JUST GOING TO GO.
GET IT OVER WITH, PROBABLY THE BEST THING.
MATTY...
WHAT HAPPENS NEXT IS GOING TO BE WRITTEN ABOUT, TALKED ABOUT, AND ANALYZED FOR YEARS TO COME. DON'T WORRY ABOUT THAT. YOU CAN'T CONTROL THAT.
JUST LISTEN TO *YOURSELF*. YOU DO THAT, I'LL SUPPORT YOU ALL THE WAY.
THEN LET'S GO.

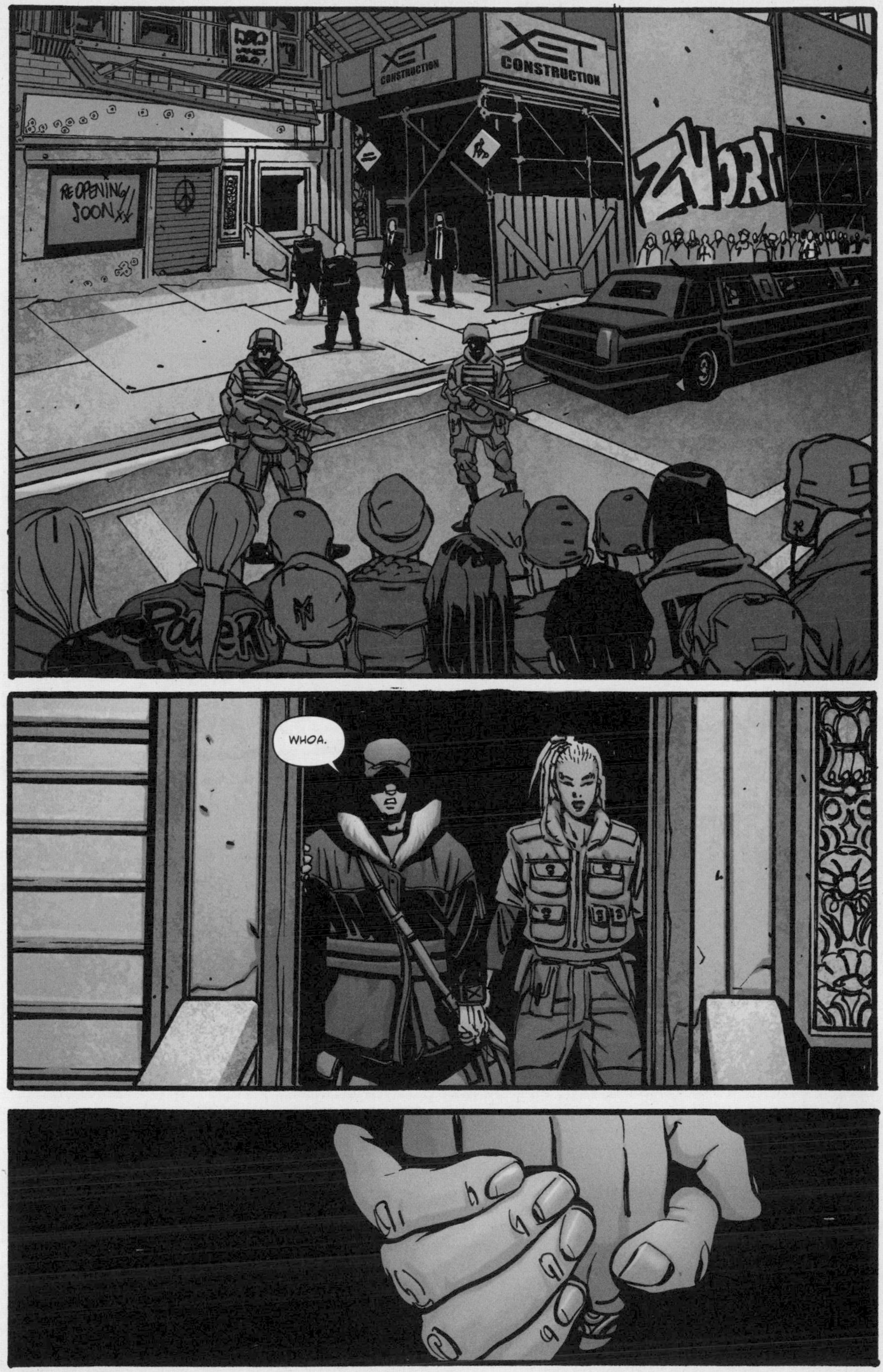
XET CONSTRUCTION
XET CONSTRUCTION
RE OPENING SOON
WHOA.

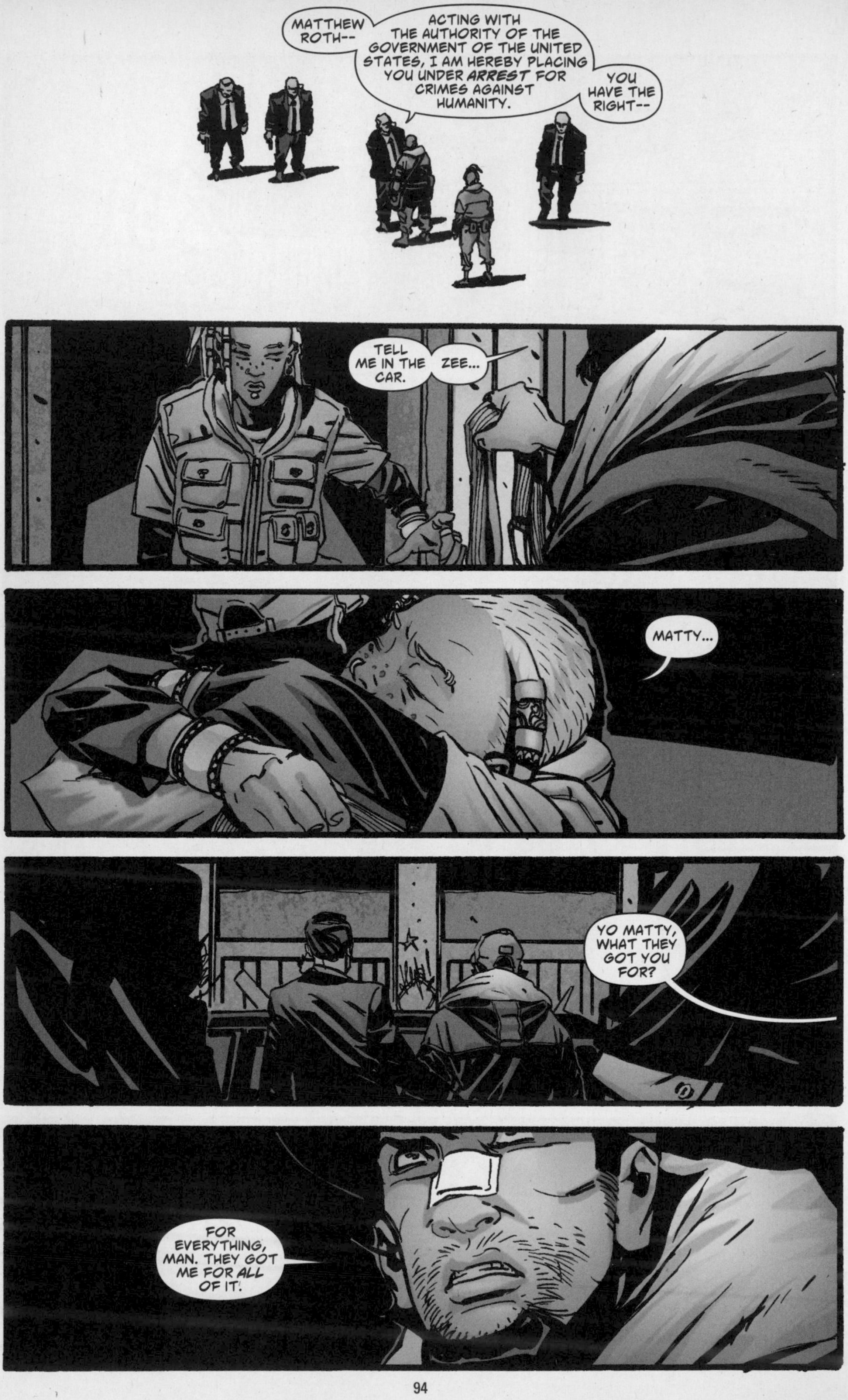
MATTHEW ROTH--
ACTING WITH THE AUTHORITY OF THE GOVERNMENT OF THE UNITED STATES, I AM HEREBY PLACING YOU UNDER ARREST FOR CRIMES AGAINST HUMANITY.
YOU HAVE THE RIGHT--
ZEE...
TELL ME IN THE CAR.
MATTY...
YO MATTY, WHAT THEY GOT YOU FOR?
FOR EVERYTHING, MAN. THEY GOT ME FOR ALL OF IT.

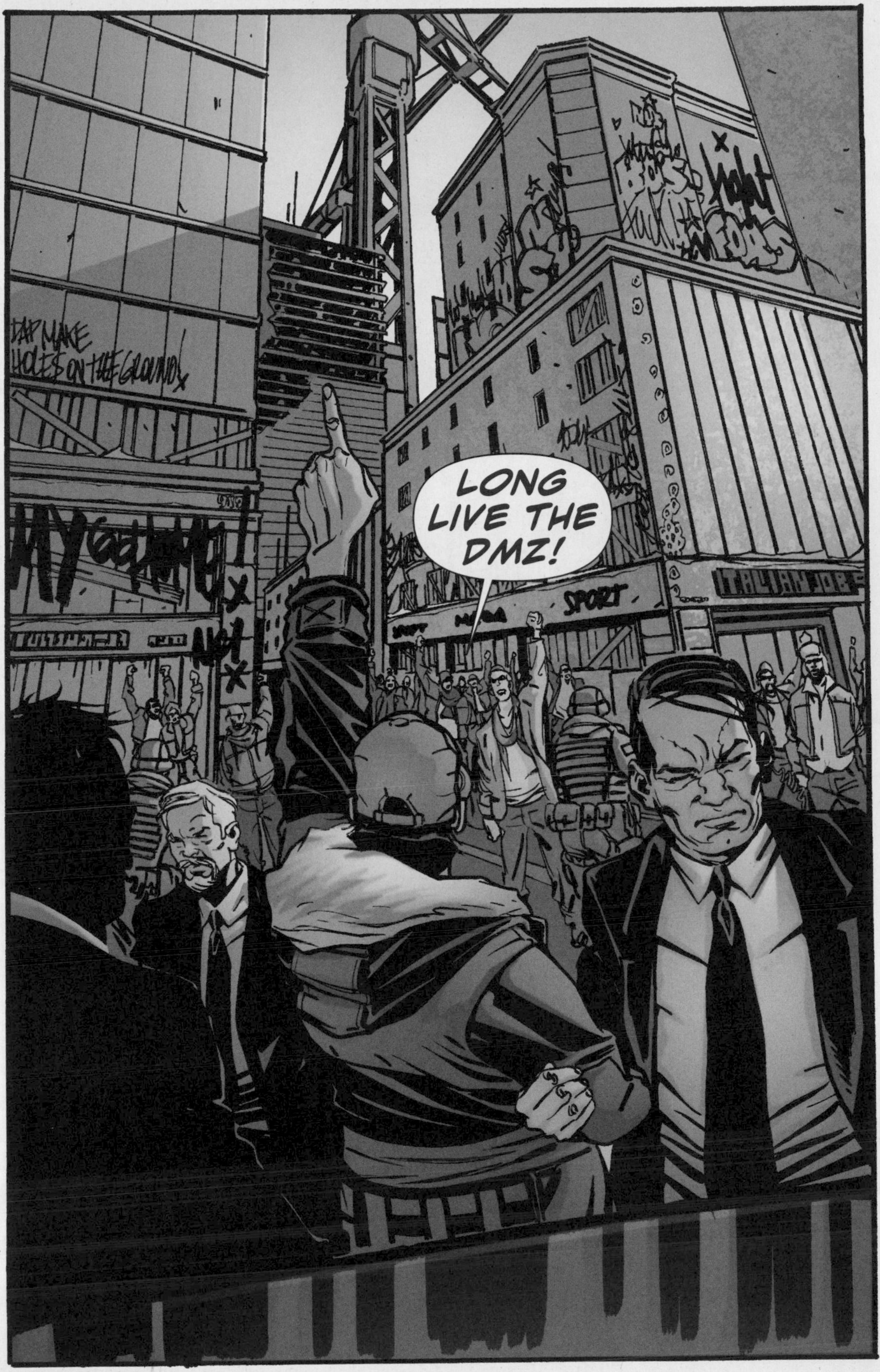
DAP MAKE HOLE$ ON THE GROUND
LONG LIVE THE DMZ!
SPORT
ITALIAN JOB

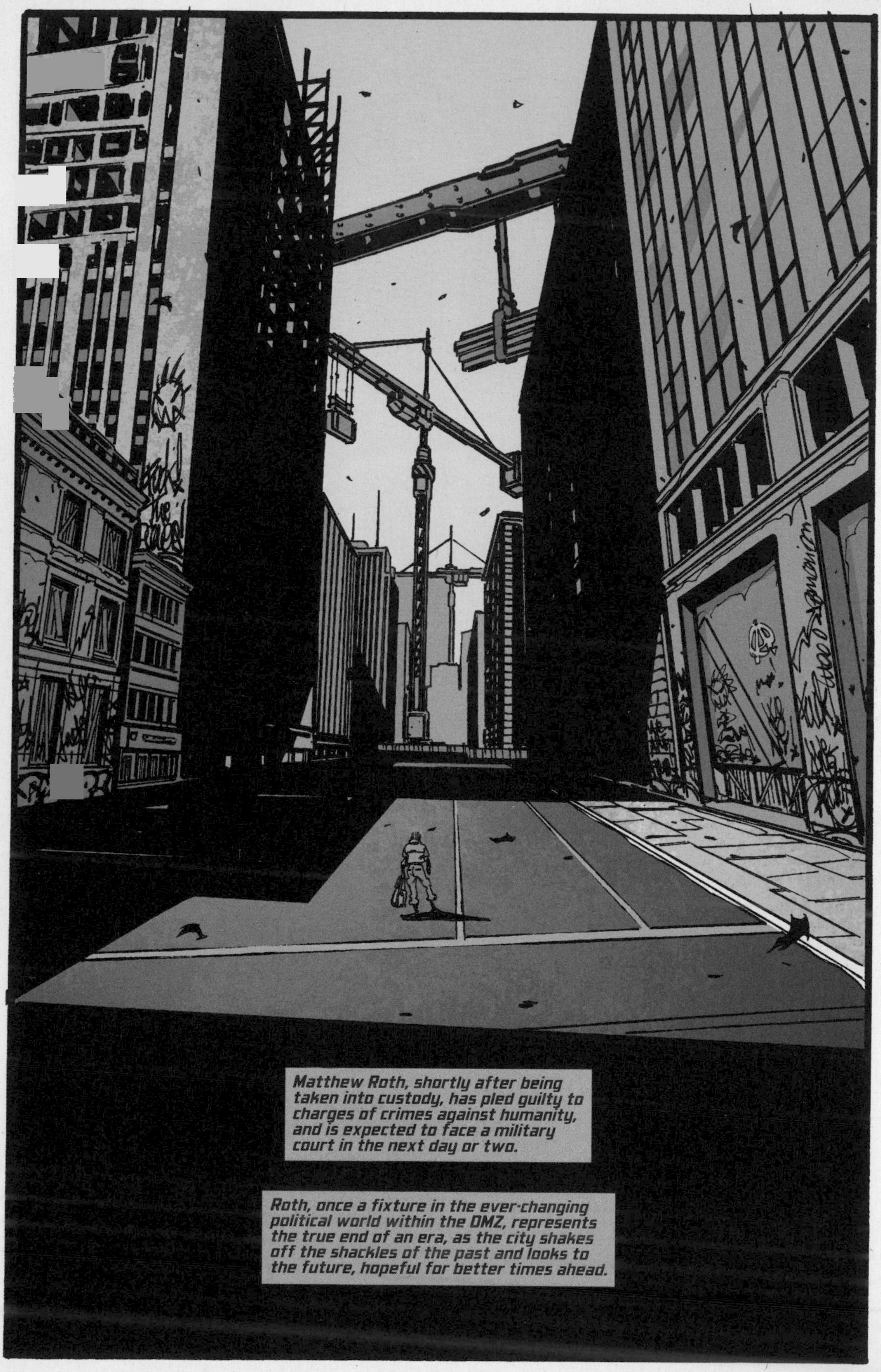
Matthew Roth, shortly after being taken into custody, has pled guilty to charges of crimes against humanity, and is expected to face a military court in the next day or two.
Roth, once a fixture in the ever-changing political world within the DMZ, represents the true end of an era, as the city shakes off the shackles of the past and looks to the future, hopeful for better times ahead.

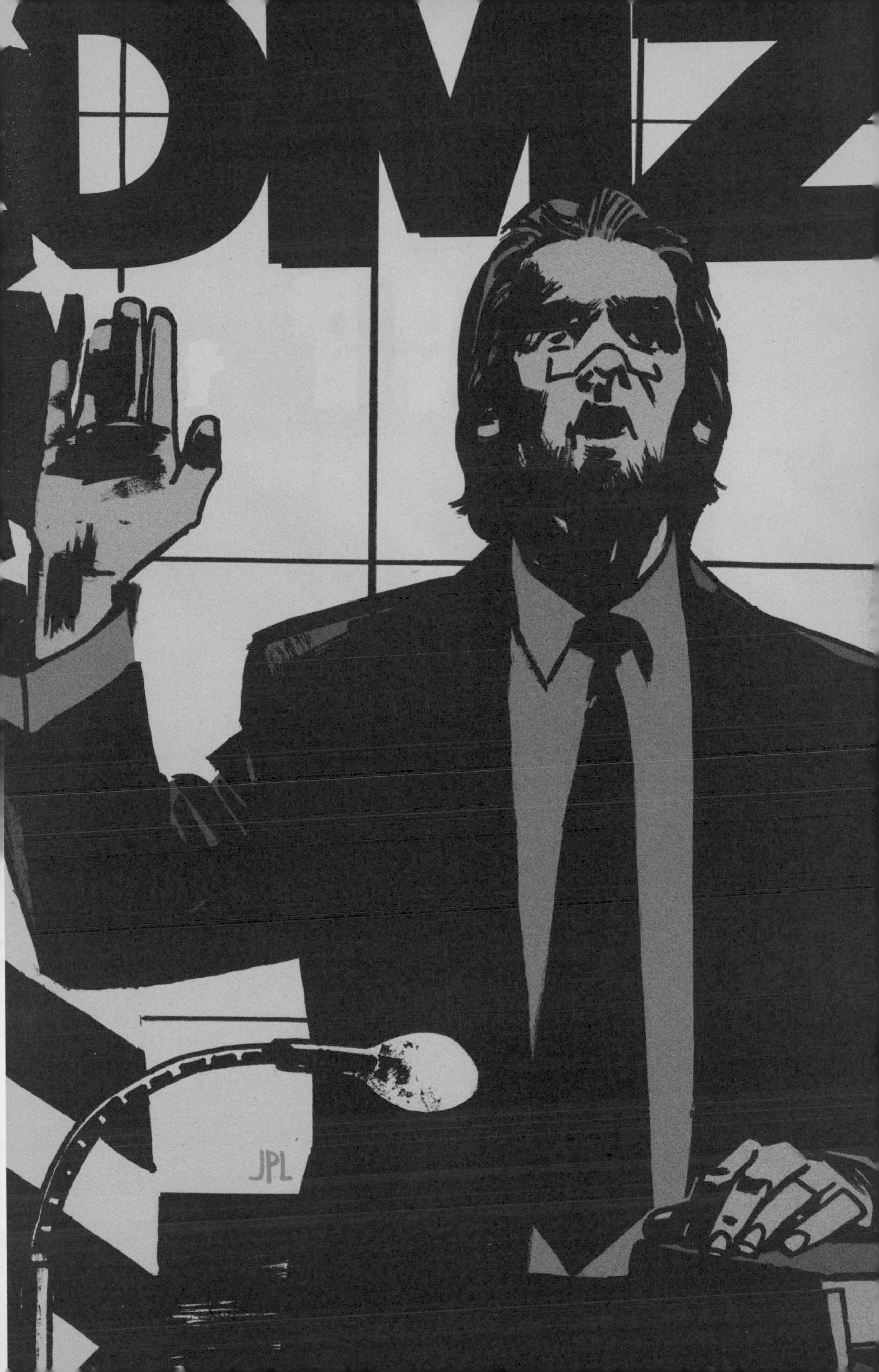
DMZ
JPL

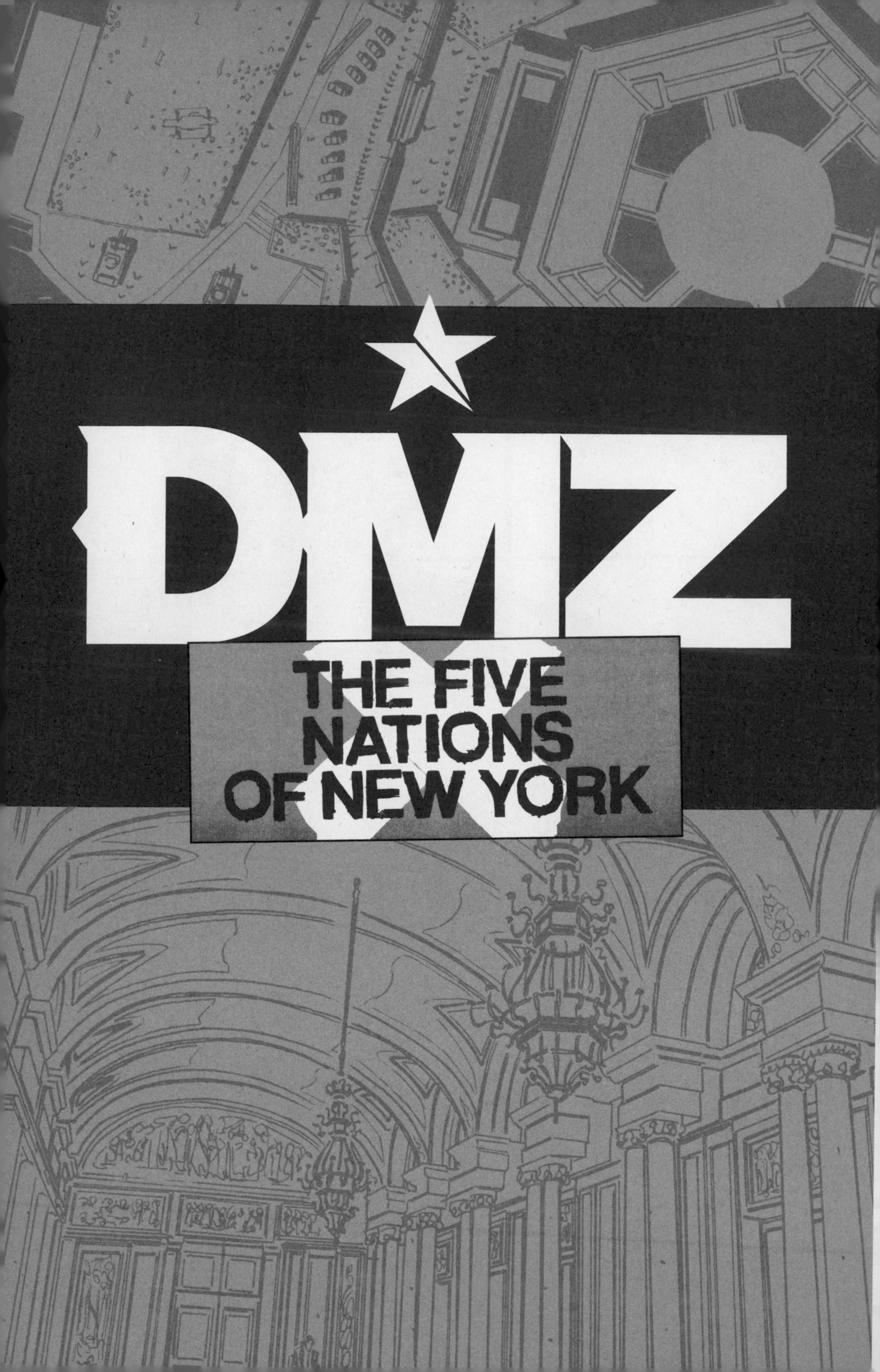
DMZ
THE FIVE NATIONS OF NEW YORK

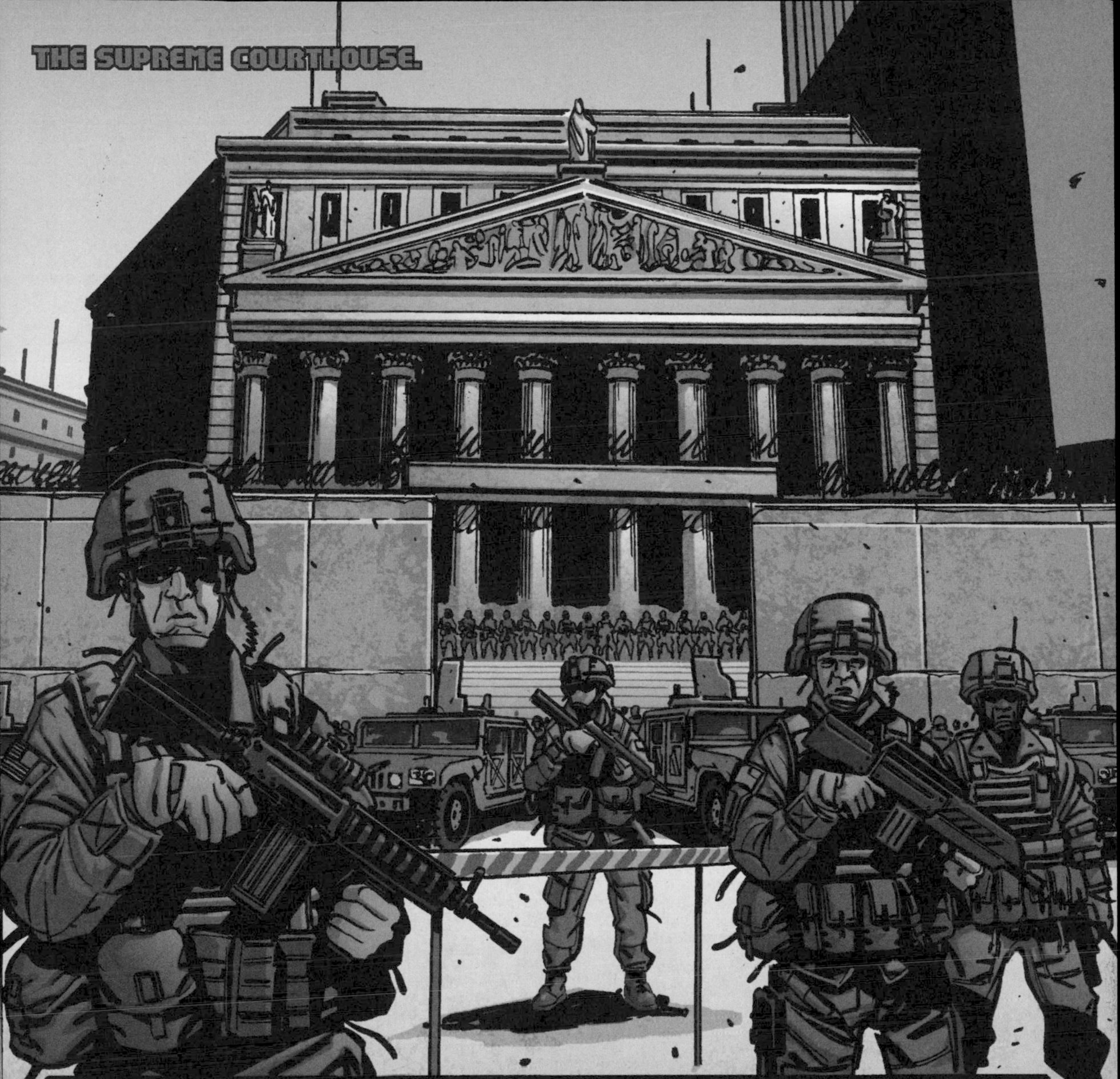
THE SUPREME COURTHOUSE.

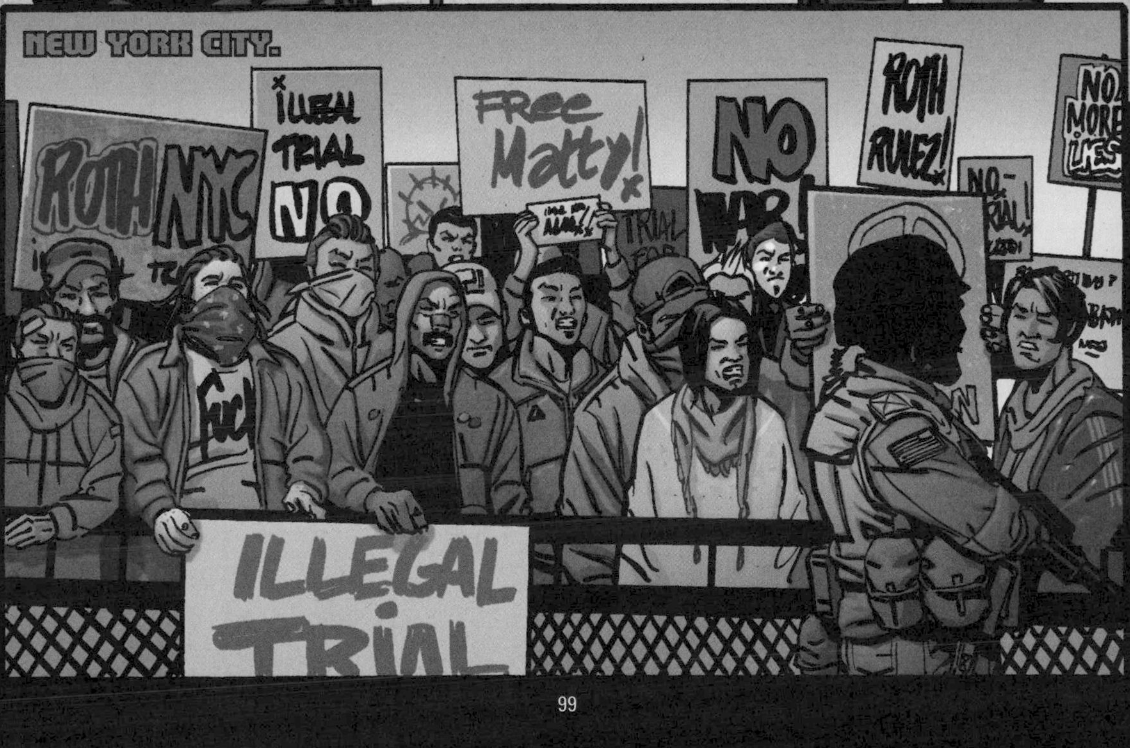
NEW YORK CITY.
ROTH NYC
ILLEGAL TRIAL NO
FREE Matty!
NO
ROTH RULEZ!
NO MORE LIES
ILLEGAL TRIAL

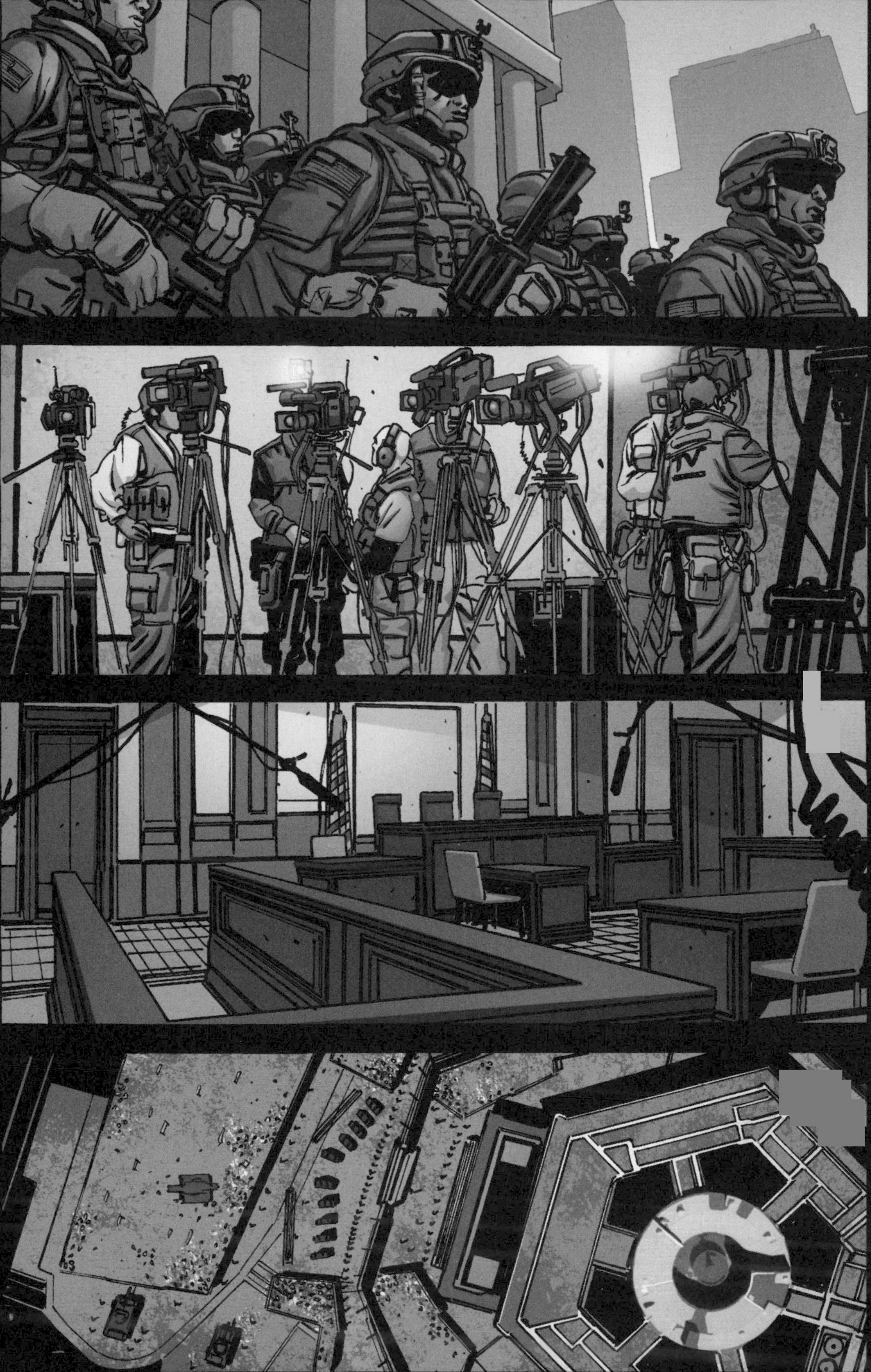
TV

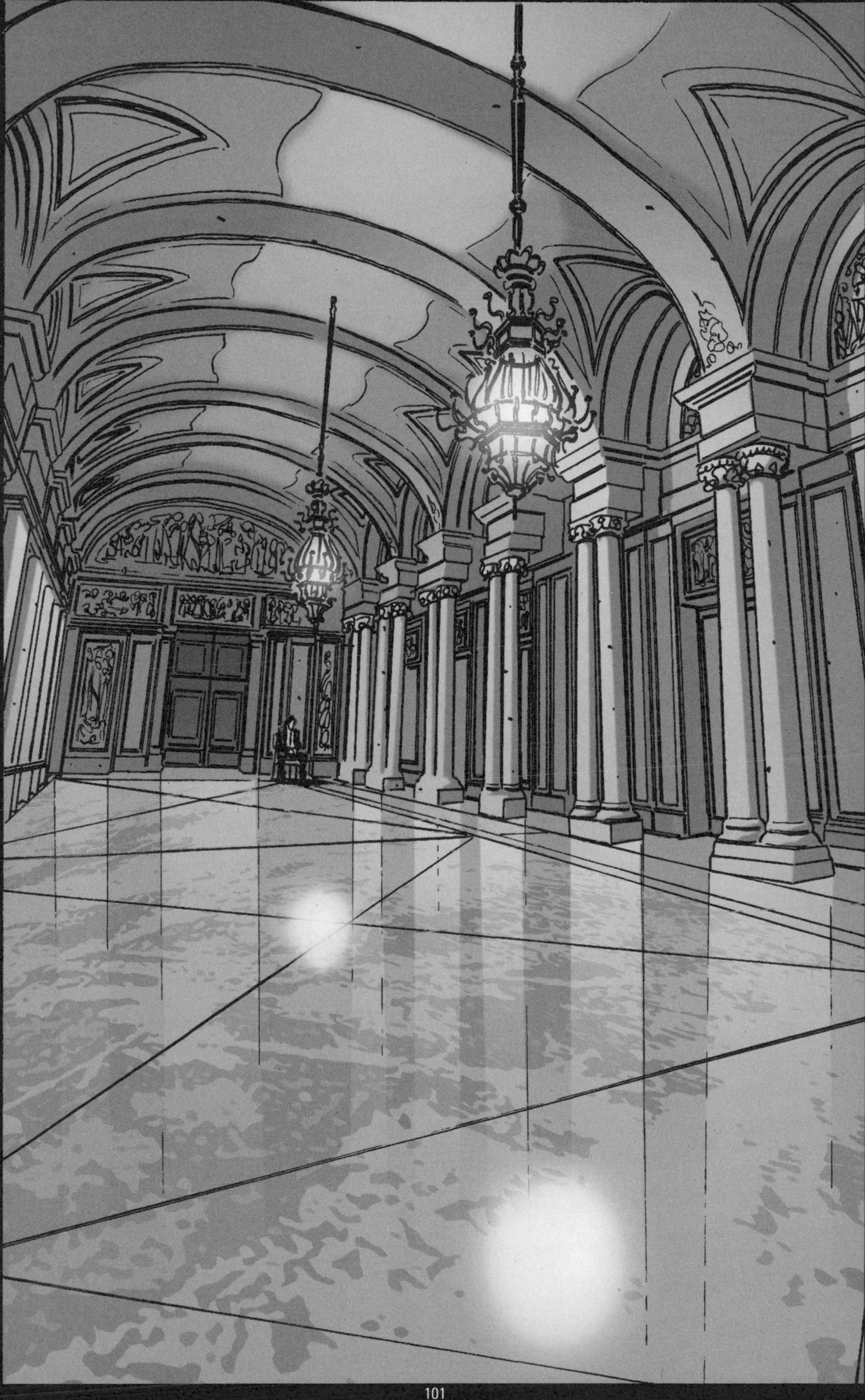

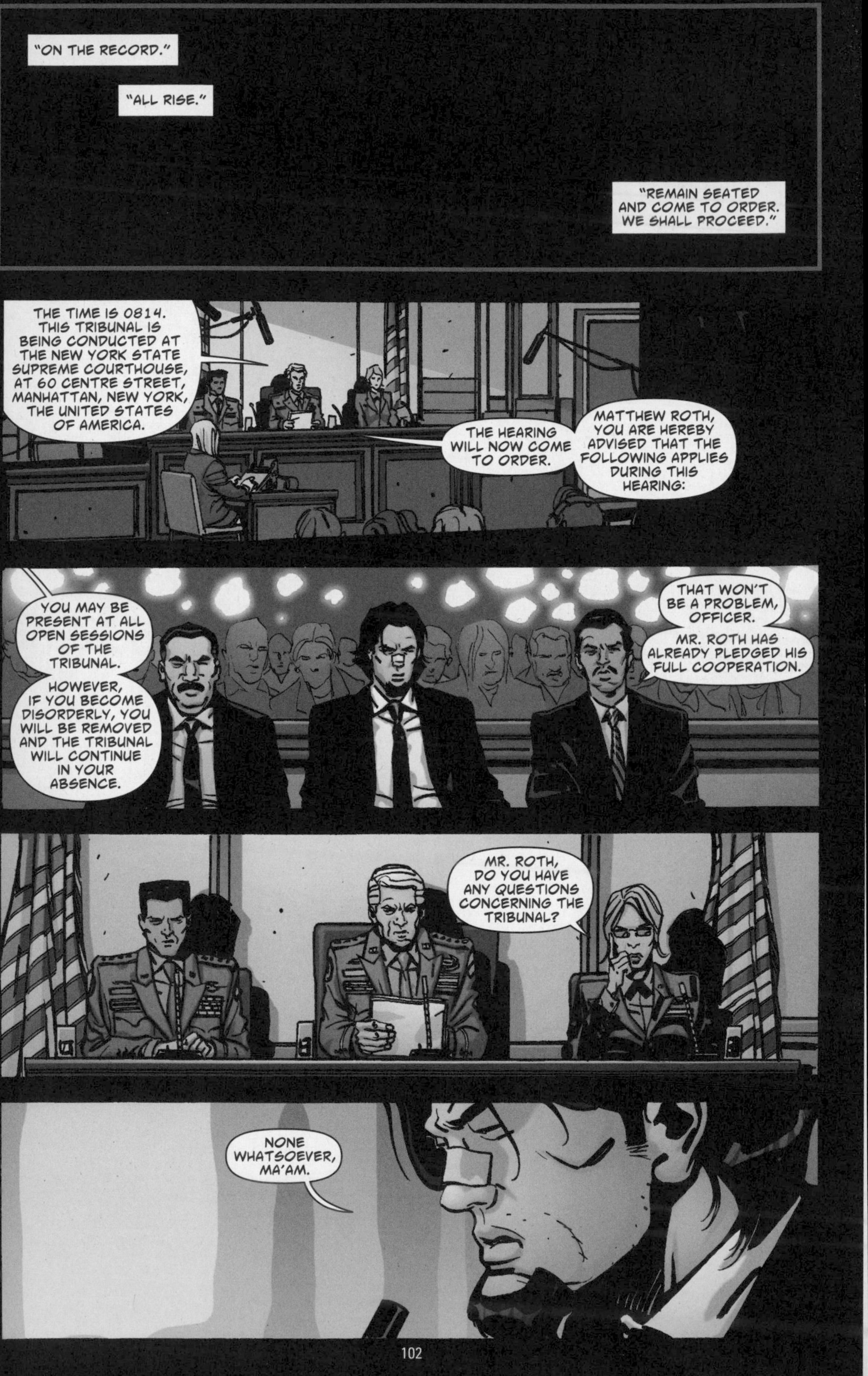
"ON THE RECORD."
"ALL RISE."
"REMAIN SEATED AND COME TO ORDER. WE SHALL PROCEED."
THE TIME IS 0814. THIS TRIBUNAL IS BEING CONDUCTED AT THE NEW YORK STATE SUPREME COURTHOUSE, AT 60 CENTRE STREET, MANHATTAN, NEW YORK, THE UNITED STATES OF AMERICA.
THE HEARING WILL NOW COME TO ORDER.
MATTHEW ROTH, YOU ARE HEREBY ADVISED THAT THE FOLLOWING APPLIES DURING THIS HEARING:
YOU MAY BE PRESENT AT ALL OPEN SESSIONS OF THE TRIBUNAL.
HOWEVER, IF YOU BECOME DISORDERLY, YOU WILL BE REMOVED AND THE TRIBUNAL WILL CONTINUE IN YOUR ABSENCE.
THAT WON'T BE A PROBLEM, OFFICER.
MR. ROTH HAS ALREADY PLEDGED HIS FULL COOPERATION.
MR. ROTH, DO YOU HAVE ANY QUESTIONS CONCERNING THE TRIBUNAL?
NONE WHATSOEVER, MA'AM.

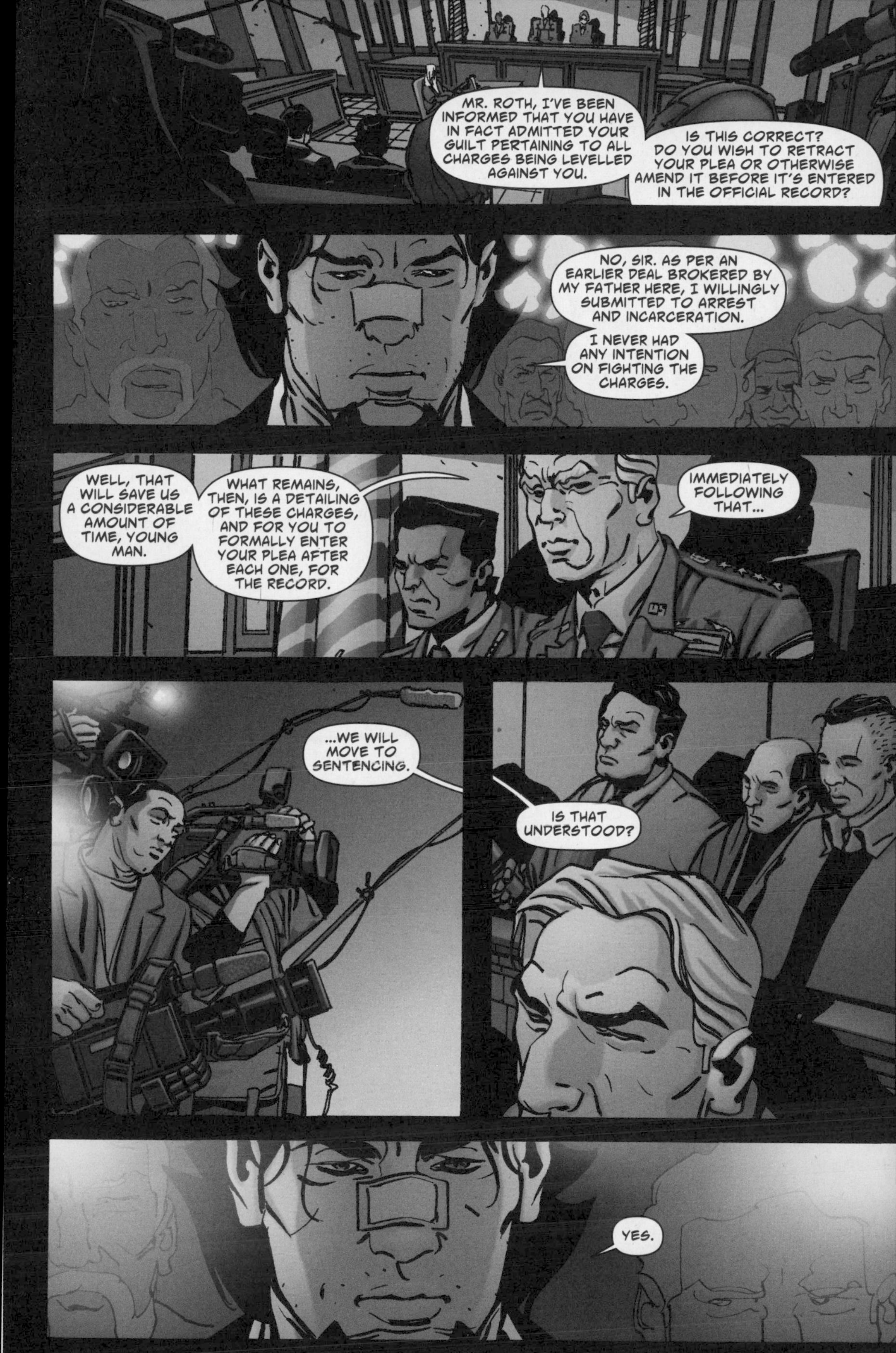
MR. ROTH, I'VE BEEN INFORMED THAT YOU HAVE IN FACT ADMITTED YOUR GUILT PERTAINING TO ALL CHARGES BEING LEVELLED AGAINST YOU.
IS THIS CORRECT? DO YOU WISH TO RETRACT YOUR PLEA OR OTHERWISE AMEND IT BEFORE IT'S ENTERED IN THE OFFICIAL RECORD?
NO, SIR. AS PER AN EARLIER DEAL BROKERED BY MY FATHER HERE, I WILLINGLY SUBMITTED TO ARREST AND INCARCERATION.
I NEVER HAD ANY INTENTION ON FIGHTING THE CHARGES.
WELL, THAT WILL SAVE US A CONSIDERABLE AMOUNT OF TIME, YOUNG MAN.
WHAT REMAINS, THEN, IS A DETAILING OF THESE CHARGES, AND FOR YOU TO FORMALLY ENTER YOUR PLEA AFTER EACH ONE, FOR THE RECORD.
IMMEDIATELY FOLLOWING THAT...
...WE WILL MOVE TO SENTENCING.
IS THAT UNDERSTOOD?
YES.

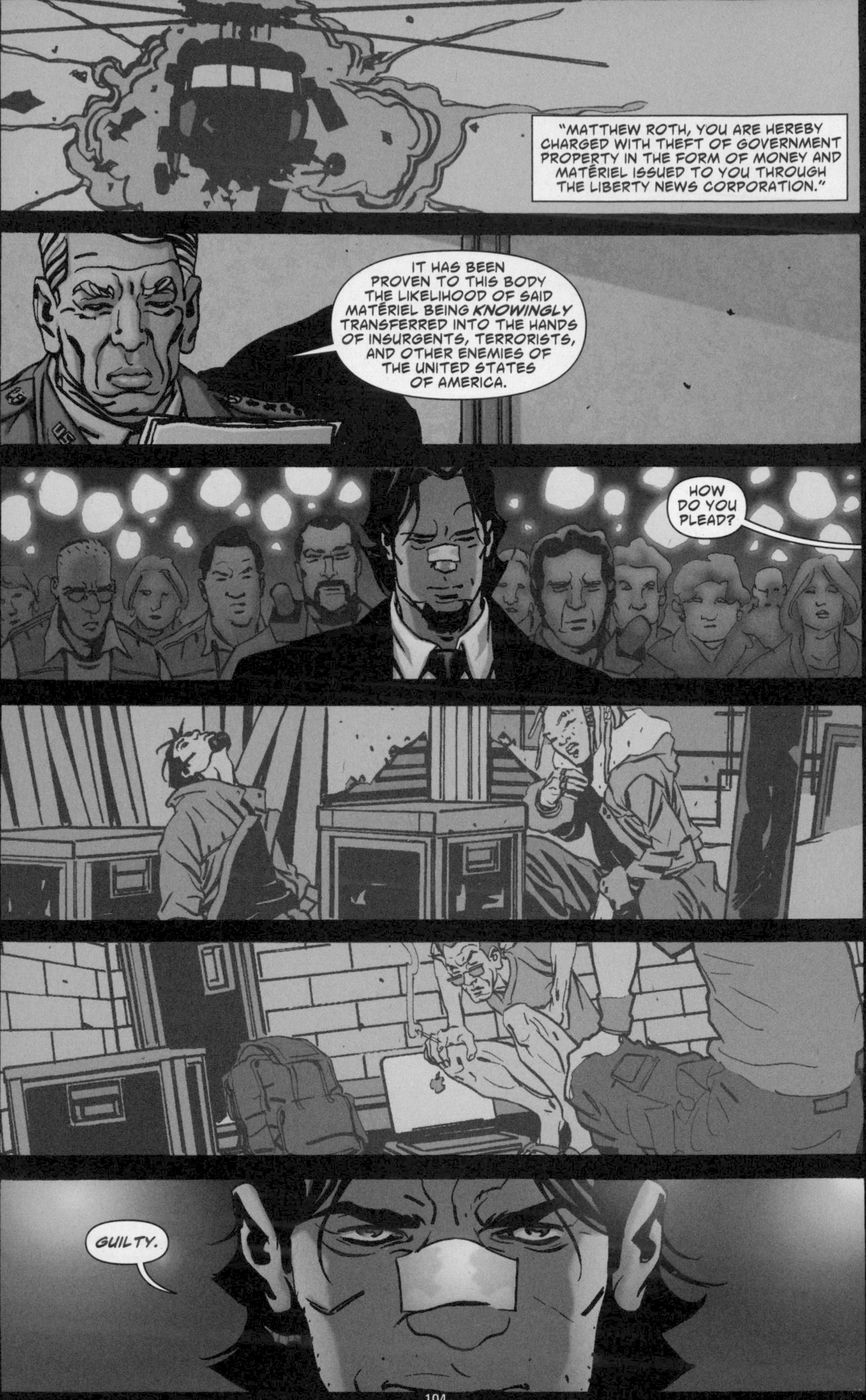
"MATTHEW ROTH, YOU ARE HEREBY CHARGED WITH THEFT OF GOVERNMENT PROPERTY IN THE FORM OF MONEY AND MATÉRIEL ISSUED TO YOU THROUGH THE LIBERTY NEWS CORPORATION."
IT HAS BEEN PROVEN TO THIS BODY THE LIKELIHOOD OF SAID MATÉRIEL BEING *KNOWINGLY* TRANSFERRED INTO THE HANDS OF INSURGENTS, TERRORISTS, AND OTHER ENEMIES OF THE UNITED STATES OF AMERICA.
HOW DO YOU PLEAD?
GUILTY.

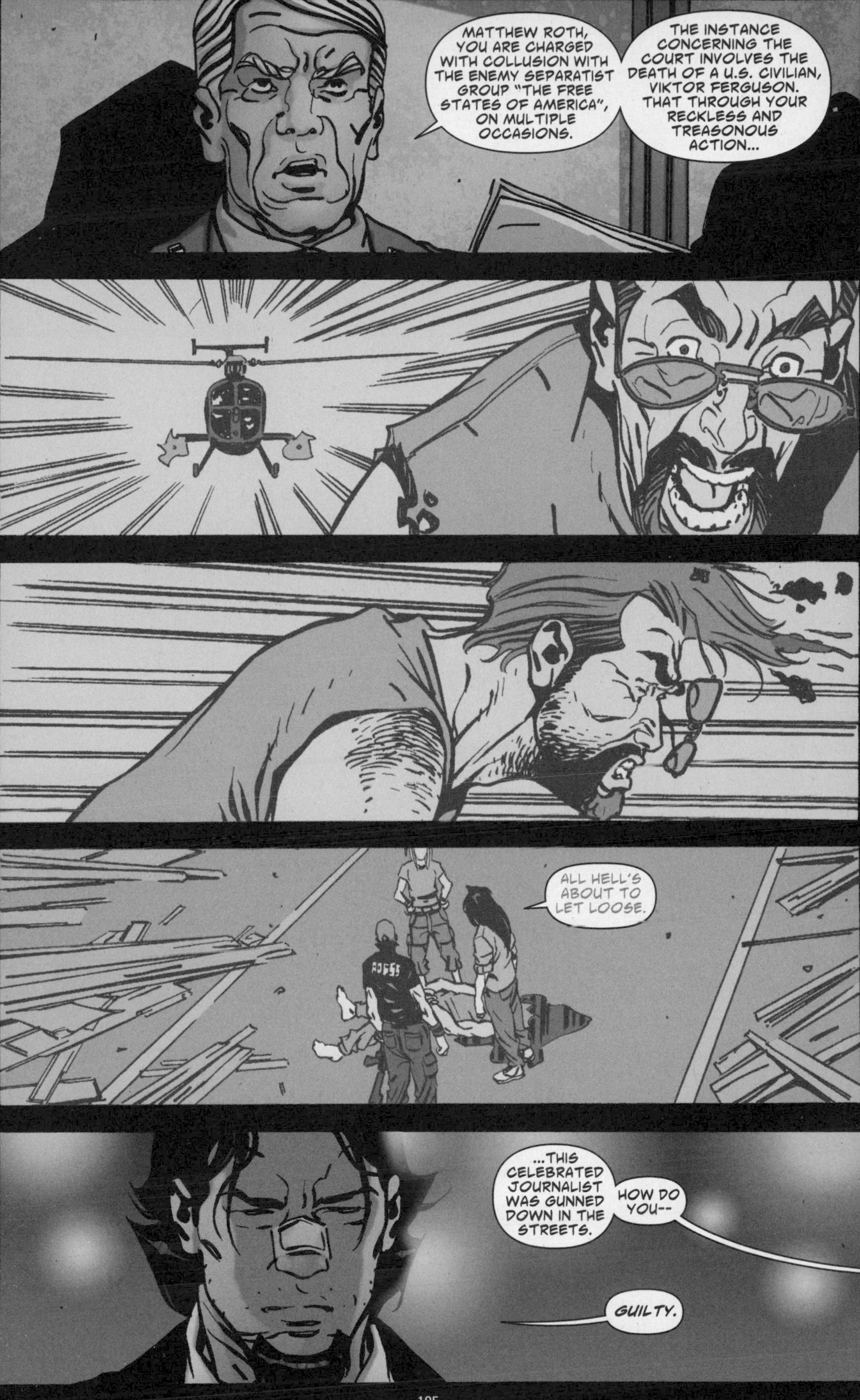
MATTHEW ROTH, YOU ARE CHARGED WITH COLLUSION WITH THE ENEMY SEPARATIST GROUP "THE FREE STATES OF AMERICA", ON MULTIPLE OCCASIONS.
THE INSTANCE CONCERNING THE COURT INVOLVES THE DEATH OF A U.S. CIVILIAN, VIKTOR FERGUSON. THAT THROUGH YOUR RECKLESS AND TREASONOUS ACTION...
ALL HELL'S ABOUT TO LET LOOSE.
...THIS CELEBRATED JOURNALIST WAS GUNNED DOWN IN THE STREETS.
HOW DO YOU--
GUILTY.

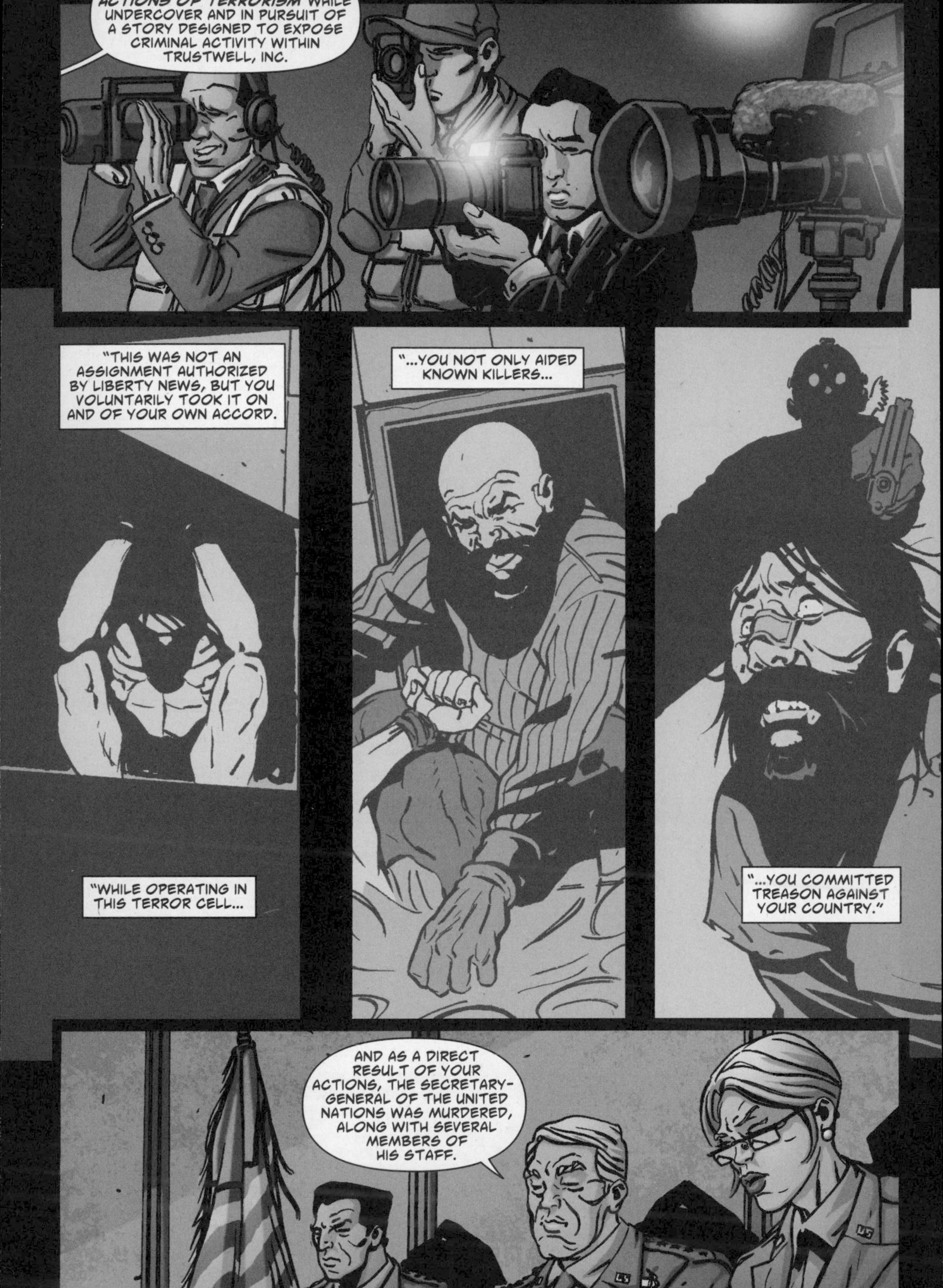
MR. ROTH, YOU ARE CHARGED WITH MULTIPLE ACTIONS OF TERRORISM WHILE UNDERCOVER AND IN PURSUIT OF A STORY DESIGNED TO EXPOSE CRIMINAL ACTIVITY WITHIN TRUSTWELL, INC.
"THIS WAS NOT AN ASSIGNMENT AUTHORIZED BY LIBERTY NEWS, BUT YOU VOLUNTARILY TOOK IT ON AND OF YOUR OWN ACCORD.
"WHILE OPERATING IN THIS TERROR CELL...
"...YOU NOT ONLY AIDED KNOWN KILLERS...
"...YOU COMMITTED TREASON AGAINST YOUR COUNTRY."
AND AS A DIRECT RESULT OF YOUR ACTIONS, THE SECRETARY-GENERAL OF THE UNITED NATIONS WAS MURDERED, ALONG WITH SEVERAL MEMBERS OF HIS STAFF.

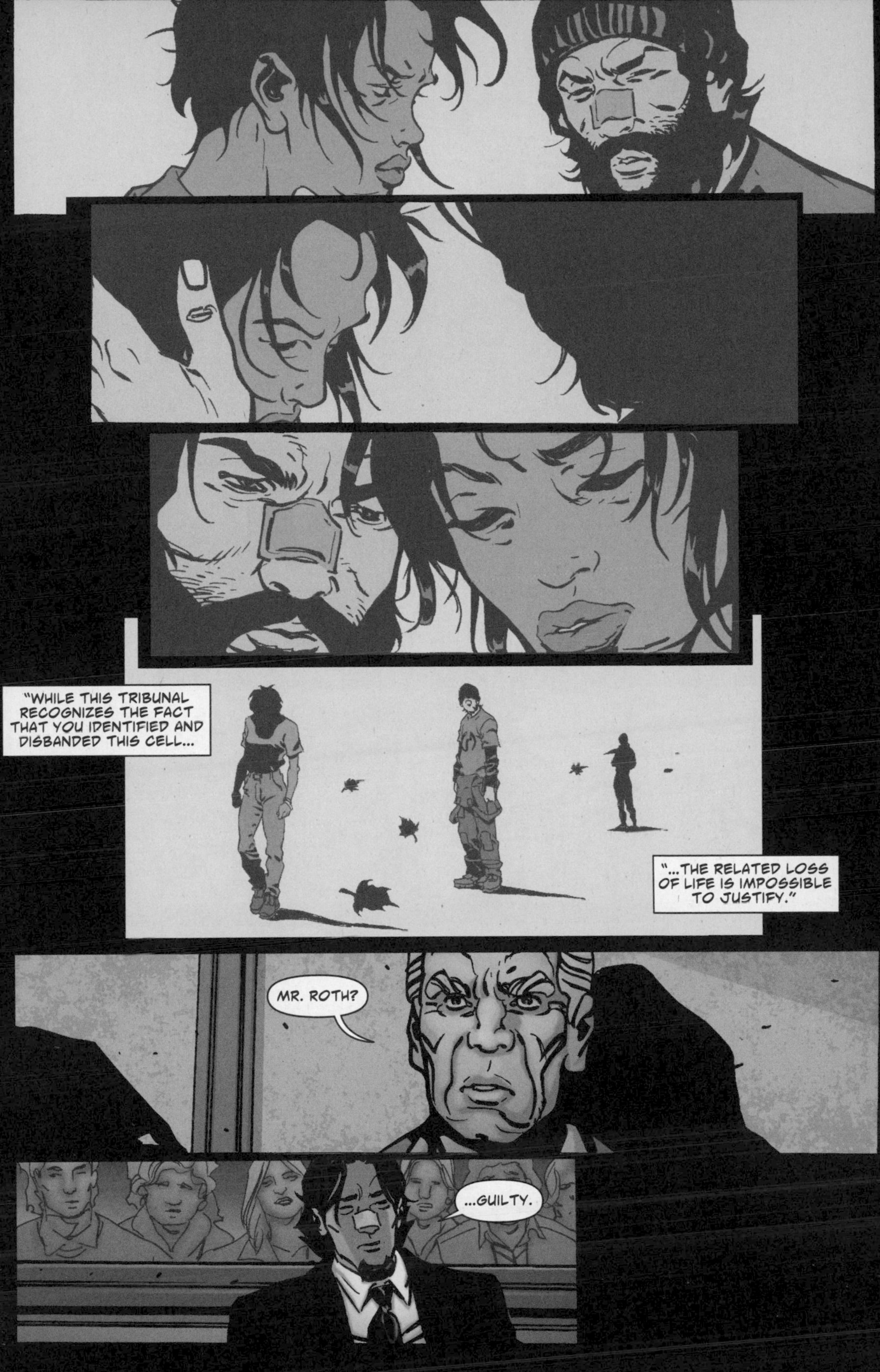
"WHILE THIS TRIBUNAL RECOGNIZES THE FACT THAT YOU IDENTIFIED AND DISBANDED THIS CELL...
"...THE RELATED LOSS OF LIFE IS IMPOSSIBLE TO JUSTIFY."
MR. ROTH?
...GUILTY.

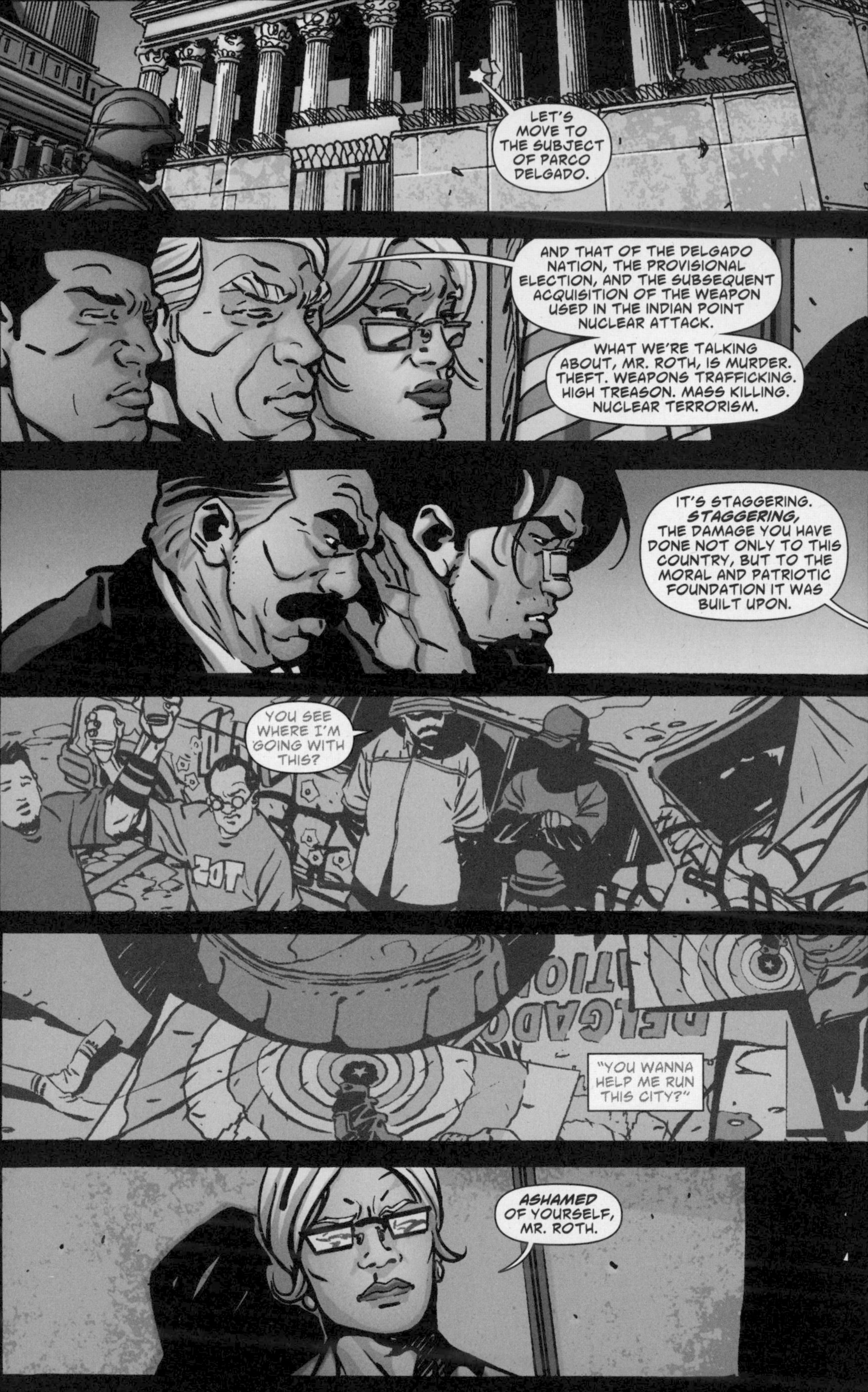
LET'S MOVE TO THE SUBJECT OF PARCO DELGADO.
AND THAT OF THE DELGADO NATION, THE PROVISIONAL ELECTION, AND THE SUBSEQUENT ACQUISITION OF THE WEAPON USED IN THE INDIAN POINT NUCLEAR ATTACK.
WHAT WE'RE TALKING ABOUT, MR. ROTH, IS MURDER. THEFT. WEAPONS TRAFFICKING. HIGH TREASON. MASS KILLING. NUCLEAR TERRORISM.
IT'S STAGGERING. STAGGERING, THE DAMAGE YOU HAVE DONE NOT ONLY TO THIS COUNTRY, BUT TO THE MORAL AND PATRIOTIC FOUNDATION IT WAS BUILT UPON.
YOU SEE WHERE I'M GOING WITH THIS?
ZOT
"YOU WANNA HELP ME RUN THIS CITY?"
ASHAMED OF YOURSELF, MR. ROTH.

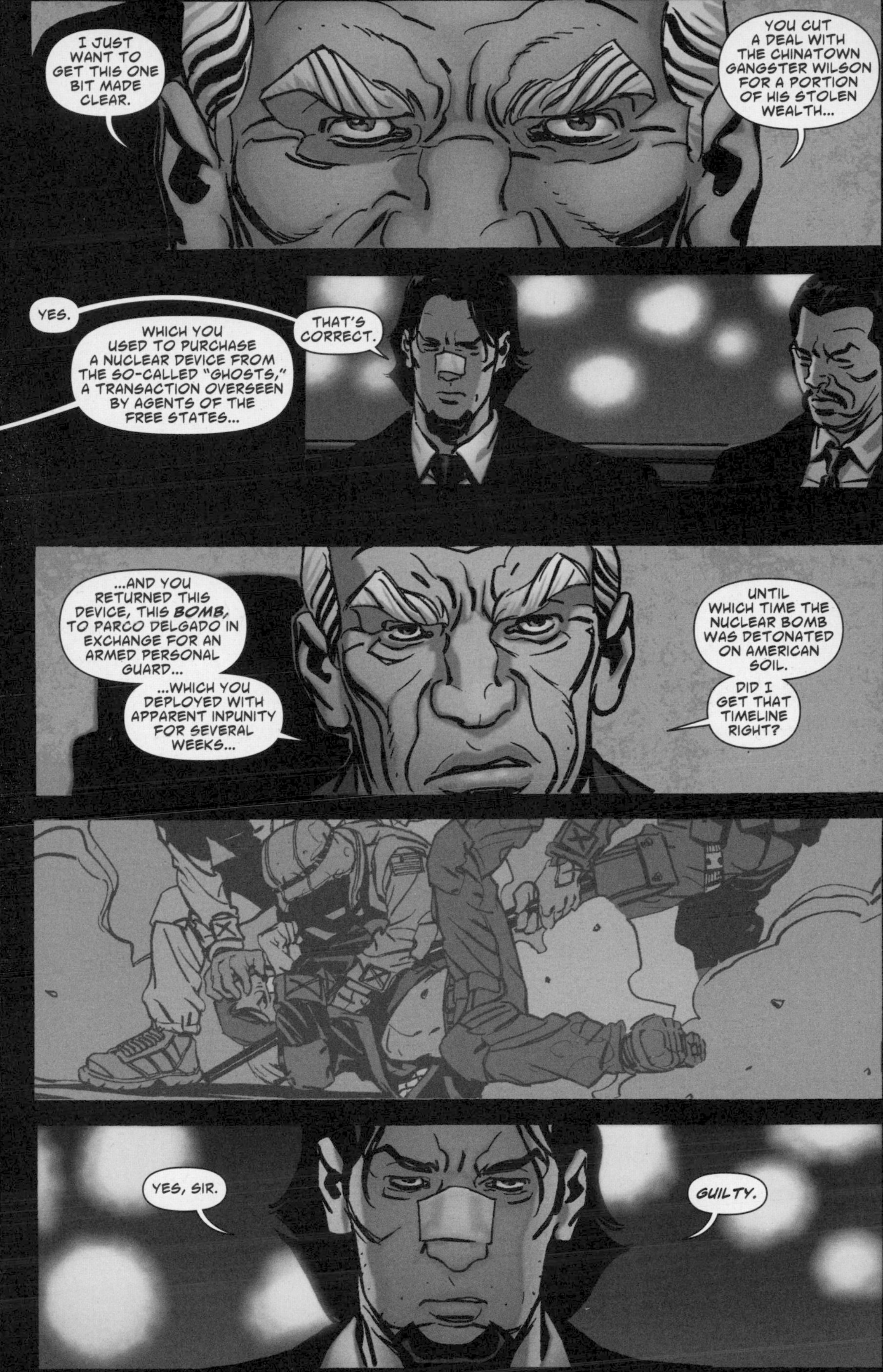
I JUST WANT TO GET THIS ONE BIT MADE CLEAR.
YOU CUT A DEAL WITH THE CHINATOWN GANGSTER WILSON FOR A PORTION OF HIS STOLEN WEALTH...
WHICH YOU USED TO PURCHASE A NUCLEAR DEVICE FROM THE SO-CALLED "GHOSTS," A TRANSACTION OVERSEEN BY AGENTS OF THE FREE STATES...
YES.
THAT'S CORRECT.
...AND YOU RETURNED THIS DEVICE, THIS BOMB, TO PARCO DELGADO IN EXCHANGE FOR AN ARMED PERSONAL GUARD...
...WHICH YOU DEPLOYED WITH APPARENT INPUNITY FOR SEVERAL WEEKS...
UNTIL WHICH TIME THE NUCLEAR BOMB WAS DETONATED ON AMERICAN SOIL.
DID I GET THAT TIMELINE RIGHT?
YES, SIR.
GUILTY.

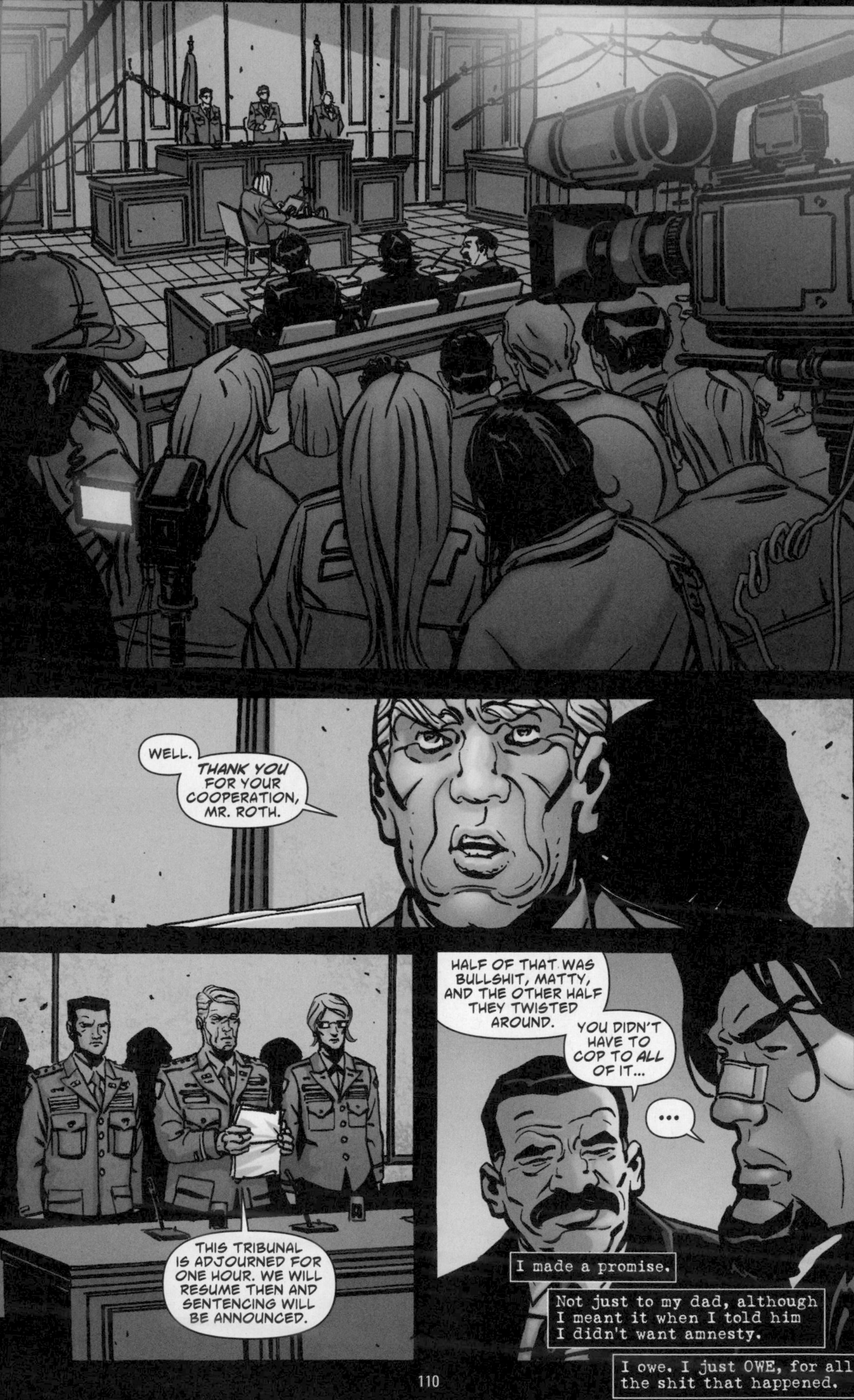
WELL.
THANK YOU FOR YOUR COOPERATION, MR. ROTH.
THIS TRIBUNAL IS ADJOURNED FOR ONE HOUR. WE WILL RESUME THEN AND SENTENCING WILL BE ANNOUNCED.
HALF OF THAT WAS BULLSHIT, MATTY, AND THE OTHER HALF THEY TWISTED AROUND.
YOU DIDN'T HAVE TO COP TO *ALL* OF IT...
...
I made a promise.
Not just to my dad, although I meant it when I told him I didn't want amnesty.
I owe. I just OWE, for all the shit that happened.

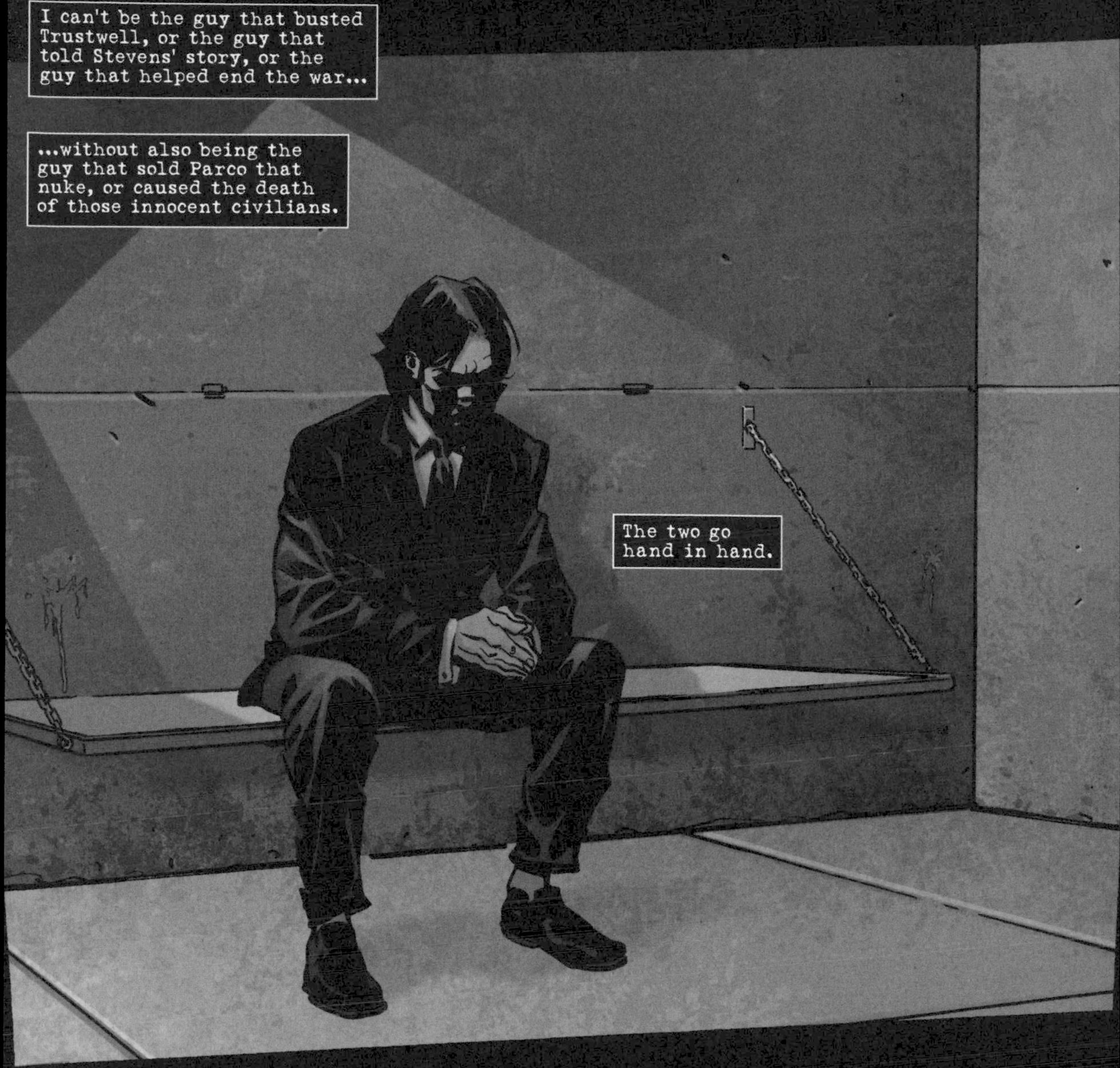
I can't be the guy that busted Trustwell, or the guy that told Stevens' story, or the guy that helped end the war...
...without also being the guy that sold Parco that nuke, or caused the death of those innocent civilians.
The two go hand in hand.

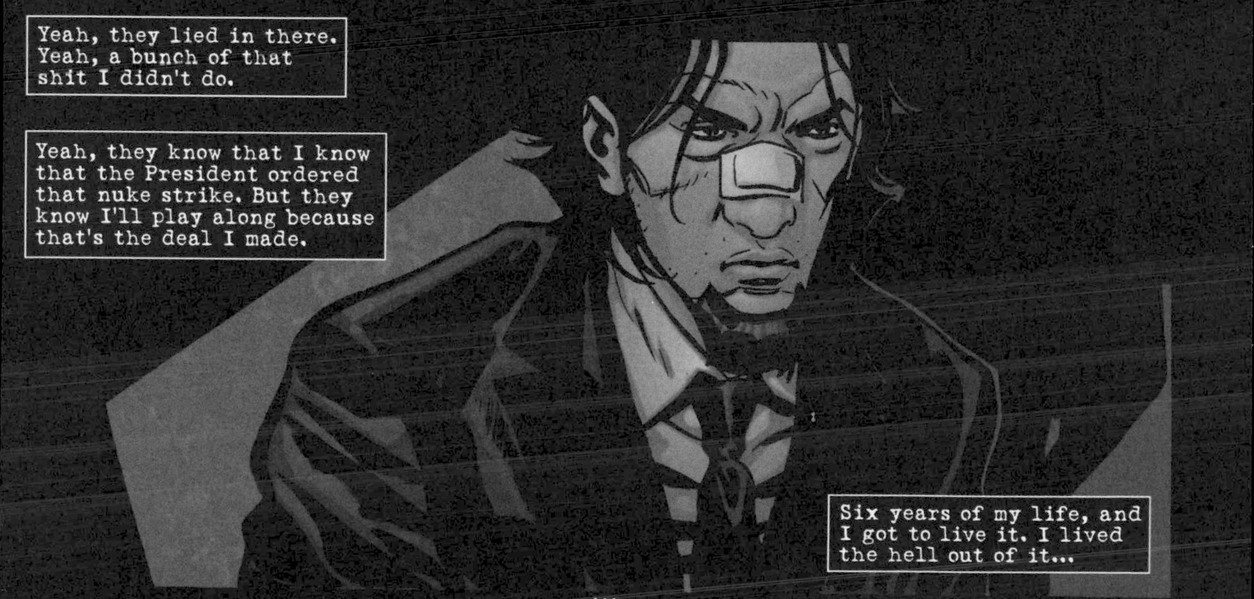
Yeah, they lied in there. Yeah, a bunch of that shit I didn't do.
Yeah, they know that I know that the President ordered that nuke strike. But they know I'll play along because that's the deal I made.
Six years of my life, and I got to live it. I lived the hell out of it...

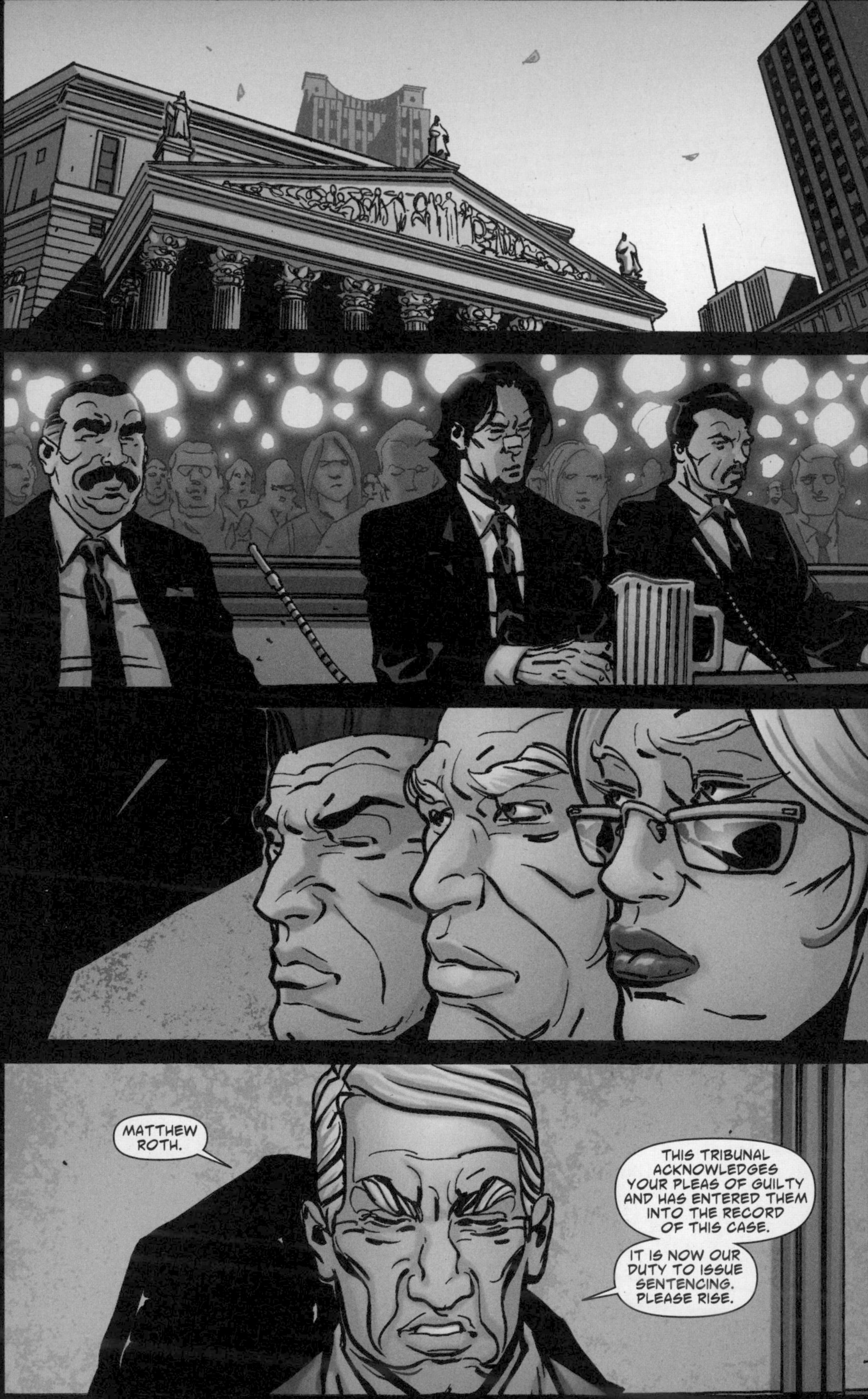
MATTHEW ROTH.
THIS TRIBUNAL ACKNOWLEDGES YOUR PLEAS OF GUILTY AND HAS ENTERED THEM INTO THE RECORD OF THIS CASE.
IT IS NOW OUR DUTY TO ISSUE SENTENCING. PLEASE RISE.

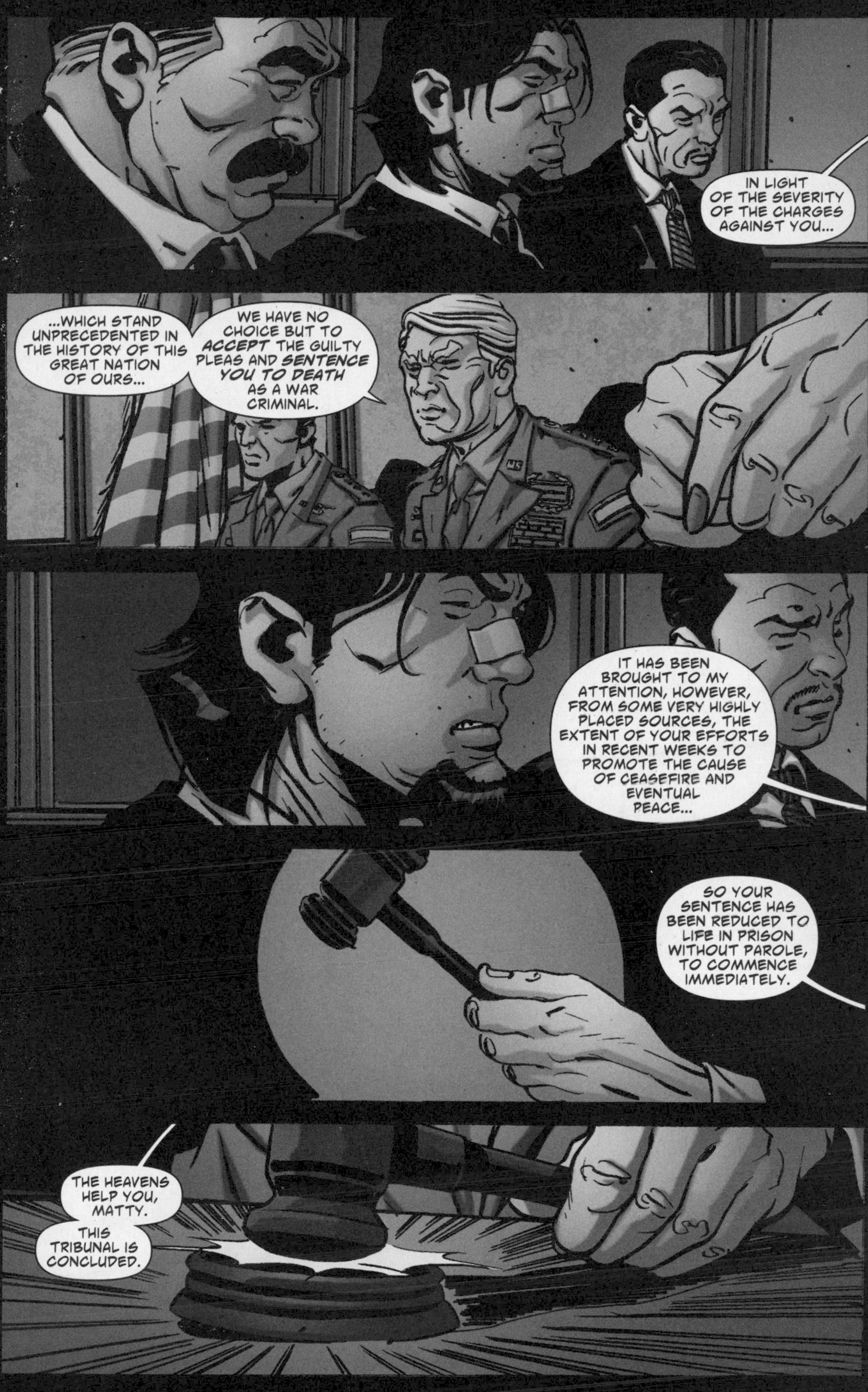

IN LIGHT OF THE SEVERITY OF THE CHARGES AGAINST YOU...
...WHICH STAND UNPRECEDENTED IN THE HISTORY OF THIS GREAT NATION OF OURS...
WE HAVE NO CHOICE BUT TO ACCEPT THE GUILTY PLEAS AND SENTENCE YOU TO DEATH AS A WAR CRIMINAL.
IT HAS BEEN BROUGHT TO MY ATTENTION, HOWEVER, FROM SOME VERY HIGHLY PLACED SOURCES, THE EXTENT OF YOUR EFFORTS IN RECENT WEEKS TO PROMOTE THE CAUSE OF CEASEFIRE AND EVENTUAL PEACE...
SO YOUR SENTENCE HAS BEEN REDUCED TO LIFE IN PRISON WITHOUT PAROLE, TO COMMENCE IMMEDIATELY.
THE HEAVENS HELP YOU, MATTY.
THIS TRIBUNAL IS CONCLUDED.

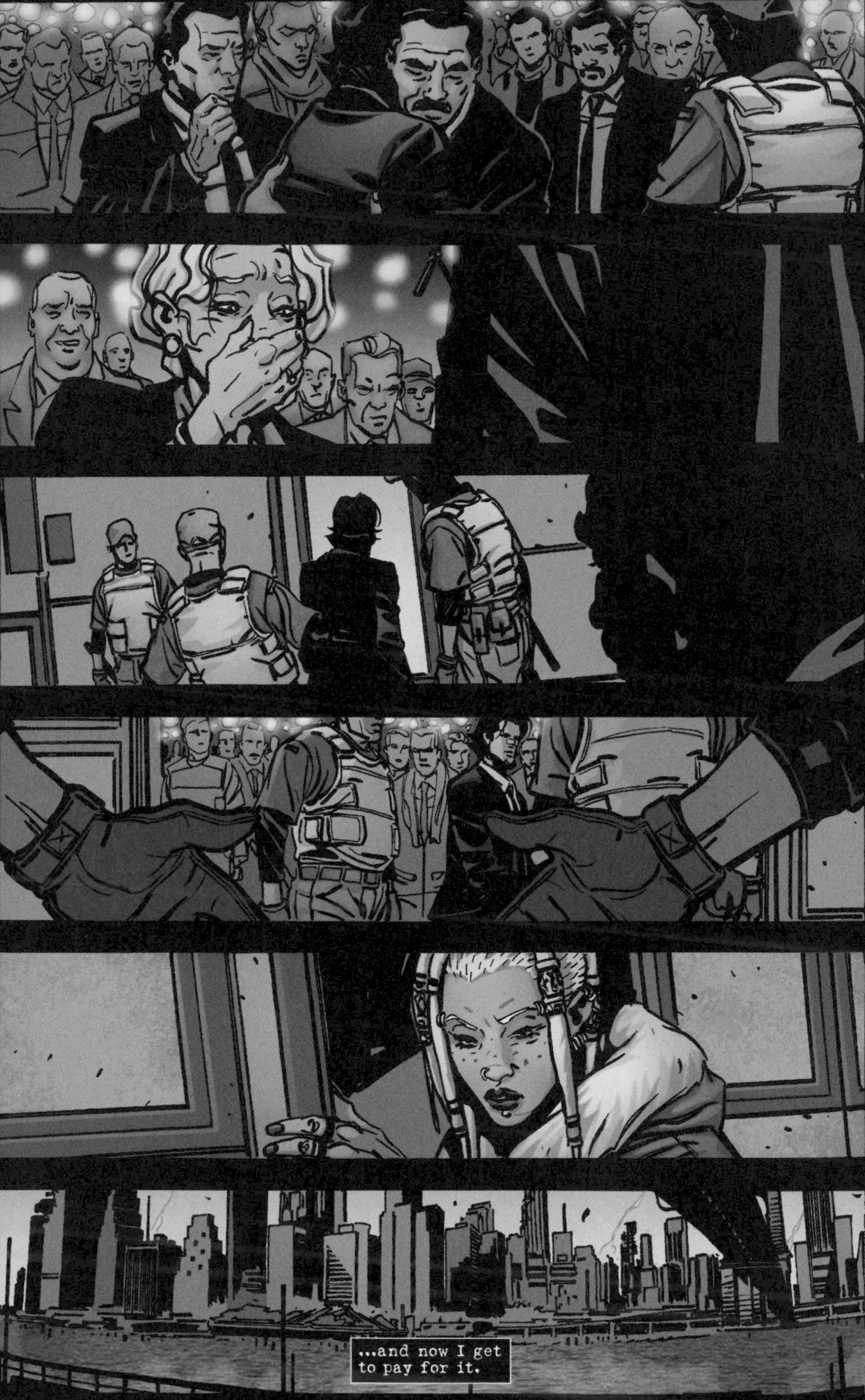
...and now I get to pay for it.

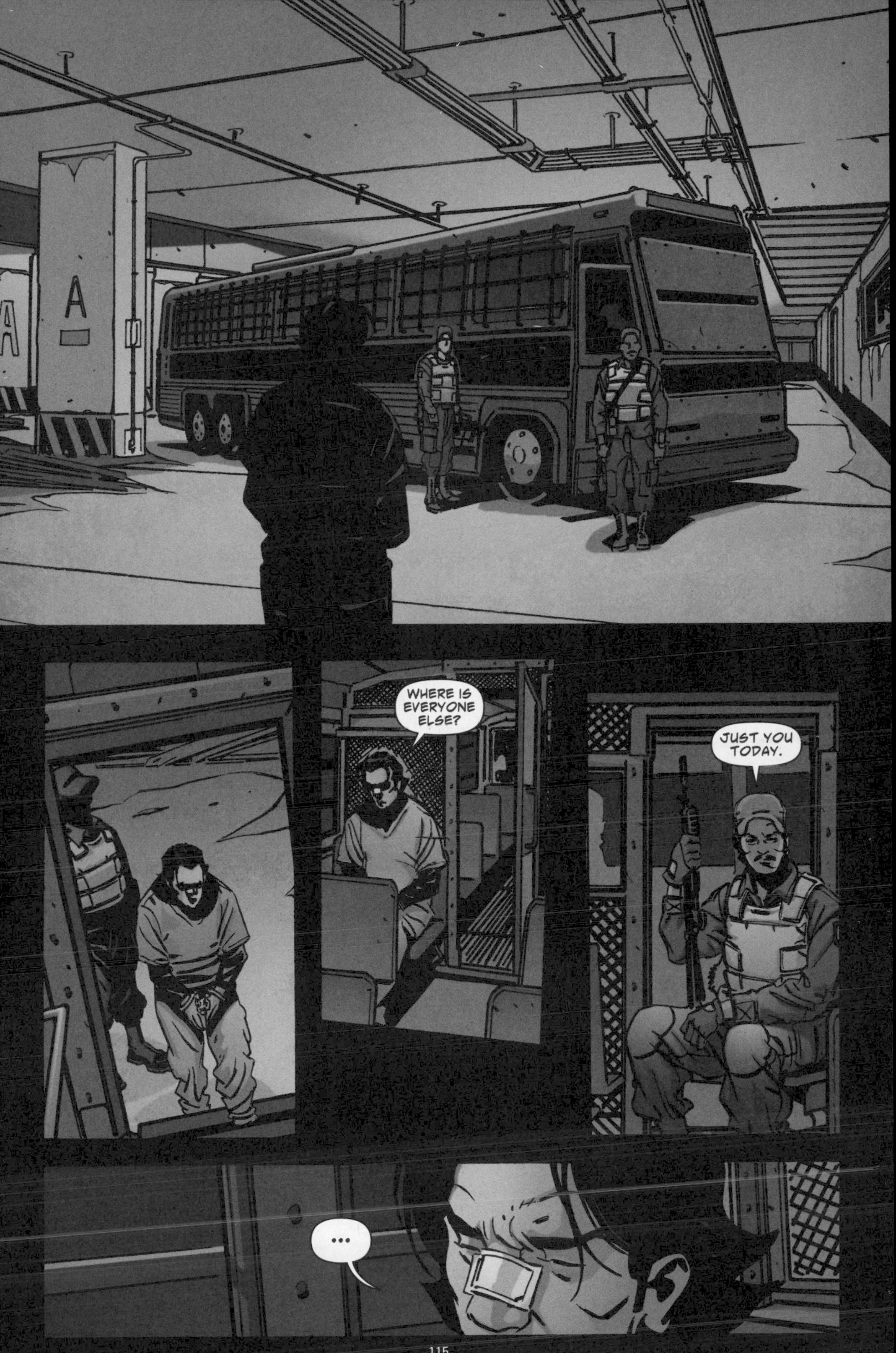
A
WHERE IS EVERYONE ELSE?
JUST YOU TODAY.
...

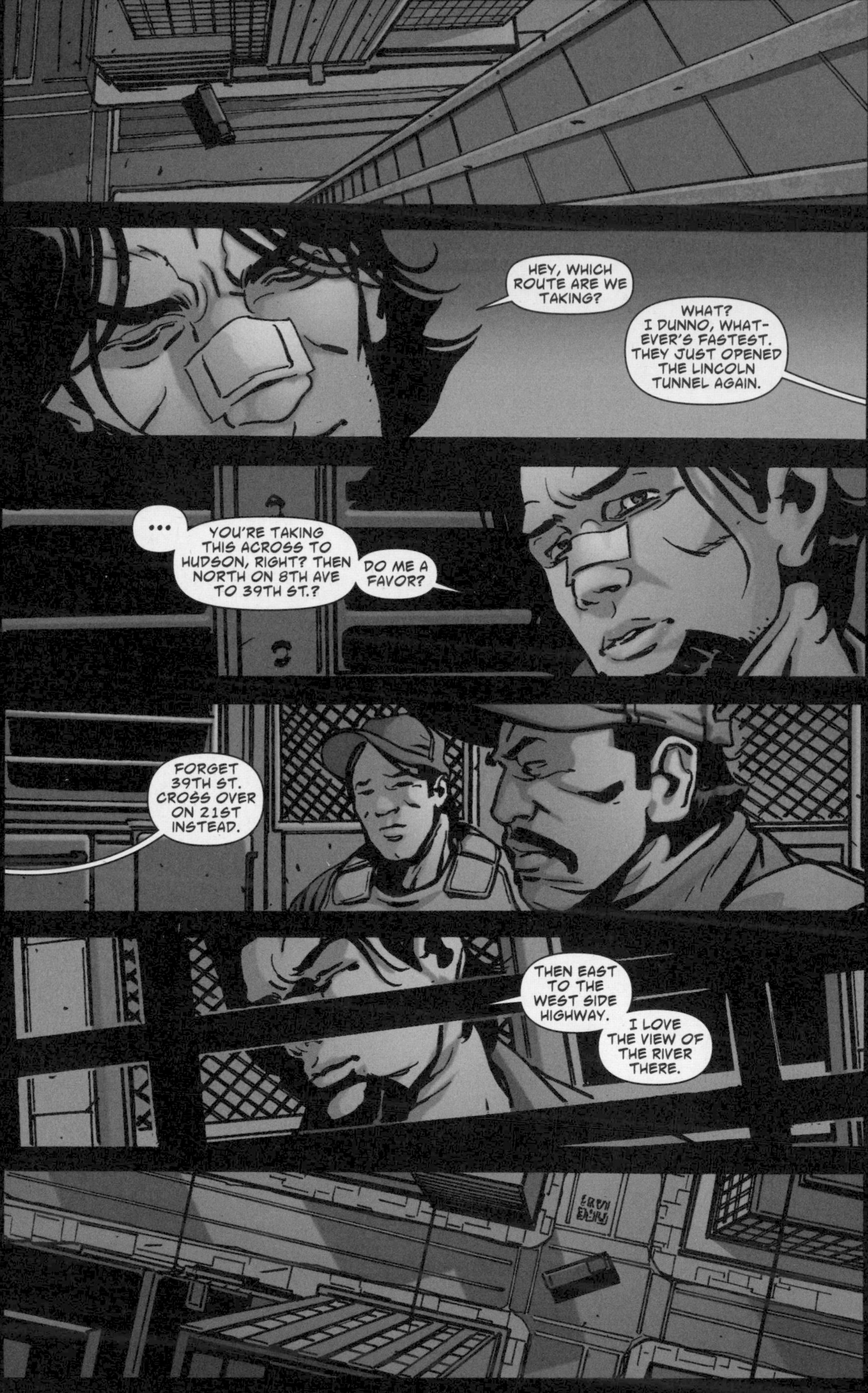
HEY, WHICH ROUTE ARE WE TAKING?
WHAT? I DUNNO, WHAT-EVER'S FASTEST. THEY JUST OPENED THE LINCOLN TUNNEL AGAIN.
...
YOU'RE TAKING THIS ACROSS TO HUDSON, RIGHT? THEN NORTH ON 8TH AVE TO 39TH ST.?
DO ME A FAVOR?
FORGET 39TH ST. CROSS OVER ON 21ST INSTEAD.
THEN EAST TO THE WEST SIDE HIGHWAY.
I LOVE THE VIEW OF THE RIVER THERE.

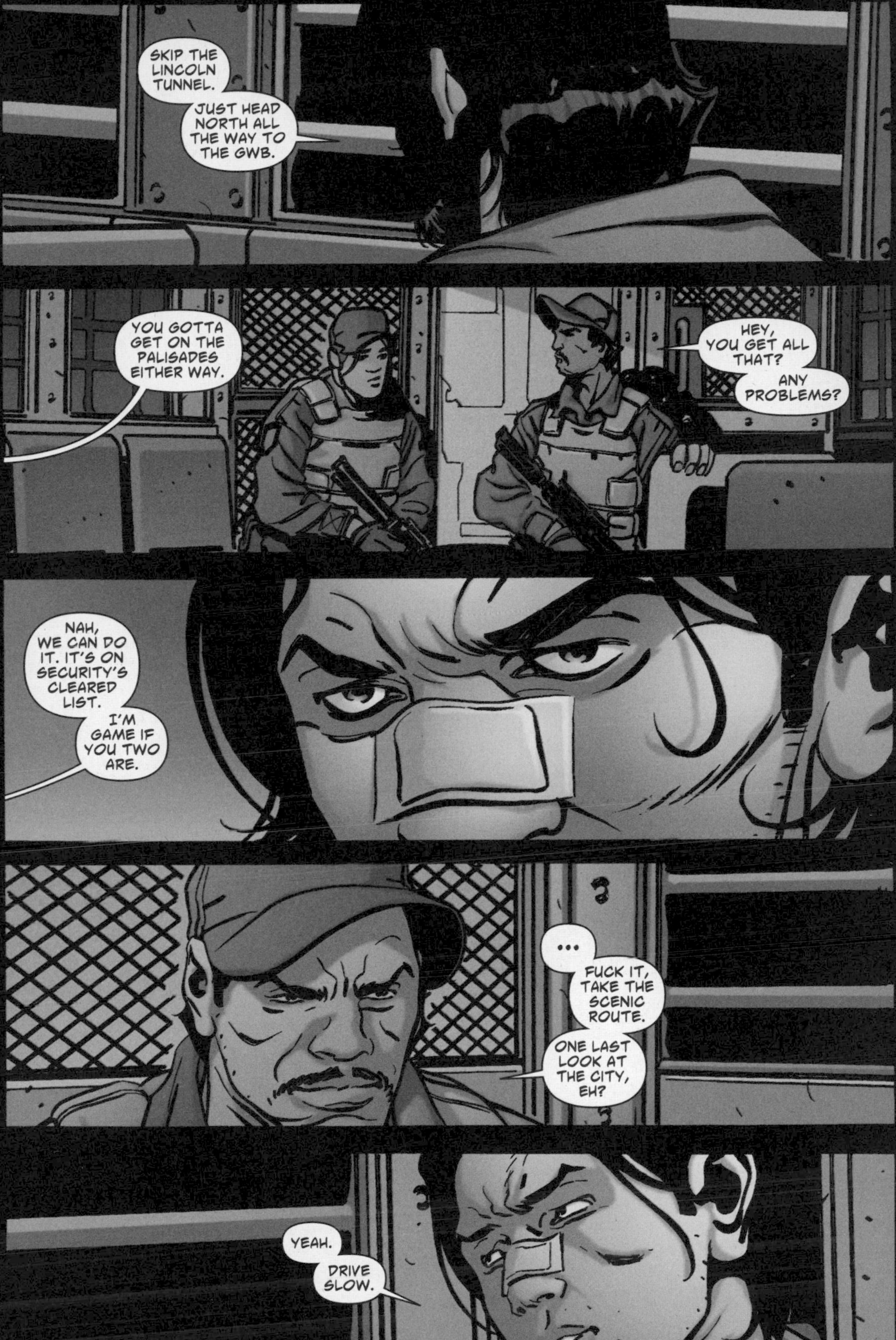
SKIP THE LINCOLN TUNNEL.
JUST HEAD NORTH ALL THE WAY TO THE GWB.
YOU GOTTA GET ON THE PALISADES EITHER WAY.
HEY, YOU GET ALL THAT?
ANY PROBLEMS?
NAH, WE CAN DO IT. IT'S ON SECURITY'S CLEARED LIST.
I'M GAME IF YOU TWO ARE.
...
FUCK IT, TAKE THE SCENIC ROUTE.
ONE LAST LOOK AT THE CITY, EH?
YEAH.
DRIVE SLOW.

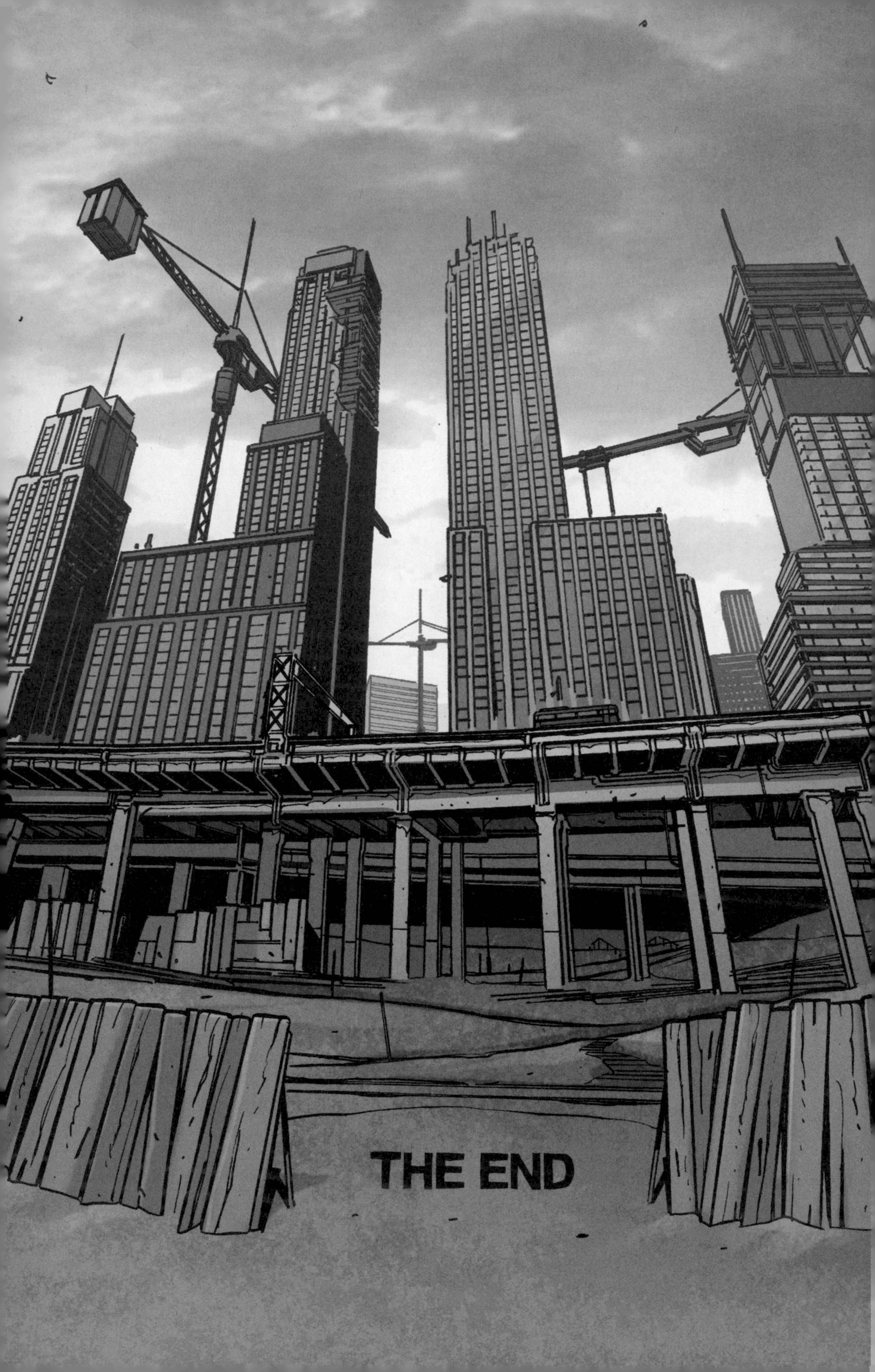
THE END

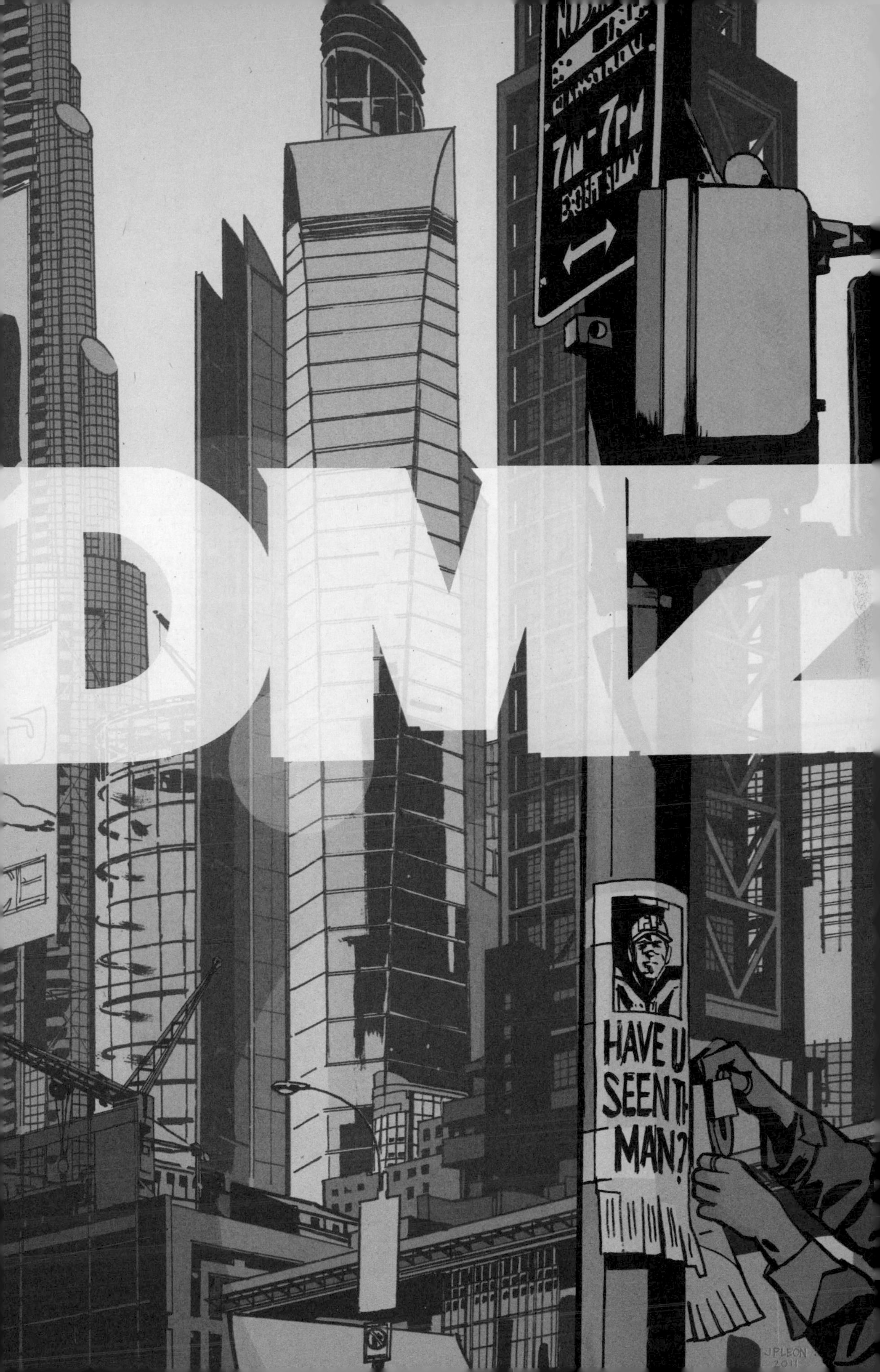
DMZ
HAVE U SEEN TH MAN?
J P LEON 2011

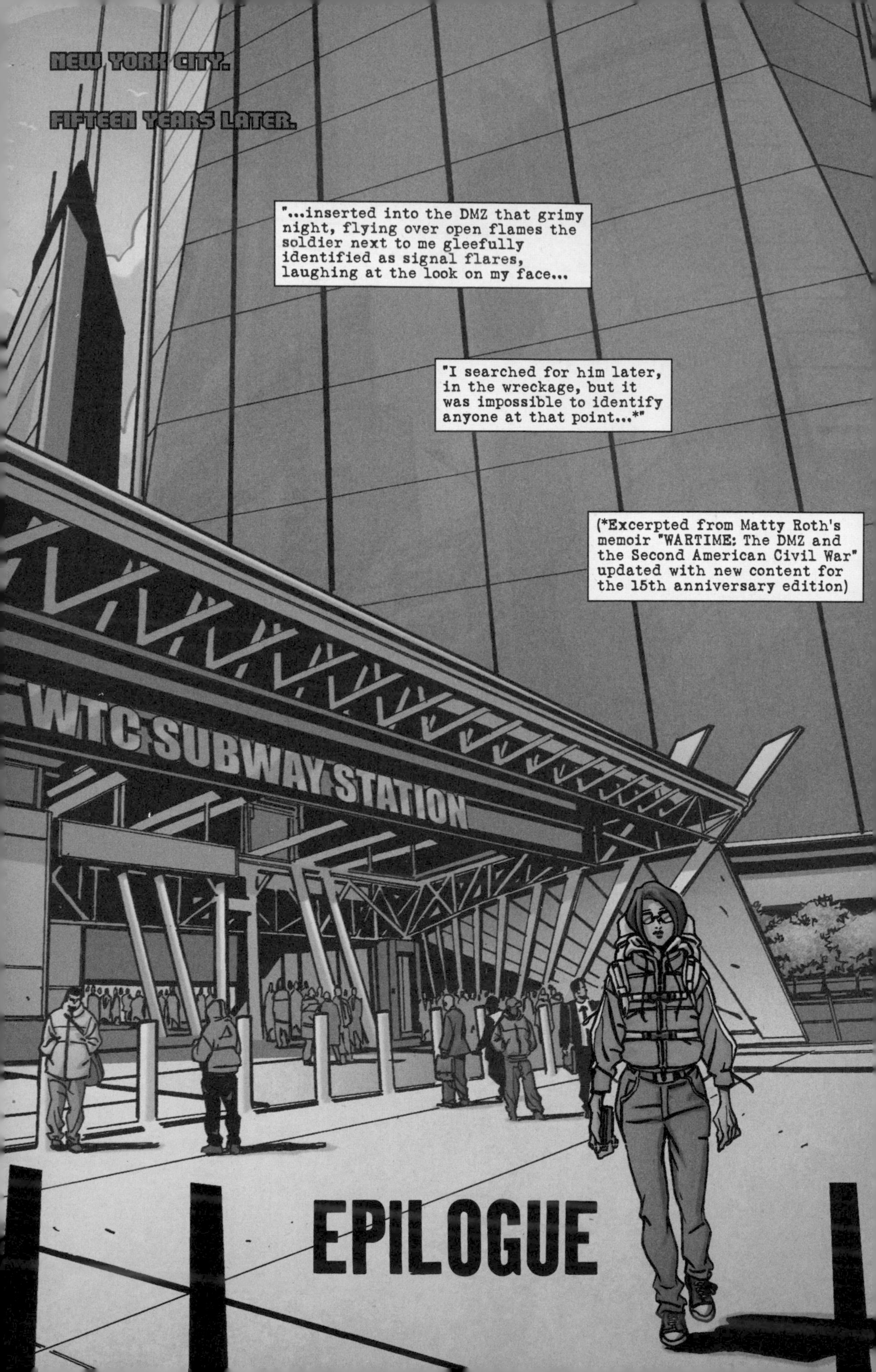

NEW YORK CITY.
FIFTEEN YEARS LATER.
"...inserted into the DMZ that grimy night, flying over open flames the soldier next to me gleefully identified as signal flares, laughing at the look on my face...
"I searched for him later, in the wreckage, but it was impossible to identify anyone at that point..."*
(*Excerpted from Matty Roth's memoir "WARTIME: The DMZ and the Second American Civil War" updated with new content for the 15th anniversary edition)
WTC SUBWAY STATION
EPILOGUE

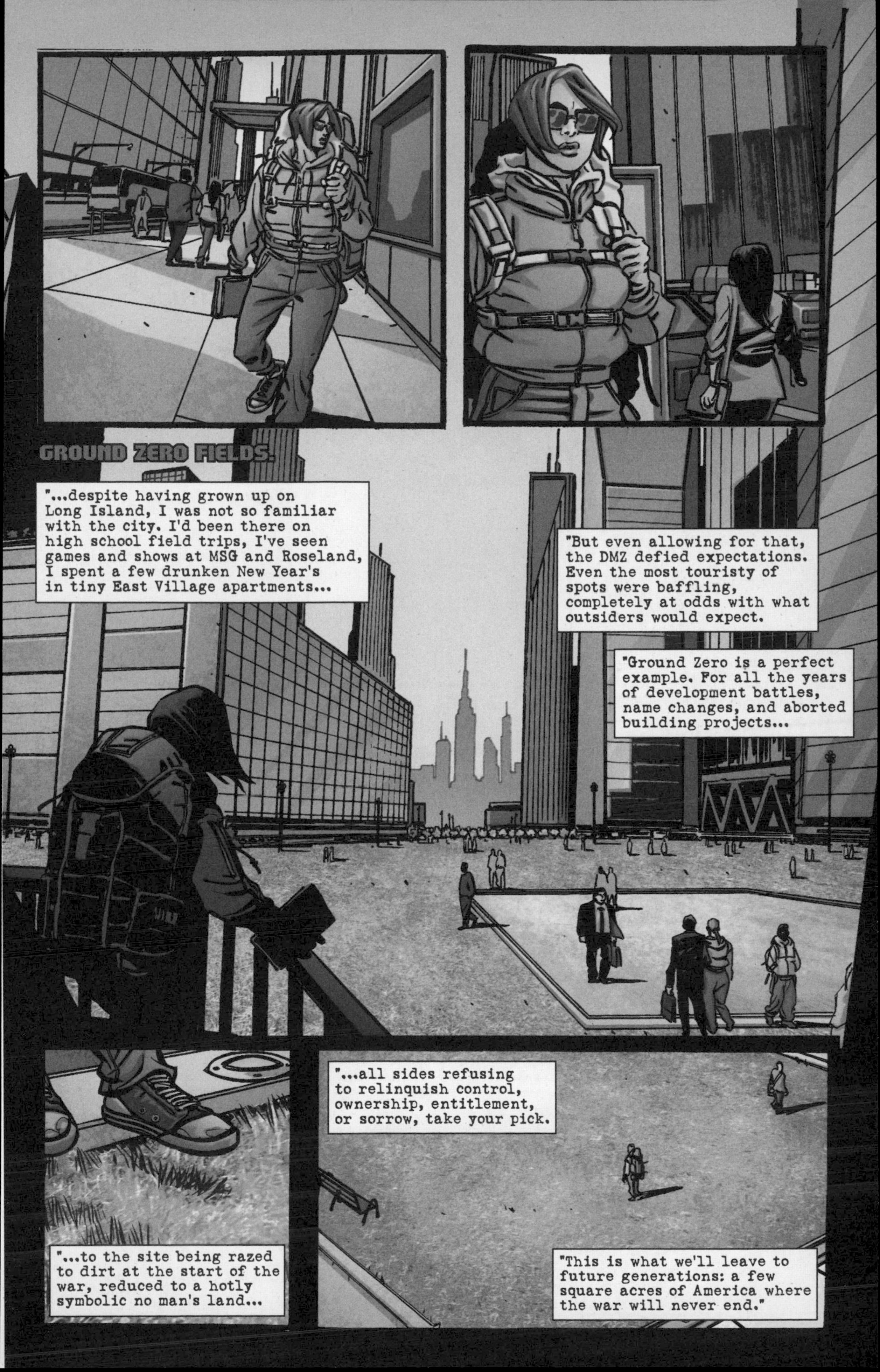
GROUND ZERO FIELDS.
"...despite having grown up on Long Island, I was not so familiar with the city. I'd been there on high school field trips, I've seen games and shows at MSG and Roseland, I spent a few drunken New Year's in tiny East Village apartments...
"But even allowing for that, the DMZ defied expectations. Even the most touristy of spots were baffling, completely at odds with what outsiders would expect.
"Ground Zero is a perfect example. For all the years of development battles, name changes, and aborted building projects...
"...to the site being razed to dirt at the start of the war, reduced to a hotly symbolic no man's land...
"...all sides refusing to relinquish control, ownership, entitlement, or sorrow, take your pick.
"This is what we'll leave to future generations: a few square acres of America where the war will never end."

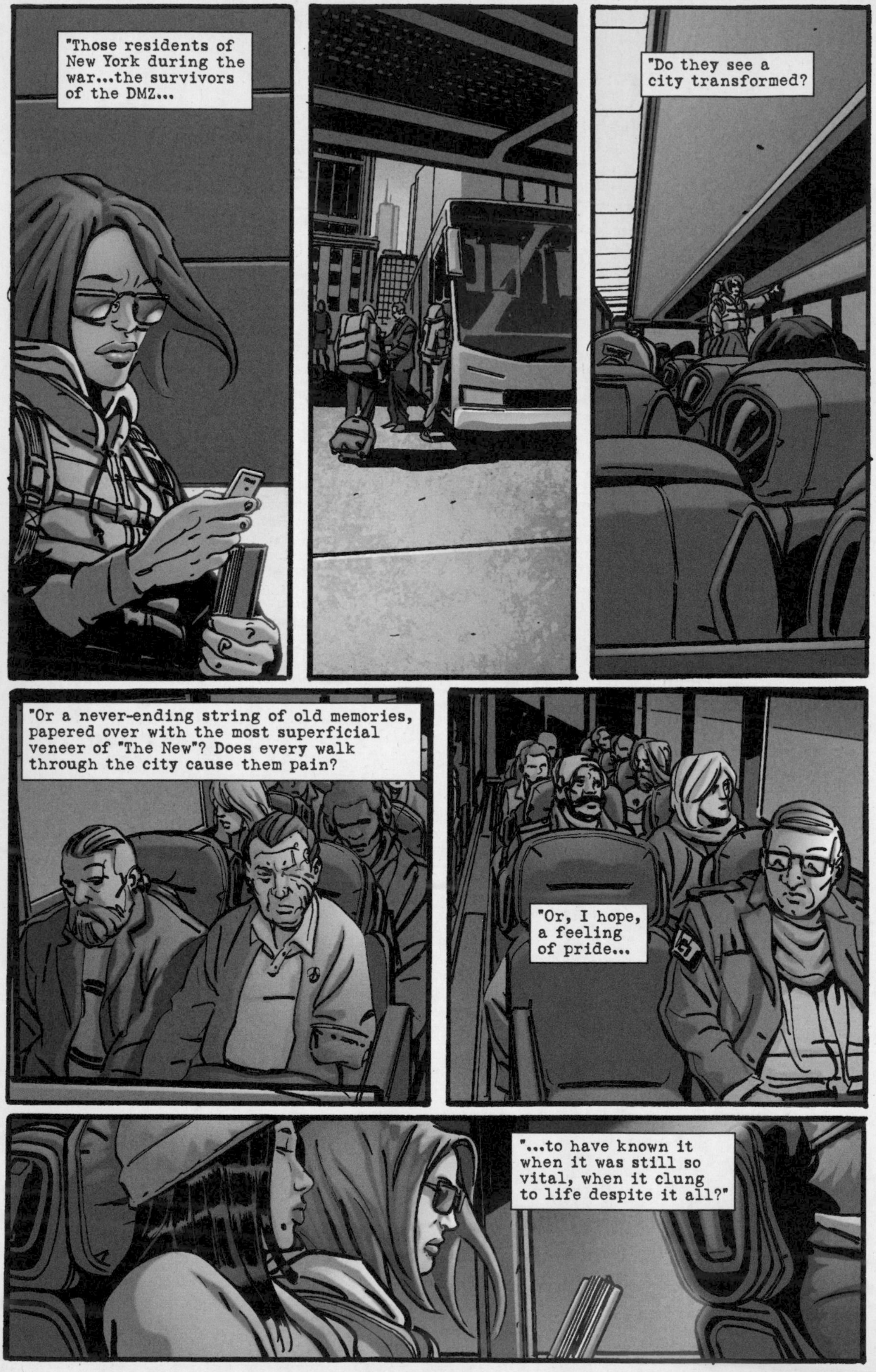
"Those residents of New York during the war...the survivors of the DMZ...
"Do they see a city transformed?
"Or a never-ending string of old memories, papered over with the most superficial veneer of "The New"? Does every walk through the city cause them pain?
"Or, I hope, a feeling of pride...
"...to have known it when it was still so vital, when it clung to life despite it all?"

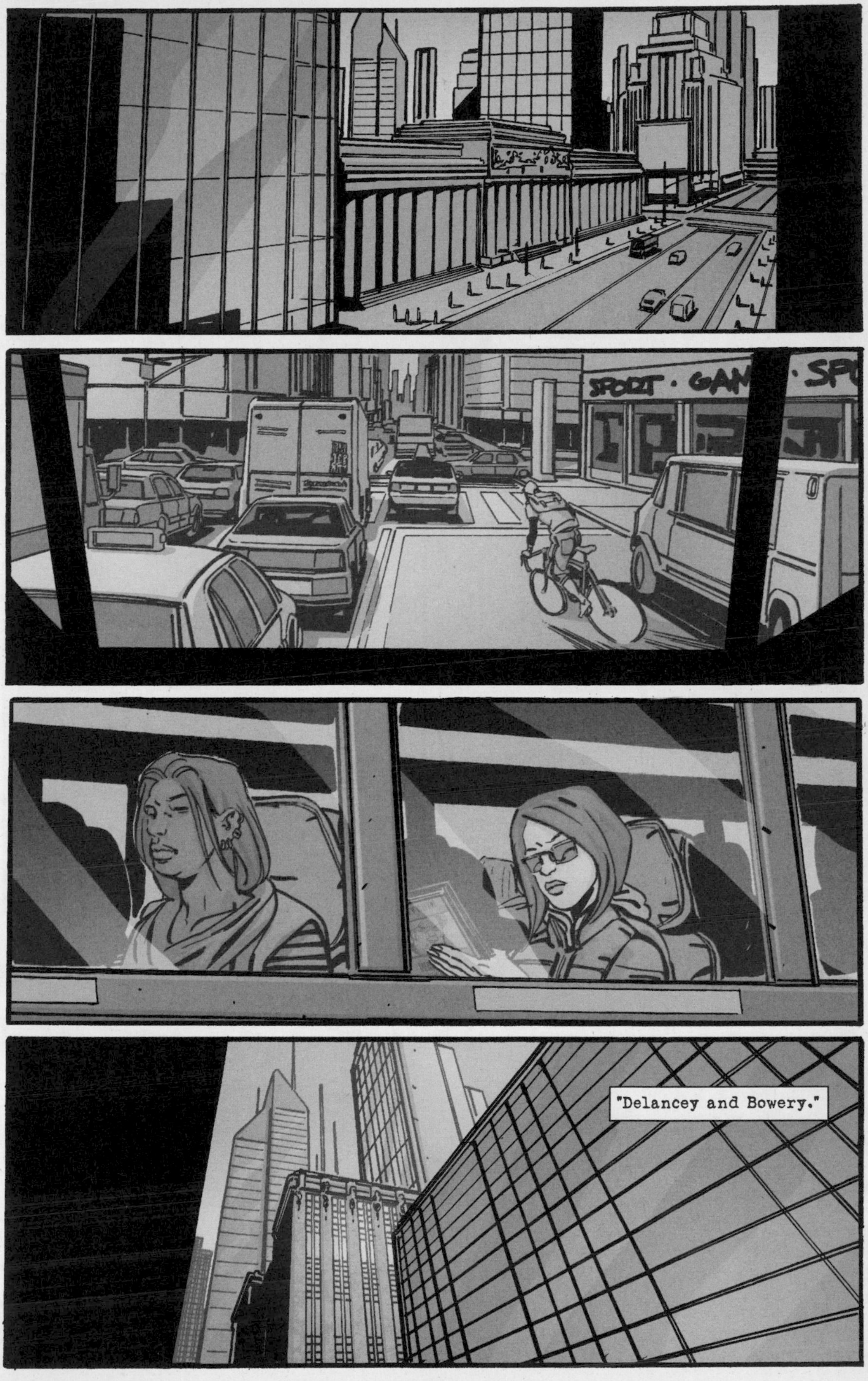
SPORT · GAM
"Delancey and Bowery."

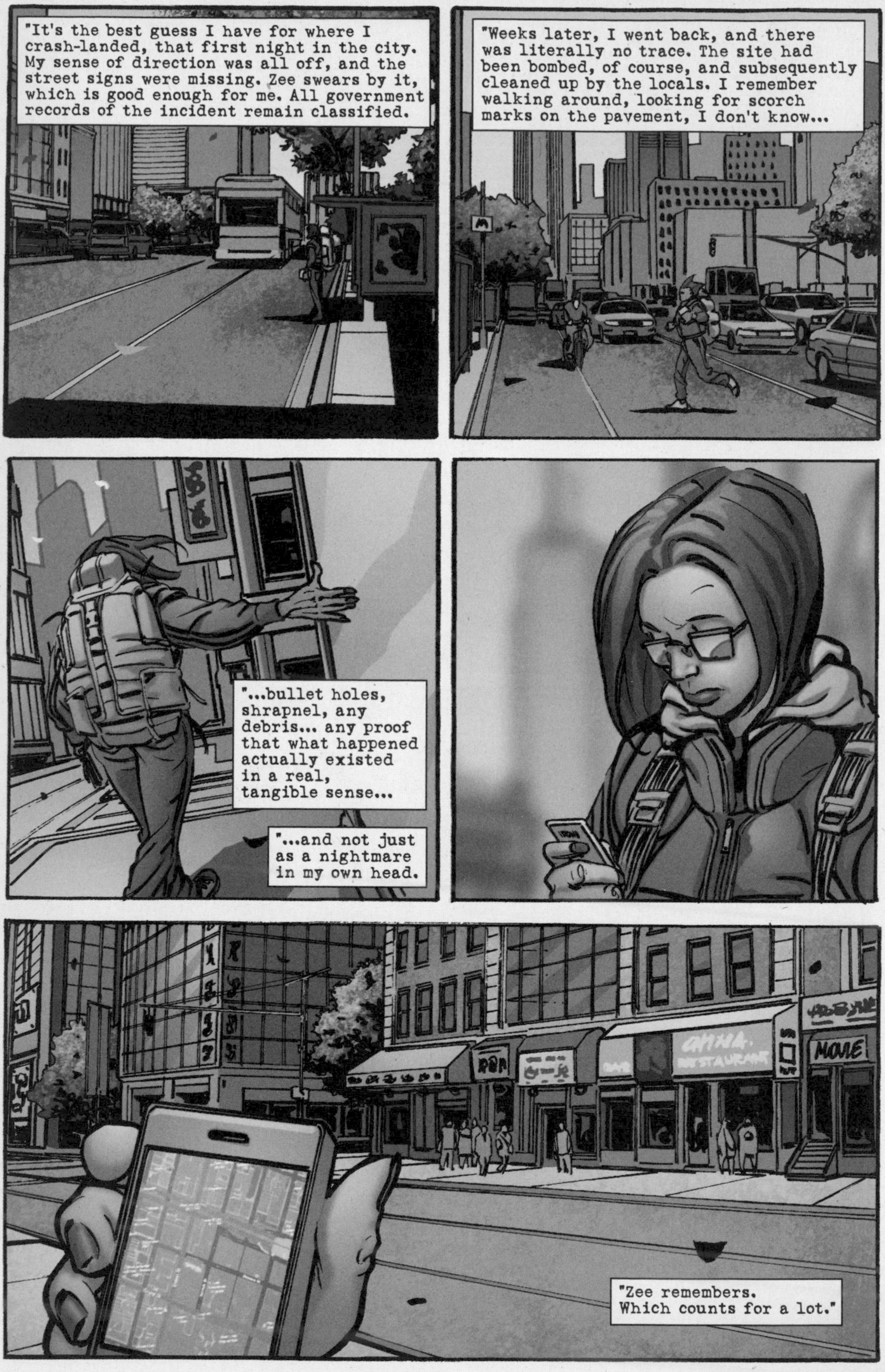
"It's the best guess I have for where I crash-landed, that first night in the city. My sense of direction was all off, and the street signs were missing. Zee swears by it, which is good enough for me. All government records of the incident remain classified.
"Weeks later, I went back, and there was literally no trace. The site had been bombed, of course, and subsequently cleaned up by the locals. I remember walking around, looking for scorch marks on the pavement, I don't know...
"...bullet holes, shrapnel, any debris... any proof that what happened actually existed in a real, tangible sense...
"...and not just as a nightmare in my own head.
MOVIE
"Zee remembers. Which counts for a lot."

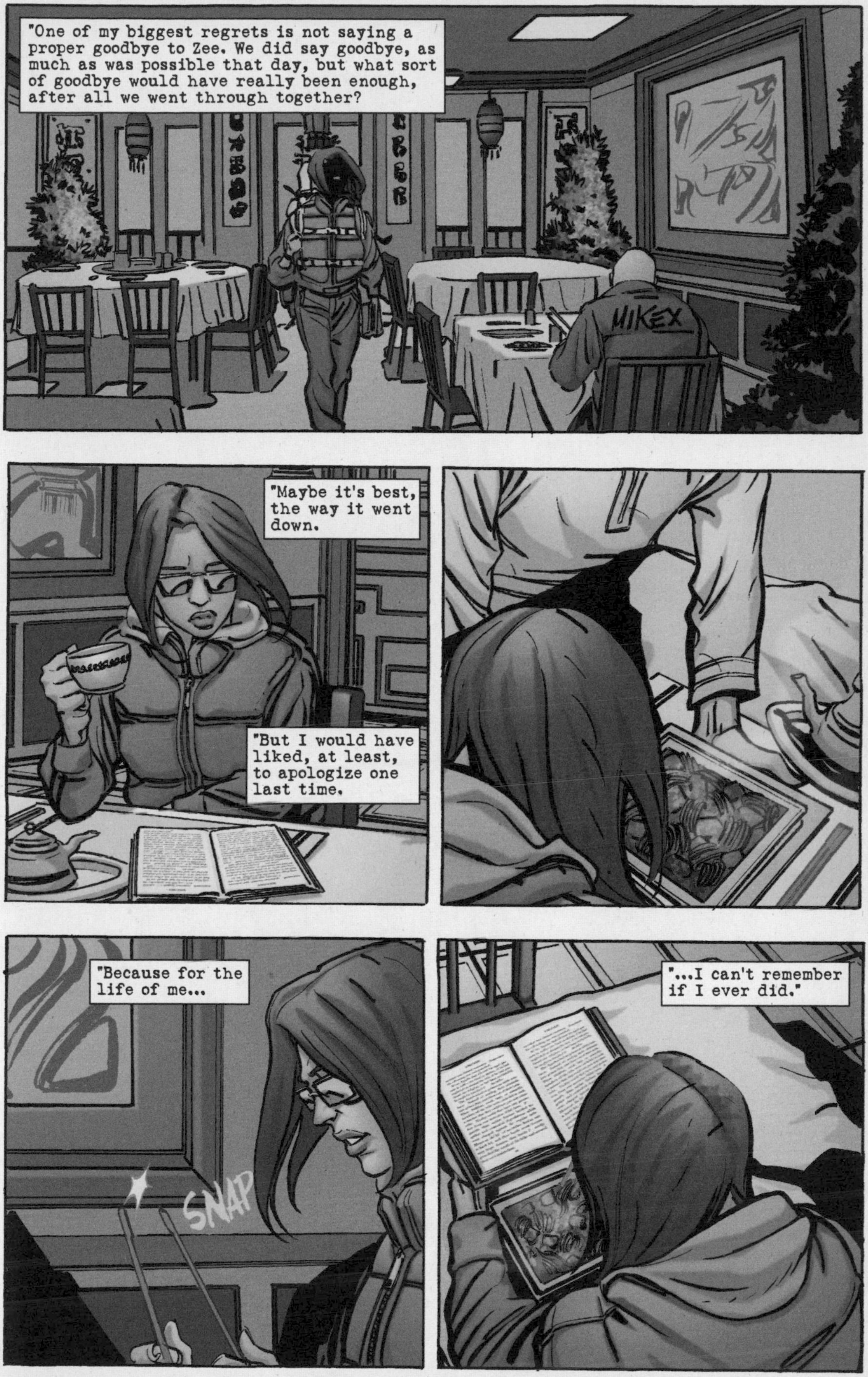
"One of my biggest regrets is not saying a proper goodbye to Zee. We did say goodbye, as much as was possible that day, but what sort of goodbye would have really been enough, after all we went through together?
MIKEX
"Maybe it's best, the way it went down.
"But I would have liked, at least, to apologize one last time.
"Because for the life of me...
SNAP
"...I can't remember if I ever did."

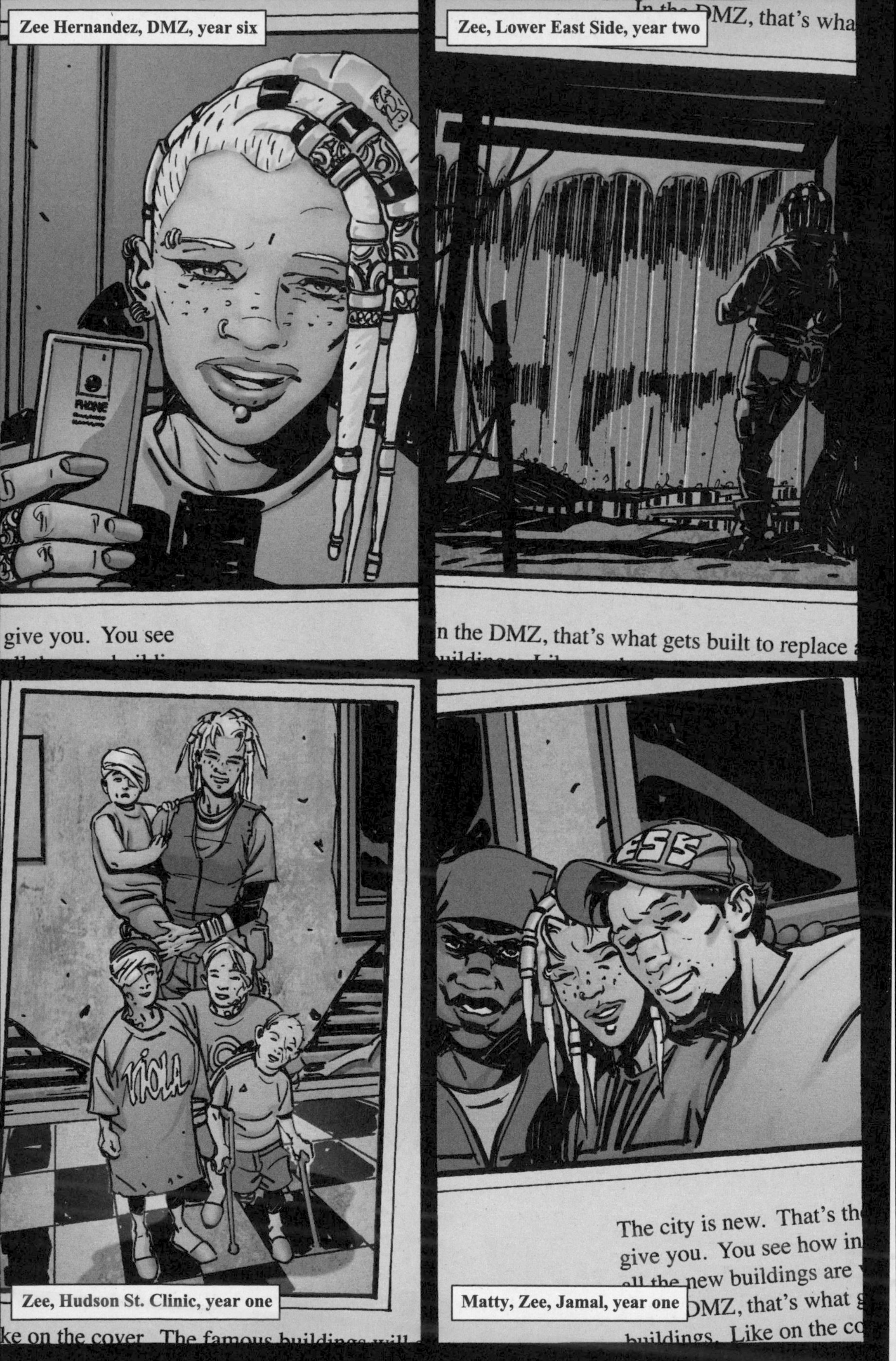
Zee Hernandez, DMZ, year six
PHONE
give you. You see
Zee, Lower East Side, year two
, that's wha
n the DMZ, that's what gets built to replace
Zee, Hudson St. Clinic, year one
VIOLA
ke on the cover. The famous buildings
Matty, Zee, Jamal, year one
The city is new. That's th
give you. You see how in
new buildings are
DMZ, that's what
buildings. Like on the co

PFC Chris Stevens, Matty, year three

Zee, Chinatown, Fourth of July, year five

He's facing away from us, and ... s, and looking out the win...

as a ped

all ind s an s big zine, wall.

Chinatown Apartment, year five

the windows at the city. us, and looking ou

Kelly Connolly, year two

Matty Roth, unknown

from us, and looking out t

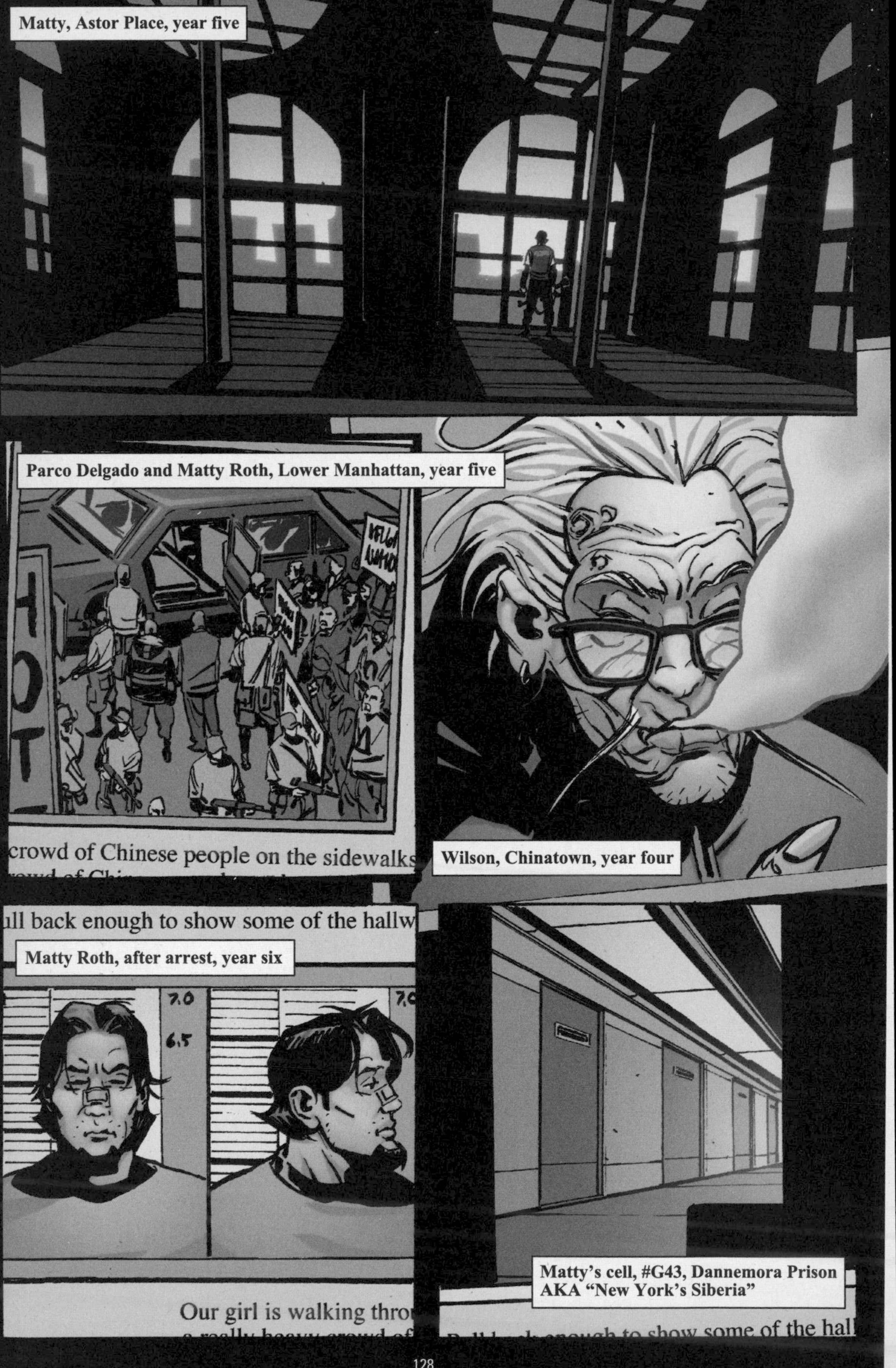
Matty, Astor Place, year five
Parco Delgado and Matty Roth, Lower Manhattan, year five
crowd of Chinese people on the sidewalks
Wilson, Chinatown, year four
ll back enough to show some of the hallw
Matty Roth, after arrest, year six
7.0
6.5
Our girl is walking thro
Matty's cell, #G43, Dannemora Prison
AKA "New York's Siberia"

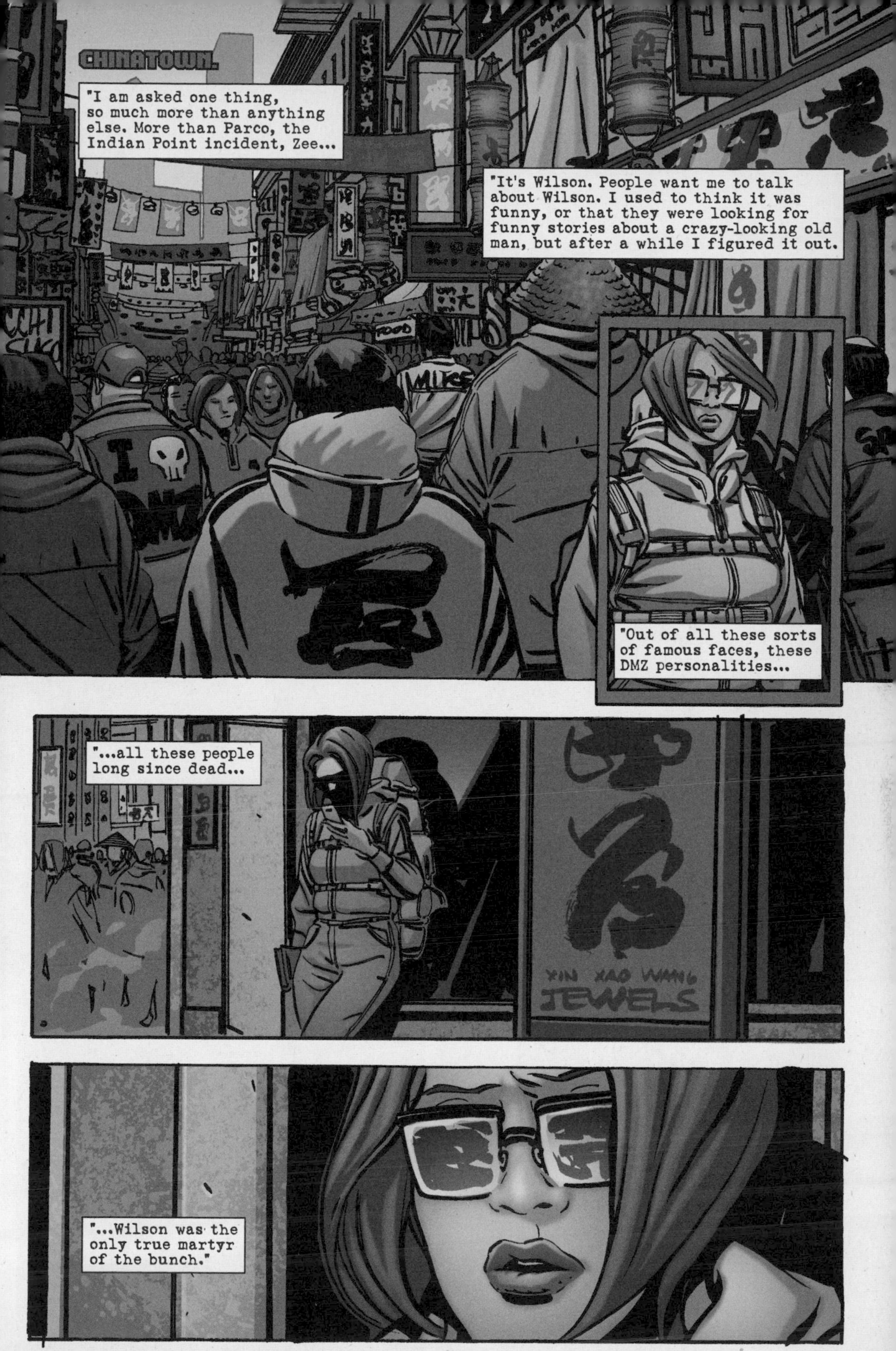
CHINATOWN.
"I am asked one thing, so much more than anything else. More than Parco, the Indian Point incident, Zee...
"It's Wilson. People want me to talk about Wilson. I used to think it was funny, or that they were looking for funny stories about a crazy-looking old man, but after a while I figured it out.
FOOD
"Out of all these sorts of famous faces, these DMZ personalities...
"...all these people long since dead...
XIN XAO WANG
JEWELS
"...Wilson was the only true martyr of the bunch."

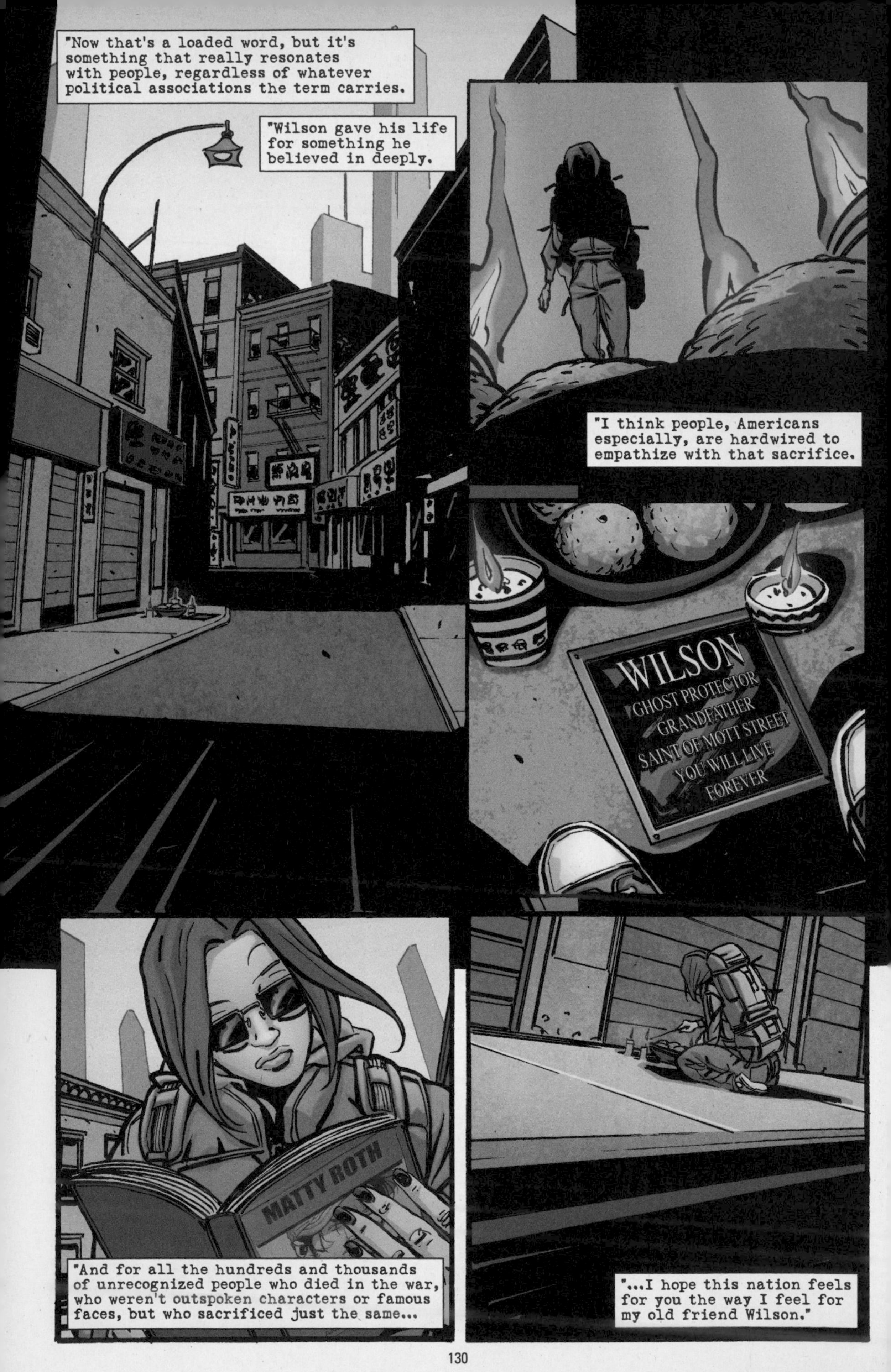
"Now that's a loaded word, but it's something that really resonates with people, regardless of whatever political associations the term carries.
"Wilson gave his life for something he believed in deeply.
"I think people, Americans especially, are hardwired to empathize with that sacrifice.
WILSON
GHOST PROTECTOR
GRANDFATHER
SAINT OF MOTT STREET
YOU WILL LIVE
FOREVER
MATTY ROTH
"And for all the hundreds and thousands of unrecognized people who died in the war, who weren't outspoken characters or famous faces, but who sacrificed just the same...
"...I hope this nation feels for you the way I feel for my old friend Wilson."

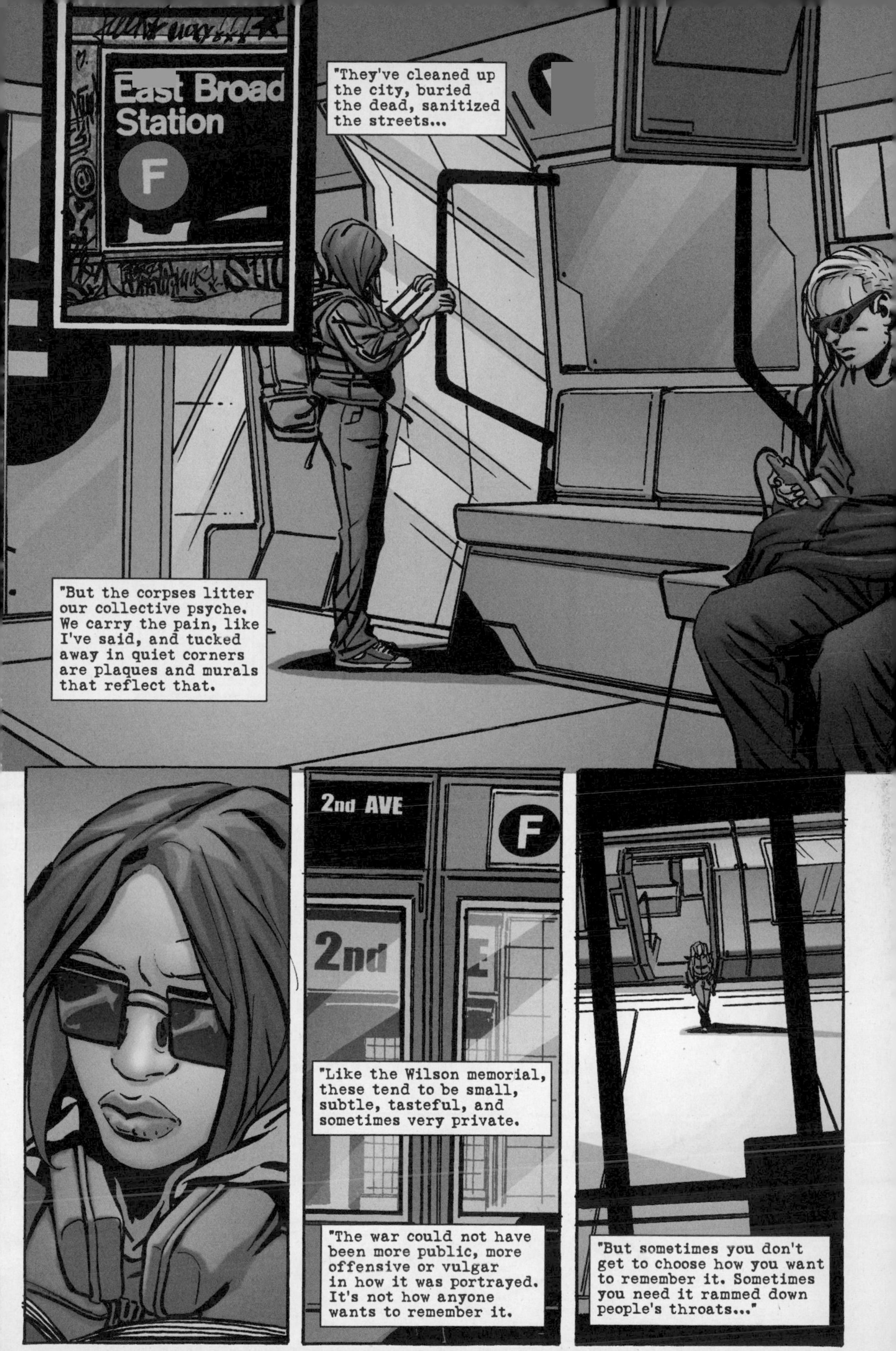
East Broad
Station
F
"They've cleaned up the city, buried the dead, sanitized the streets...
"But the corpses litter our collective psyche. We carry the pain, like I've said, and tucked away in quiet corners are plaques and murals that reflect that.
2nd AVE
F
2nd
"Like the Wilson memorial, these tend to be small, subtle, tasteful, and sometimes very private.
"The war could not have been more public, more offensive or vulgar in how it was portrayed. It's not how anyone wants to remember it.
"But sometimes you don't get to choose how you want to remember it. Sometimes you need it rammed down people's throats..."

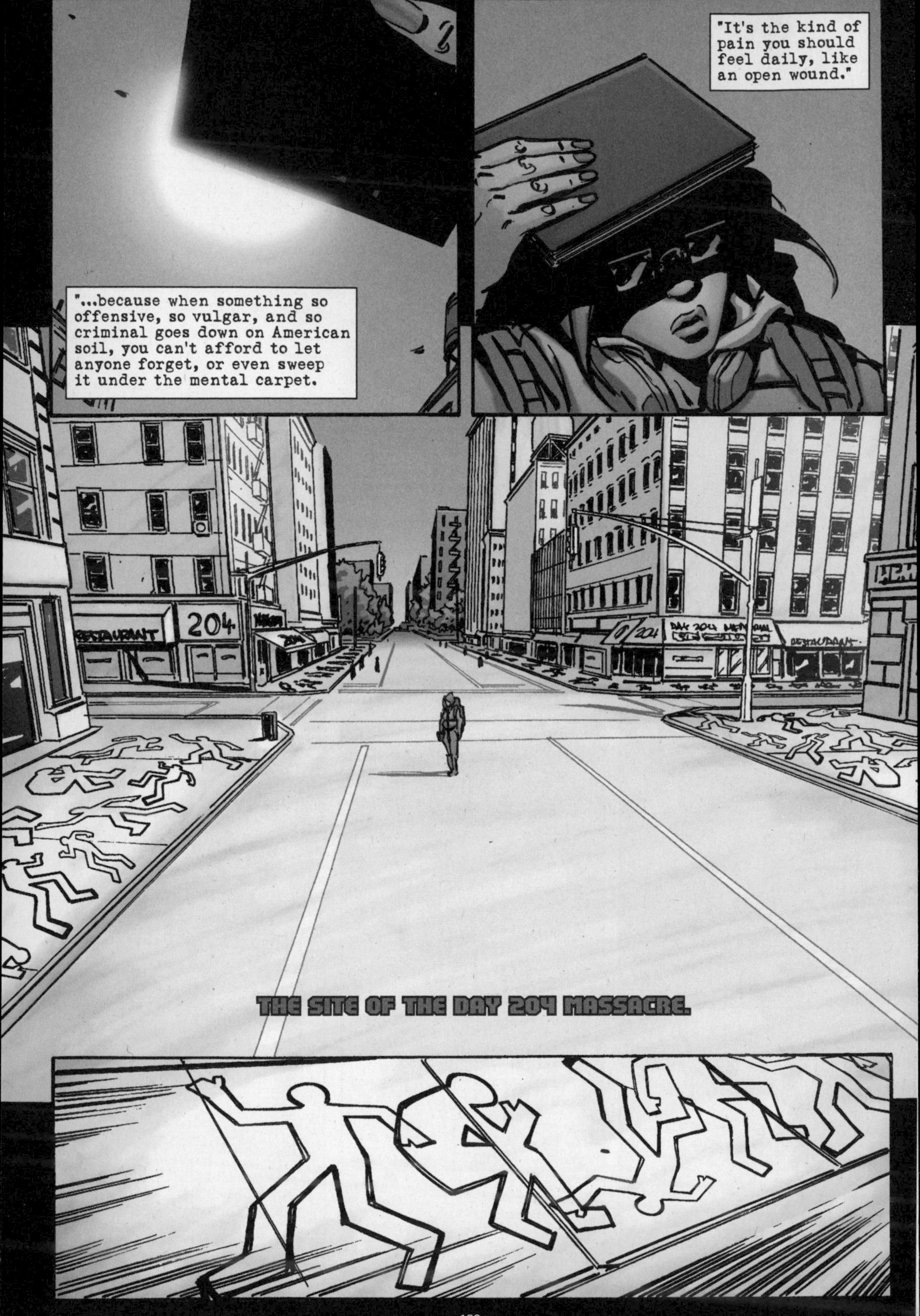
"It's the kind of pain you should feel daily, like an open wound."
"...because when something so offensive, so vulgar, and so criminal goes down on American soil, you can't afford to let anyone forget, or even sweep it under the mental carpet.
204
THE SITE OF THE DAY 204 MASSACRE.

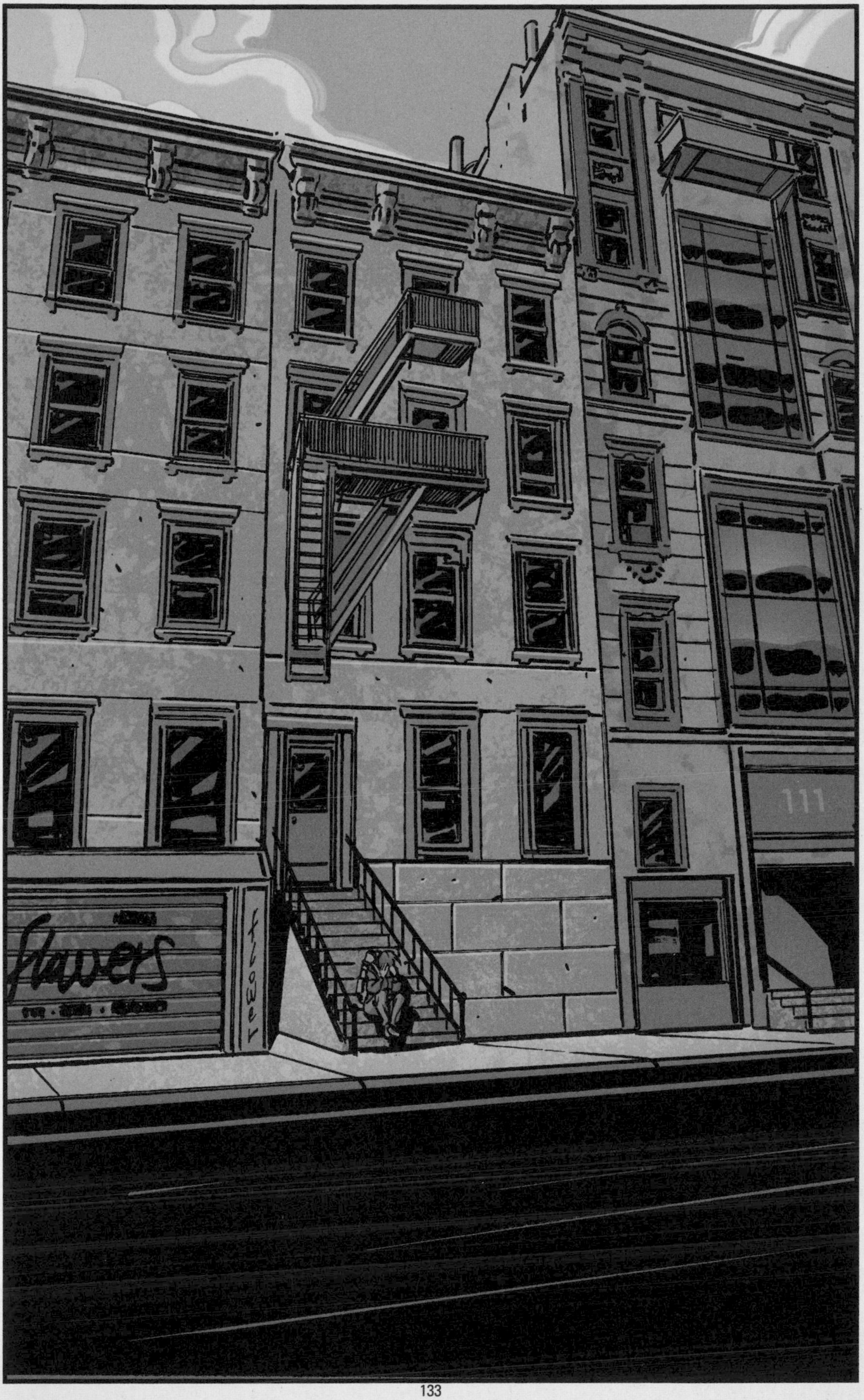
flowers
flower
111

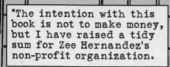

"The intention with this book is not to make money, but I have raised a tidy sum for Zee Hernandez's non-profit organization.

"I've long since decided against any sort of legal appeals or parole attempts, so I have no expenses to speak of. I will not earn a dime from this volume.

"As of the date of this latest edition coming off the presses, they have not made a move in that direction.

"The money paid to me from Liberty News went largely unspent, and what was has been paid back. I know there is talk that all the material in this book belongs to them, as per the contract I was pressed into signing, way back on Day 1.

"I am frequently asked if I will write anything else, if I have another book in me."

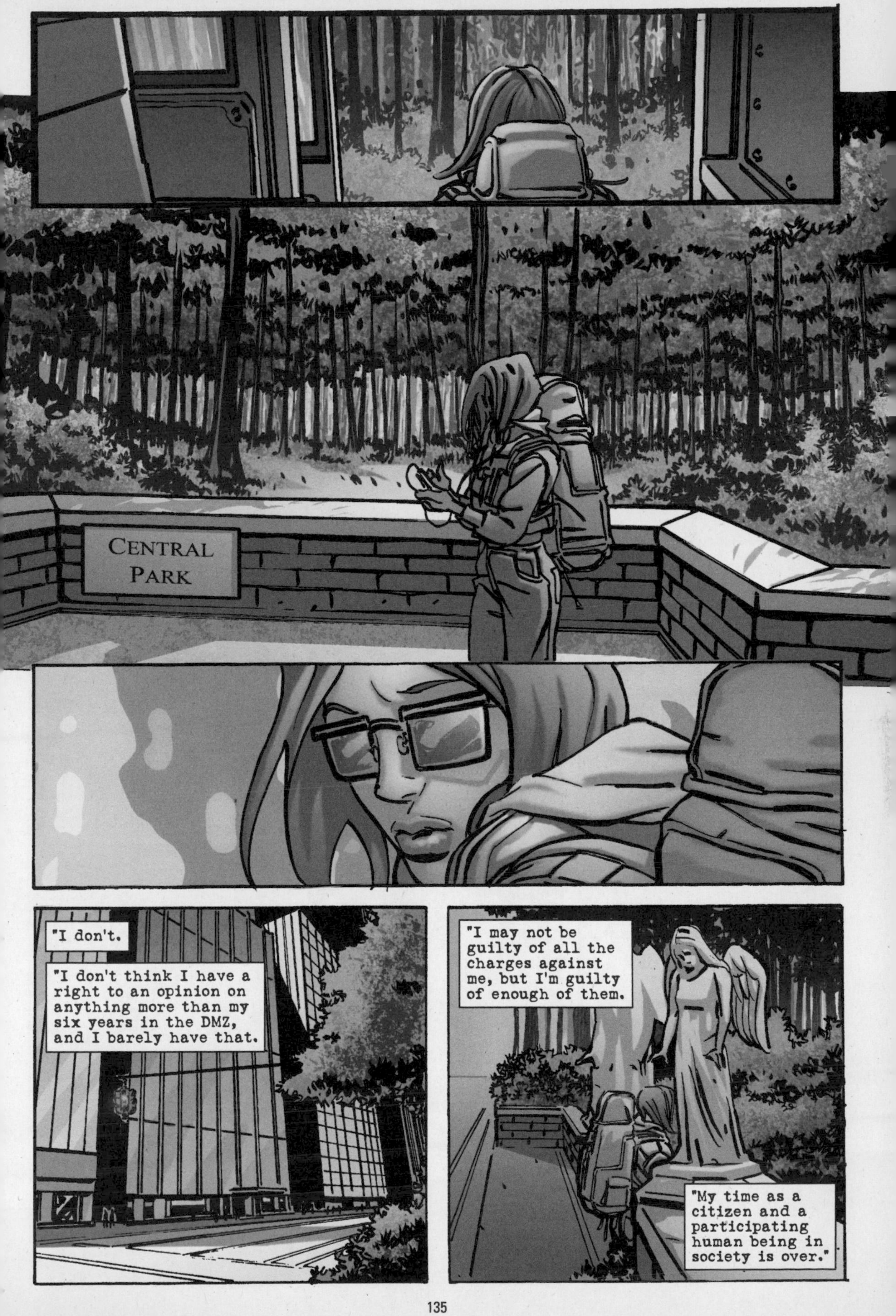
CENTRAL PARK
"I don't.
"I don't think I have a right to an opinion on anything more than my six years in the DMZ, and I barely have that.
"I may not be guilty of all the charges against me, but I'm guilty of enough of them.
"My time as a citizen and a participating human being in society is over."

"My life has ceased to have a positive value. My contribution to the world ended the day I shipped the manuscript for this book off to my mother.

"So there will be no other books from me.

"What you hold in your hands is...

"...I believe...

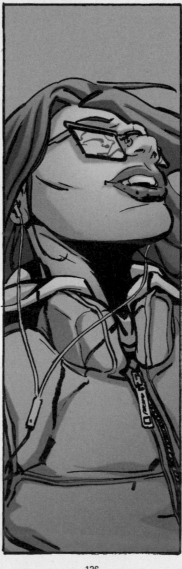

GHOSTS WERE RIGHT!

"...the total sum of the purpose of my life."

MATTY ROTH

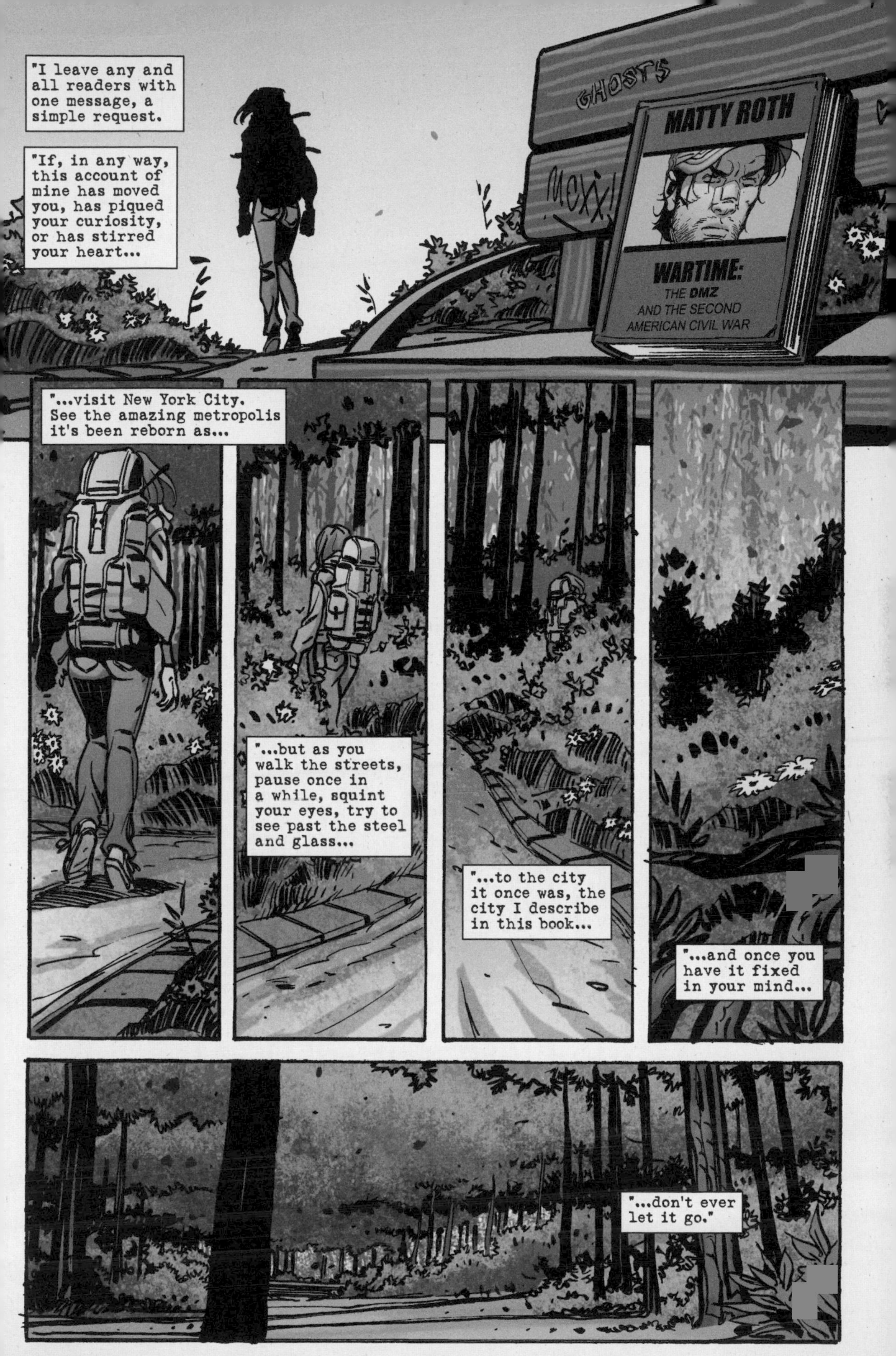
"I leave any and all readers with one message, a simple request.
"If, in any way, this account of mine has moved you, has piqued your curiosity, or has stirred your heart...
GHOSTS
MATTY ROTH
WARTIME:
THE DMZ
AND THE SECOND
AMERICAN CIVIL WAR
"...visit New York City. See the amazing metropolis it's been reborn as...
"...but as you walk the streets, pause once in a while, squint your eyes, try to see past the steel and glass...
"...to the city it once was, the city I describe in this book...
"...and once you have it fixed in your mind...
"...don't ever let it go."

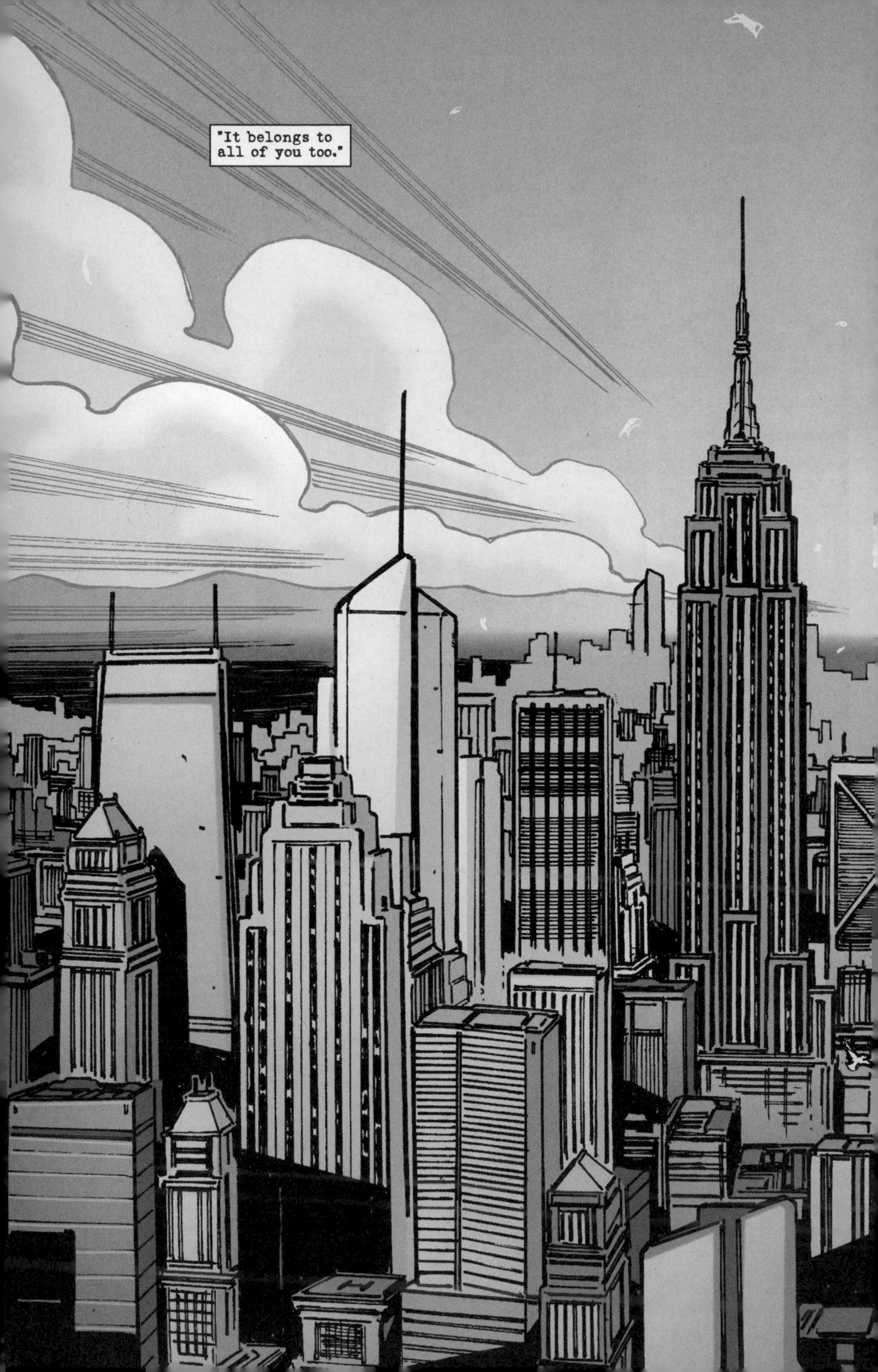
"It belongs to all of you too."

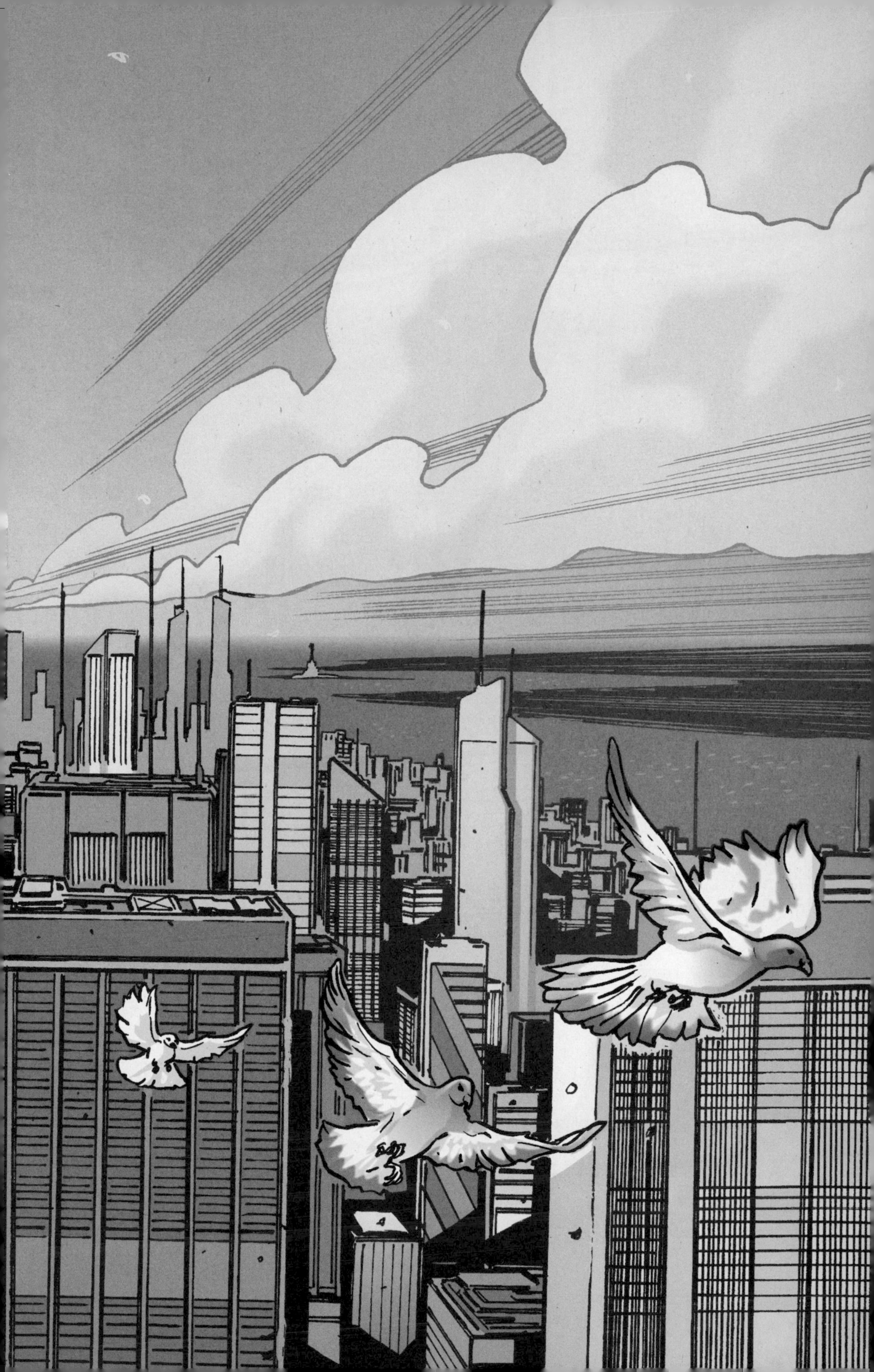

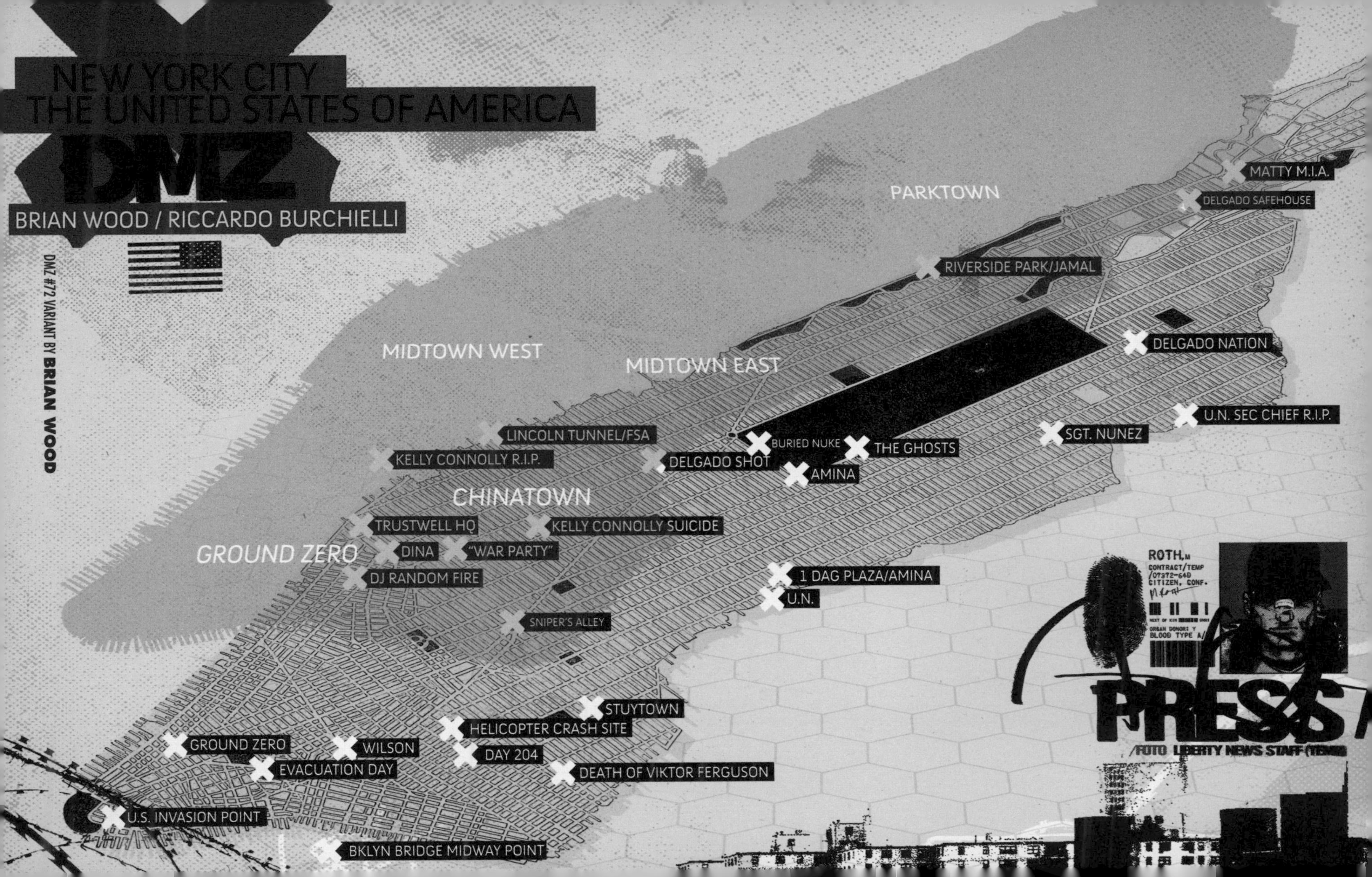

DMZ #72 VARIANT BY **BRIAN WOOD**

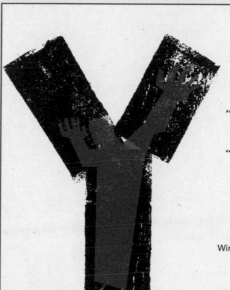

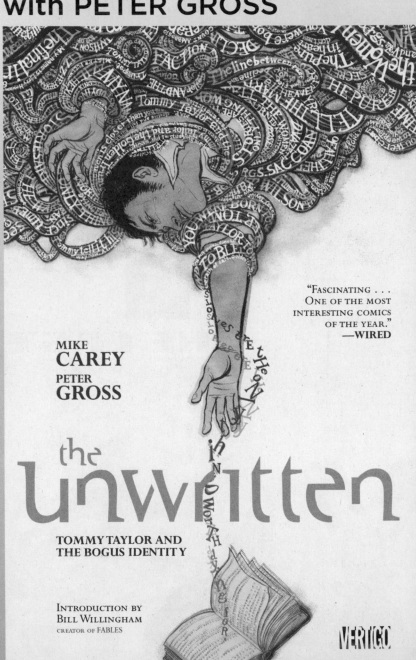

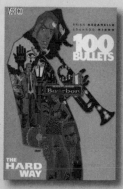
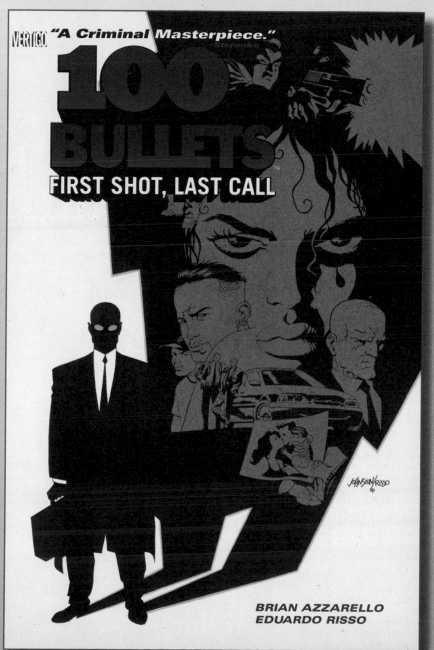

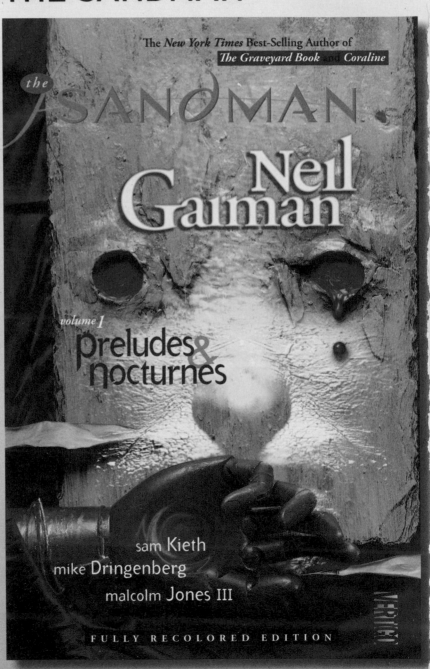